C0065 73595

D0260608

JAMES ROBERTS & MARTYN WHITTOCK

TRUMP
AND THE
PURITANS

HOW THE EVANGELICAL RELIGIOUS RIGHT PUT
DONALD TRUMP IN THE WHITE HOUSE

Biteback Publishing

First published in Great Britain in 2020 by
Biteback Publishing Ltd
Westminster Tower
3 Albert Embankment
London SE1 7SP
Copyright © James Roberts and Martyn Whittock 2020

James Roberts and Martyn Whittock have asserted their rights under the Copyright, Designs and Patents Act 1988 to be identified as the authors of this work.

All rights reserved. No part of this publication may be reproduced, stored in a retrieval system or transmitted, in any form or by any means, without the publisher's prior permission in writing.

This book is sold subject to the condition that it shall not, by way of trade or otherwise, be lent, resold, hired out or otherwise circulated without the publisher's prior consent in any form of binding or cover other than that in which it is published and without a similar condition, including this condition, being imposed on the subsequent purchaser.

Every reasonable effort has been made to trace copyright holders of material reproduced in this book, but if any have been inadvertently overlooked the publisher would be glad to hear from them.

ISBN 978-1-78590-508-7

10 9 8 7 6 5 4 3 2 1

A CIP catalogue record for this book is available from the British Library.

Set in Adobe Caslon Pro and Trade Gothic

Printed and bound in Great Britain by
CPI Group (UK) Ltd, Croydon CR0 4YY

MIX
Paper from
responsible sources
FSC
www.fsc.org
FSC® C020471

To Claire, Antonia and Ann-Marie.
Greatest gifts, greatest blessings, my daughters.
JAMES ROBERTS

To John Chettleburgh, Steve Oldrieve,
Stuart Brown and Andrew Sharland,
who share my interest in theology and
politics and the interaction of the two.
With thanks for their friendship.
MARTYN WHITTOCK

CONTENTS

ACKNOWLEDGEMENTS

We are grateful to many people who assisted in the writing and production of this book. We wish to especially thank Ali Hull, with whom we first discussed the connection between Trump and the Puritans over an animated lunch at Clevedon, on the Somerset coast; and James Macintyre, whose introduction made this possible.

James: I would especially like to thank: Glenn Edwards, photographer – together we have seen the worst. Colleagues and friends, disputatious yet congenial: Brendan Walsh, Alban McCoy, Clifford Longley, Christa Pongratz-Lippitt, David Harding, Mike Holland, Catherine Pepinster, Ruth Gledhill, Liz Dodd, Maggie Fergusson, Christopher Lamb, Iain Millar, Joanna Moorhead, Rose Gamble, Ignatius Kusiak, Guy Keleny, Isabel Gribben, Pippa Lee, Marcus Tanner and Raymond Whitaker. My wife Remi, who knows the last shall be first.

Martyn: I would like to especially thank my wife Christine, for her never-failing support, interest, patience and willingness to listen to my latest ideas. And our daughters Hannah and Esther, who have been members of many an animated discussion and whose interest in politics and theology greatly inform such conversations.

We also wish to thank Robert Dudley, our agent, Olivia Beattie and James Lilford and the team at Biteback for all of their advice, encouragement and support.

PREFACE

The 'Trump phenomenon' is often described as the US version of a populist trend that has impacted on many areas of contemporary global politics. Exploring it is a key part of understanding the modern world and its complexity. As the US gears up for the 2020 presidential election – and as the polarisation of US politics increases – the nature of this phenomenon, its origins, its impact on the USA and its long-term effects are the subjects of analysis, speculation and heated debate. We hear it and read it via the broadcast news, in our newspapers, across the internet and on social media. Again and again people ask: 'What is going on in the USA? Why is it happening?'

Despite the global political similarities, Donald Trump's success is also rooted in a peculiarly American experience, since a very large and influential part of his support base lies among Christians of the so-called 'evangelical religious right'. The influence of US evangelical Christians on national politics has never been more pronounced than it is today. From the appointment of Supreme Court judges, to US relations with Israel, from support for the wall, to abortion legislation, the power of this extraordinary lobby is seen in the changing politics and policies of the nation. In this, religious faith has an impact that is quite unique to the USA among 21st-century Western states; and it stands in comparison with the impact of Islam in other countries. There is clearly something distinctive about US culture and politics that sets it apart from comparatively developed democratic societies and states.

Remarkably, 2020 is not only the year of the next US presidential election, it is also the 400th anniversary of the arrival of the *Mayflower* Pilgrims in North America and the beginnings of Puritan New England. In addition, both the election and anniversary occur in the month of November. Is this mere coincidence, synchronicity or a providential arrangement of events? While readers will have their own opinions, there are clearly those in the modern USA who would consider this juxtaposition of dates as being something more than mere random chance. To them, God's providence is shaping the pattern of modern history. But, regardless of differing conclusions reached concerning the significance of the autumnal coming together of events in 2020, there is undeniably an historical link between the origins of Puritan settlement of North America and the remarkable events that have shaken the nation since 2016. What is going on in the modern USA has very deep roots. They are roots that stretch back into the almost mythological origins of the nation in the seventeenth century.

That is the contention of this book. The evidence we explore reveals how the original Puritan settlers (at Plymouth Colony and, especially, in Massachusetts Bay Colony) contributed something undeniably potent to the development of the eventual United

States, which emerged in the eighteenth century, expanded in the nineteenth and became a superpower in the twentieth. In the twenty-first century, modern America is still negotiating a way through the legacy of these events of 400 years ago. And this is so, despite the huge ethnic, demographic, political, constitutional, cultural and religious changes that have occurred in the intervening years. In short, huge numbers of US voters are still, in effect, doing 'Puritan politics'.

As a result, this book provides an exploration of one of the most important forces driving the support for Donald Trump, which is delivering millions of election-winning votes: America's Puritan heritage. Support for Trump among evangelicals is the latest manifestation of this key strand within the cultural DNA of the USA. As a direct result, the long-term influence of the Puritans makes the USA different to any other Western democracy; it motivates and energises a key part of the Trump base; and it has played a major role in delivering political power to the President.

Our exploration will bring together historic evidence and the latest journalistic analysis. The Mayflower Compact meets the tweets of @realDonaldTrump and New England Puritan ideology meets the political goals of modern evangelical conservatives. It is through untangling these ancient narratives and tracing their path through four centuries of history that we can begin to understand that, while aspects of the Trump phenomenon can be compared to wider global developments, what is occurring is still unique to the modern United States.

We believe that anyone wanting to fully understand what is currently happening in the USA must take this into account if they are to fully appreciate what is going on. *Trump and the Puritans* takes readers from the formative years of the seventeenth century to the remarkable events that have led to the current situation in the USA.

In carrying out this exploration we are grateful to a huge range of people, sources, assessments and evidence streams, which have made this possible. We have endeavoured to formally identify our sources in our endnotes. We have also attempted to be fair and balanced in a field of politics that has become increasingly heated over recent years. We hope that we have achieved this and that readers will gain a deeper (and historically more connected) insight into this crucial area of US politics. It goes without saying that all errors are our own.

James Roberts
Martyn Whittock

INTRODUCTION

A RATHER UNEXPECTED ALLIANCE

AN IDEA THAT WENT BADLY WRONG

In the US presidential election year of 2004, *The Guardian* dreamed up a scheme to recruit thousands of readers to persuade American voters in swing states to reject sitting President George W. Bush and vote, instead, for the Democratic candidate, Senator John Kerry. 'Operation Clark County' would involve recruiting 50,000 readers to write letters to voters in Clark County, Ohio. In 2000, Bush defeated Democrat Al Gore in the tightest of races. Four years later *The Guardian* wanted to help the Democrats oust him. In 2000, Gore won Clark County by a mere 1 per cent – just over 300 votes. So, *The Guardian* contacted the director of the Clark County board of elections and paid $25 for a copy of the electoral roll. The scheme seemed set to change US history.

Unfortunately for *The Guardian* and 'G2' editor, Ian Katz, who came up with the idea, soon after the first 14,000 letters started arriving in the county in the rural Midwest, an un-anticipated response took shape. It was expressed succinctly in a headline in the local newspaper, the *Springfield News-Sun*: 'Butt Out Brits, voters say'. 'Each email someone gets from some arrogant Brit telling us why to not vote for George Bush is going to backfire, you stupid, yellow-toothed pansies', was one reaction. Clearly, the scheme was not exactly going to plan. In late October *The Guardian* called a halt to 'Operation Clark County'. In November, Bush won 51 per cent of the vote there, with a swing of 1,600 votes in his favour. The hapless Katz said afterwards that it would be 'self-aggrandising' to think *The Guardian*'s intervention made any difference to the result, but one wonders. Influencing voters by telling them how they should vote can be a far from straightforward venture, but some of those committed to such an approach have not been deterred.

Twelve years later, interventions by 'Brits' on behalf of Democratic hopeful Hillary Clinton against the Republican candidate Donald Trump were more sophisticated. Birmingham-born and Cambridge-educated comedian John Oliver successfully imported a very British brand of mockery to the US. His late Sunday night HBO TV show, *Last Week Tonight with John Oliver*, was launched in 2014 and rapidly garnered an audience of over 4 million. Donald Trump was manna from heaven for Oliver's satire and, after ignoring the billionaire tycoon in the early primaries, he turned to deploying all the comic savagery he could muster once it was clear Trump might win the Republican nomination. Oliver's fans found his show fearless, and it was widely applauded: it was nominated in six categories at the Emmys in 2016 and went on to win three awards. On the online news forum Daily Beast in February 2016, Marlow Stern declared that Oliver had 'destroyed' Trump. But Oliver hadn't destroyed him. After Trump's victory over the favourite, Hillary

Clinton, in November 2016, Oliver urged his viewers to spend their time and money to help 'support organisations that are going to need help under a Trump administration', including the major abortion provider, Planned Parenthood. A horrified Oliver declared that 'a Klan-backed misogynist internet troll is going to be delivering the next State of the Union address, and that is not normal'.[1]

Oliver was discovering that while there was a large sector of the American population – particularly in New York where he had made his home – who viewed the world with his level of knowing, not to say, British style of comedic sophistication, there was an equally large population in the so-called 'flyover states' that was suspicious of this apparent sophistication and was unconvinced by its presumption of moral superiority. The geographical and social pattern of 'east/west versus the middle' and 'city and suburbs versus the countryside' that would become even more entrenched in the November 2018 mid-terms had claimed another victim. However, by the time Oliver had become aware of this phenomenon – and long before 2018 – Hillary Clinton had made her own spectacular contribution to dividing the USA. And, unwittingly, to her own defeat.

A DEFINING MOMENT
– THE BIRTH OF THE 'DEPLORABLES'

On 9 September 2016, while addressing the LGBT Gala at the Cipriani Club in New York City, from a podium bearing the words 'Stronger Together', Hillary Clinton let the cat out of the bag. After praising her warm-up speaker for 'her advocacy on behalf of the transgender community, particularly transgender women of colour', she moved on to attack the running-mate of her rival for the presidency, Donald J. Trump. She described how Mike Pence, whom she did not refer to by name, had 'signed a law that would have allowed businesses to discriminate against LGBT Americans'. As the audience understandably booed their disapproval, she expanded on her point:

> And there's so much more that I find deplorable in his [Trump's] campaign: the way that he cosies up to white supremacists, makes racist attacks, calls women pigs, mocks people with disabilities – you can't make this up. He wants to round up and deport sixteen million people, calls our military a disaster ... Our campaign slogan is not just words. We really do believe that we are stronger together.[2]

Clinton nodded to the gender issues that were already starting to provoke debate in the US and in the UK, musing that 'somewhere not far from here ... is a young girl who is just not sure what her future holds because she just doesn't feel like she's herself and no one understands that'. Then she went on to make a number of campaign promises:

> So, together we're gonna pass the Equality Act to guarantee full equality. We're going to put comprehensive, quality, affordable healthcare within reach for more people, including for mental health and addiction. We're gonna take on youth homelessness, and as my wonderful, extraordinary, great daughter [Chelsea Clinton] said, we are going to end the cruel and dangerous practice

of conversion therapy [whose proponents claim to 'cure' gays of their homosexuality]. We're going to keep working toward an AIDS-free generation, a goal that I set as secretary of state, and with your help we're going to pass comprehensive gun laws...

The chants of 'Hill-a-ry! Hill-a-ry!' bounced around the hall, and she seized the moment: 'We are living in a volatile political environment. You know, to just be grossly generalistic, you could put half of Trump's supporters into what I call the basket of deplorables. Right?'

The laughter and applause allowed her to pause, before she rose to a triumphant climax:

The racist, sexist, homophobic, xenophobic, Islamophobic – you name it. And unfortunately there are people like that. And he has lifted them up. He has given voice to their websites that used to only have 11,000 people – now have 11 million. He tweets and retweets their offensive hateful mean-spirited rhetoric. Now, some of those folks – they are irredeemable, but thankfully they are not America.

So, there were some Trump supporters – half of them – who were 'not America'; but the other half were redeemable, and could still belong to Hillary's America if they came to see the error of their ways.

But the other basket ... that other basket of people are people who feel that the government has let them down, the economy has let them down, nobody cares about them, nobody worries about what happens to their lives and their futures, and they're just desperate for change. It doesn't really even matter where it comes from. They don't buy everything he says, but he seems to hold out some hope that their lives will be different. They won't wake up and see their jobs disappear, lose a kid to heroin, feel like they're in a dead-end. Those are people we have to understand and empathise with as well.

In other words, Hillary calculated that if she could win over the votes of the half of Trump's supporters who might be wavering, she would become the next President of the United States. It seemed a reasonable calculation, but she had just made a terrible tactical error. The ensuing applause at the Cipriani Club covered up the fact that she had made a disastrous miscalculation. Because there, more exultant than anyone in the hall, was Steve Bannon, co-founder of the hard-right news website Breitbart News, who the previous month had been named chief executive officer of the Trump campaign. He knew the group she was referring to. He was well acquainted with those Clinton had named 'the basket of deplorables'. He knew they despised the Washington elites, both Republican and Democrat, because they considered them as serving just two masters: their own self-interest, and Wall Street. Since the financial crash of 2008, caused by Wall Street financiers and bankers who had been rescued from ruin by trillions of dollars of public money – and who had by-and-large emerged relatively unscathed from the catastrophe of their own making – many of those in 'the basket of deplorables' had held this elite – politicians and their Wall Street allies – in contempt. They believed, not without some cause, that the hardship they were now enduring was a direct result of the financial rescue of the billionaires. The bitterness was tangible and Bannon knew all about it. And he knew how to use it.

The 'continuing progress' that Clinton claimed America was rooted in was not progress as far as these Trump supporters were concerned, with its 'Equality Act' and emphasis on group identities. This liberal-secular agenda, which President Barack Obama had promoted for eight years, was not their agenda. As Clinton noted, they had seen their communities decline inexorably and could do nothing about it. The values that they had been taught were the route to success in an America they believed in – blue-collar fathers and mothers making sacrifices to raise their family in the hope that their children would have a better life, an easier life, than the life of their parents – no longer applied. They could sacrifice as much as they liked, and dream as much as they could dream, but the odds were now so heavily stacked against them that the hope that had nourished their striving was, in this new America, a fantasy. The door to the American Dream was locked and bolted. Across the so-called 'Rust Belt' of the USA – from Pennsylvania, through Ohio and Michigan, to northern Indiana and eastern Illinois and Wisconsin – the abandoned factories spoke eloquently of their ex-perience of America. The same could be said of the boarded-up shops in the small towns of West Virginia whose coal mines had closed. But it was not only in these states that the mood was angry and alarmed. In the white picket-fenced, small-town communities across much of the Midwest, emotions were also running high. And, for many, the frustration with the economic situation was matched by a deep ideological disquiet, which was becoming anger.

To many living outside the seaboard states, it seemed that the foundation of their traditional hope – their Christian faith that was mirrored in the public conversations of what they still considered to be 'a Christian country' – was now held in contempt in most of the media that hosted the national conversation. To them, for every voice upholding traditional Christian faith and traditional morality, there seemed to be two that derided it. Hillary Clinton's politics explicitly embraced every minority group imaginable but failed to see the ones – in their view – that were the least complaining and most deserving: themselves. As they saw it, in a world of liberal identity politics they had been denied an identity that they them-selves would recognise. Her invitation to them to join her was seen immediately for what it was: an attempt to split the Trump vote. From their perspective, her attempt was risible and presumptuous. Clinton had posted her invitation into a chasm.

Unbeknown to her, however, she had presented this part of the electorate with a priceless gift. She had provided them with a group identity. From now on all Trump supporters, 'redeemable' or 'irre-deemable', would feel the power of belonging. They had a team. They were the 'deplorables'. The term quickly became a badge of honour that was worn with pride. Inadvertently Clinton had given them a label and it unwittingly assisted them in focusing much of their anger on the kind of America that had gained public approval since 2008.

After the passing into law of what Hillary and her supporters in the US and elsewhere called 'marriage equality' – a term that many 'deplorables' regarded as a form of Newspeak – President Barack Obama ordered that the White House be bathed in the colours of the rainbow. In the eyes of many this was a tender act of solidarity. After centuries of the darkening of marriage through prejudice and exclusion, America had taken a step towards a new era of equality, perhaps the most important one since the Supreme Court's Roe *v.* Wade ruling in 1973, which affirmed a woman's right to abortion.

In the eyes of the 'deplorables', however, the rainbow White House was a transparent act of liberal-secular passive aggression. Under the guise of inclusiveness, the government was excluding the huge section of traditionally Christian Americans who believed that marriage was, by definition and nature, an institution that joined together one man and one woman. Hillary Clinton took it for granted that she and her supporters were on the right side of history; implying that humanity was on a path from lesser to greater moral virtue and that she and her allies were leading the way. However, she and her supporters collided with an entrenched position that had millennia of history in Judaeo-Christian scripture and tradition behind it: 'In the image of God he created them; male and female he created them.'[3] To the most active defenders of this belief system, it seemed that the liberal secularists had thought that they could overthrow this ancient natural order without looking back. The future belonged to liberal secularism. But now 'they', the ones left behind by history, Americans who felt they had had 'the land of the free and the home of the brave' pulled from under their feet, to be replaced by an a-patriotic and unrecognisable patchwork of banners and loyalties, suddenly had a flag around which they could rally, along with the Stars and Stripes. The battle was joined over traditional Christianity, US patriotism and economic anger. And its articulation as a distinct cause gave the opposition to Clinton the sudden appearance of 'a crusade'. Albeit a crusade whose banner was being held aloft by a rather unlikely Christian crusader: Donald Trump. Homemade roadside signs, such as that observed outside Luverne, Alabama, read: 'THANK GOD WE ARE DEPLORA-BLE.'[4] It would prove to be a heady and unorthodox kind of moonshine that was being distilled in the 'flyover states'.

THE MYSTERY OF DONALD TRUMP, THE 'CHRISTIAN CRUSADER'

Across much of the world Donald Trump is a hate figure. The people who floated the Trump balloon above Westminster in London in July 2018 and the 100,000 who demonstrated against his UK visit, which was marked both by a meeting with the Queen and by the launching of the balloon, were hardly able to explain their hatred beyond saying that Trump was 'horrible' – a word frequently used when those protesting against the presence of the US President were asked to explain why they disliked him. He excited similar levels of opposition when he visited London again in 2019.

Harvard students who were so traumatised – the day after the presidential election – that they were excused completion of their assignments were similarly unable to explain why they were so incapacitated. But what was clear was that behind the opposition and the trauma was a mystery and an enigma. How could a man with such well-documented personal failings, whose personality traits were so unappealing to so many, be elected President of the United States?

And, as the identity of his supporters was examined more closely, how could it be that self-described 'evangelical' Christians could see such a man as their political saviour? These Christians would be asked many questions along the lines of: 'Aren't you all about forgiveness? About loving your enemies? About helping the poor? How do you reconcile these teachings of Jesus with backing a man like Trump?' And their answers were sometimes as simple and instinctive as the views of those who launched the Trump balloon in London. But not often. For the most part, evangelicals who were Trump supporters knew exactly why they voted for him.

The phrase 'it's the economy, stupid' was coined by James Carville, Bill Clinton's election strategist in 1992, as part of a Democratic strategy to remind voters about the weak George H. Bush economy. However, the world has moved on since then. It is now clear that voters care about other things too, and they care about some things even more than the economy, and whether they will be better or worse off. They care about what they consider to be the distinctive culture and values of the country in which they live, and if they think these values are under attack or being eroded, they will vote to defend them even if this defence carries an economic price. Trump's slogan 'Make America Great Again' brilliantly referenced both the American economy – he would bring jobs lost as a result of globalisation back to the United States – and American culture. Being American, he insisted, was no longer something to be apologetic about: he would bring back pride in being American (as he and his supporters defined it). As they saw it, the 'American way of life' was something that could be defended before the whole world because it was the best way of life that the world had so far produced. Among these Americans, there had always been an ill-disguised suspicion that the patriotism of the previous President,

Barack Obama, had not run very deep.[5] This made Obama popular in the UK and Europe, where patriotic nationalist fervour had long been regarded as a rather suspect emotion among more educated people, particularly following two nationalistic world wars that had torn Europe apart. But in America it became clear that patriotism had been bottled up, rather than diffused or deflected. And in Europe, too, it is rapidly becoming clear that the potency of competing nationalisms is far from being defused.[6] When Trump uncorked that particular bottle in the USA, the energy released was – in rally after rally – quite appalling, or quite magnificent, depending on one's viewpoint.

In Britain, the Brexit vote uncovered a hidden nationalist patriotism on the part of many Britons. Those whose loyalty to a more narrowly defined version of country and culture took precedence over their acceptance of British-European identity and an administration based in mainland Europe (that might or might not deliver greater prosperity) momentarily had a chance to speak in the referendum of June 2016. They duly delivered a kicking to the leaders of most UK parties, their EU partners and the other half of a deeply divided electorate, taking many by surprise. But even here there was a fundamental difference between the US election of that same year and the Brexit vote. In the US election, God was an acknowledged player. In the Brexit vote, he wasn't. That is not entirely true, however. A fringe group of numerically small, but energetic, UK Christians made much of their claims that the EU represented an anti-Christian fulfilment of biblical prophecy.[7] It was an extreme (and much disputed) millenarianism that would have been understood across the Atlantic but would have mystified the vast majority of Leave voters, had they even been aware of these particular accusations against the EU. Things were – and are – different in the USA.

The presidential inauguration of Donald Trump, on 20 January 2017, featured six religious leaders, more than any other inauguration in history. One of the five Christians who prayed with Trump was Paula White, a televangelist who had been his spiritual adviser since 2002. 'Let these United States of America be that beacon of hope to all people and all nations under your dominion, a true hope for human kind,' she prayed, 'in the name of Jesus Christ. Amen.'[8] Seven months later, on *The Jim Bakker Show*, she said that Trump had been 'raised up by God', and that 'we are scaring the literal hell out of demonic spirits'. This was spoken in the context of Trump's nomination of the so-called 'originalist' Neil Gorsuch to the Supreme Court. 'Originalists' interpret the US constitution as stable and unchanging, in a political version of the biblical fundamentalism espoused by many traditional Christians in the USA. Paula White's enthusiasm revealed that a major hope among those often termed the 'Christian Religious Right' or 'evangelicals', regarding the Trump presidency, was for nominees whose rulings would accord with their faith. 'If we get two more [Supreme Court justices] we will be able to overturn demonic laws and decrees that have held this nation in captivity,' White declared.[9]

Franklin Graham, son of Billy and head of the Billy Graham Evangelistic Association, took his inauguration text from the New Testament letter, 1 Timothy 2: 5–6a: 'For there is one God and one mediator between God and mankind, the man Christ Jesus, who gave himself as a ransom for all people.'[10] Many in the UK (whether of faith or no faith) would have struggled to see this as a preparation for an endorsement of President Trump. In the USA, too, the approach has been questioned. As the presidency progressed, Graham was persistently challenged to defend Trump from a Christian point of view. While not defending Trump's history of alleged immoral behaviour and intemperate comments, Graham held that God had placed Trump in the White House, despite his character flaws, because he was the man who could get God's work done at this – in Graham's view – absolutely critical point in US and world history. US liberals were incredulous.

It was indicative of what some contemporary evangelical Christian commentators have called the 'Cyrus Factor' – a reference to a king of Persia described as an instrument of God in the Old Testament – whereby God might choose to use an imperfect person in order to accomplish a divinely ordained task. We shall return to this view of Donald Trump as we explore and seek to understand other areas of support for him within the so-called 'evangelical religious right', for it is one of the powerful forces driving support for him from within this influential section of US society. It also helps to explain some, otherwise inexplicably sanguine, approaches to his actions and alleged behaviour that shock many other observers. As such, we need to put a marker on it now, because referring to it will help explain many of the more puzzling areas covered in this book. For, so long as Donald Trump promises to deliver on areas considered as quintessentially 'home territory' to traditional right-leaning evangelical voters, other areas (alleged or self-evident) of his life – conduct, speech and policies (that might otherwise give cause for concern) – can be ignored or marginalised.

Meanwhile, Britain has drifted ever further away from its cousin across the water. Franklin Graham was invited by the Lancashire Festival of Hope to preach at Blackpool's Winter Gardens in September 2018. In July, Blackpool Transport banned adverts for the event being placed on the side of the town's buses, citing 'heightened tensions'. Gordon Marsden, Labour MP for Blackpool South, called on the government to deny Graham a visa. 'Graham's visit to Blackpool is likely to cause considerable offence,' he said. The Muslim Council of Britain said the government had a duty to deny Graham a visa. Otherwise, it claimed, 'it will send a clear message that it is not consistent in challenging all forms of bigotry'. Two more MPs, Paul Maynard and Afzal Khan, opposed the visit, while the Blackpool Methodist Circuit said it 'cannot support any preaching or teaching that promotes homophobia or is likely to be damaging to interfaith dialogue'.[11] Three Blackpool churches planned to parade a four-metre model of Jesus wearing a rainbow sash through the town centre on the weekend of the visit. The differences between the UK and USA could not have been more clearly articulated. A report in *The Guardian* on 9 September 2018 described Graham as 'a prominent US evangelical preacher with links to Donald Trump and a track record of Islamophobic and homophobic statements'. Graham has said that Islam is evil, and that Satan is the architect of same-sex marriage and LGBT rights.[12]

In Britain in the week before the November 2018 mid-term elections in the US, the broad position of most commentators regarding Trump was less heated than the opposition to the Graham visit, but still hopeful that the President would be reined in. A Democratic majority in the House of Representatives would do this job nicely, was the rough consensus. The astonishing successes of the US economy since Trump's election were acknowledged, but praise and enthusiasm for these achievements were distributed with care.

Trump, meanwhile, embarked on what must have been an exhausting programme of carefully targeted rallies at which he appeared to draw energy from the massive turnout they all commanded. His aim was to endorse candidates in tight races, hopefully swinging the vote to the Republicans and thereby maintaining the party's majority in both Houses of Congress.

At Pensacola, Florida, on 3 November, he gave his full and en-thusiastic support to Ron DeSantis for governor against Andrew Gillum, and to incumbent governor Rick Scott running against three-term Democratic incumbent Bill Nelson in the Senate race. He duly disparaged Gillum and Nelson. But he saved his most ex-traordinary rhetoric for the end:

> For years you watched as your leaders apologised for America. That's what they did. They apologised for us. They apologised for your great country. Now you have a President who is standing up for America … We love our country. We really love our country … Reject the Democrat politics of anger and division.

'Reclaim our proud and righteous destiny as Americans,' he told the crowd. Florida was a place, he claimed, of 'pioneers and visionaries, who raised up gleaming cities by the sea'. Several times he urged his supporters to get out and vote in order to defend the America that he was describing. For the people of the past did not make the sacrifices of blood, sweat and tears that had built the state just so that people today could 'sit at home, while others try to erase their legacy, tear down our history and destroy our very proud American heritage'.

Getting further into his stride, he delivered exactly what the crowd had been waiting for:

> For the sake of our freedom and for the sake of our children, we are going to work, we are going to fight and we are going to win, win, win. We will not bend, we will not break, we will never give in, we will never give up, we will never back down, we will never surrender. And we will always fight on to victory. Always. Because we are Americans and our hearts bleed red, white and blue. We are one people, one family and one glorious nation under God.[13]

For Britons, the exaggerated (almost Churchillian) register is recognisably Trump. Less recognisable is another set of references: 'pioneers', 'visionaries', 'gleaming cities', 'righteous destiny', 'one glorious nation under God'. These ideas reverberate in American history from well before the Second World War, when Churchill honed his own form of rhetoric. Trump's words evoked a much older tradition; one that can be traced back to the Puritan settlers. In this way he was appealing to a Puritan heritage in a way that is unthinkable and incomprehensible on the UK side of the Atlantic. And when Trump says 'we will never surrender', he was stating that this legacy will never be abandoned. It will never be replaced by an ideology that sees America as anything less than exceptional and a 'righteous shining city' (as he and his supporters define it), that can inspire the less fortunate, less virtuous, darker world to follow its guiding light. In this he was plugging into a 400-year-old tradition and forging an unlikely connection with the Puritans. For, among the many factors which explain the Trump phenomenon, the support of evangelical Christians is a vitally important one. About 81 per cent of American evangelical Christians, or about 33.7 million people, voted Trump in 2016.[14] This base remained solid, even after two turbulent and controversial years, with a Fox News poll, prior to the November 2018 mid-terms, indicating that the approval rating for Trump remained as high as 73 per cent among this group of voters.[15] In understanding the power of this highly influential lobby and its outlook, we need to view things through the lens of the seventeenth century and its consequences.

The Trump presidency is seeing nothing less than a struggle for the soul of America. In 2017, Mike Huckabee (Governor of Arkansas 1996–2007 and a Republican presidential candidate in 2008 and 2016) asserted that 'he [Trump] truly understands and welcomes godly advice and he sees the value of prayer'. Furthermore, Huckabee stated: 'I believe Trump's historic battle for the White House in 2016 metaphorically reminds us that America too is in a historic battle not only for its political future but also for its very soul.'[16]

The aim of this book is to show how the four-centuries-old Puritan legacy serves to illuminate both the parameters of the 'struggle', and the 'soul' itself that is being so bitterly contested in the USA.

CHAPTER ONE

CREATING A PURITAN BRAND

The year 2020 is a defining one in the USA. For a start, it is the year of a much-anticipated presidential election. Will the controversial incumbent of the White House win a second term as leader of the most powerful nation on earth? After four bitterly contested years as President, the matter is once again to go before the US electorate. Furthermore, Donald Trump's call for a return to 'civility' in the political debate – in the run-up to the mid-term elections in November 2018 – only led to gasps of disbelief among his opponents (including ex-President Barack Obama) as they claimed that he was the one who had so effectively coarsened it in the first place. Things have not got calmer since. America is once again at a political crossroads.

However, as if that was not enough to make 2020 stand out in modern US history, the year also marks the 400th anniversary of the arrival of the *Mayflower* Pilgrims in the New World and their establishment of a 'godly' colony in what was for them the 'American wilderness'. Many millions of Americans will not see this as a random juxtaposition of events, since for them Donald Trump is the one chosen by God to implement a 21st-century programme of godly rule and the restoration of American spiritual exceptionalism that is directly rooted in those far-off events, when Puritan settlers (who followed in 1630) first established a semi-theocratic 'New Jerusalem' in the 'New World'. For millions of key voters, the link is providential, not random. These are Christians of the evangelical religious right. And if we fail to grasp this, then key elements of the Trump phenomenon and key motivations within powerful sections of his support base will remain a mystery to us.

The alliance between Trump and the evangelical religious right is of great importance due to the large numbers of voters involved (as we saw in the Introduction). For, in a way surprising to many outside the USA and despite recent numerical decline, the number of Americans identifying as Christian remains huge. The USA is home to more Christians than any other nation on earth. In 2014 an extensive programme of research revealed that 70.6 per cent of US adults identified as being Christian. And of the total US adult population, 25.4 per cent identified as 'evangelicals'.[1] While the meaning of this term may be open to interpretation, those who use it in the USA as an identifier generally subscribe to a broad raft of beliefs: acceptance of the Bible as the inspired 'word of God' (which often has a fundamentalist and literal interpretation of the scriptures); traditional concepts of marriage, family and gender; and traditional attitudes towards the practice of sexuality, almost always involving classifying homosexual practice as sinful, with acceptable (heterosexual) sexual relations being reserved for within marriage. This is a collection of beliefs that would have been both recognised and accepted by most seventeenth-century Puritan believers. As a result, 'Christian politics' is a game-changer in any US election. And for those classified as 'evangelicals' this remains broadly recognisable as 'Puritan politics'.

For people in the UK the latter point will be even more surprising than the former, since while the Christian Church is no longer a major influence in UK politics, the idea of anything remotely resembling 'Puritanism' deciding the future of government would be incomprehensible. This is because US and UK Christians have drawn hugely different lessons from their common history and understanding about 'Puritans doing politics'. In the UK, the Puritans are a tainted brand – to put it mildly. We might admire their dedication to 'purifying' the church and their love of the Bible, but all that stuff about banning Christmas, plays, music and sport on a Sunday afternoon looks very joyless, judgemental and dull. Not to mention the slaughtering of Catholics in Ireland, which has left a legacy of bitterness that is still with us in 2020; and continues to deeply divide the way that that island views its history. And anyway, British people might say (assuming they have thought much about it at all) surely all that 'Puritan politics stuff' fell apart when King Charles II was restored in 1660. Indeed, in 1659 one contemporary commentator said of the Puritans, who had dominated politics since the execution of King Charles I in 1649, 'the Lord has blasted them and spit in their faces'.[2] On 30 January 1661, which was the twelfth anniversary of the execution of Charles I at Whitehall in 1649, the body of Oliver Cromwell was exhumed from its grave in Westminster Abbey.[3] The corpse was then put through the indignities of a posthumous 'trial' for high treason and 'executed'. This took the form of the body being hanged in chains at Tyburn, as a common criminal, and afterwards disposed of by burial in unconsecrated ground. When one of the surviving regicides was on his way to suffer retribution at the hands of exultant royalists, following a predictable trial verdict, somebody in the crowd yelled out: 'Where now is your Good Old Cause?'⁴ It seemed a reasonable question, if rather unkind to pose it in such a blunt fashion to a man on his way to be hanged, drawn and quartered. But, all in all, it was clear that Puritans and politics had parted ways. Puritans were a thing of the past; and the future, in what would become the United Kingdom, would have little time for its Puritan past. After the restoration of the Stuart monarchy in 1660, dissenting non-conformists (the heirs of the Puritans) focused on rather less ambitious projects, such as social reform. British Puritans – and their association, in the popular consciousness at least, with drab-coloured clothes, stiff white collars and joyless souls – have been confined to the history books. And only a minority of 21st-century British people mourn their disappearance.

This is not so on the other side of the Atlantic. There the Puritan brand is still doing very well indeed. This is because it was Puritans (of one form or another) who set up their own version of an ideal community in New England in the seventeenth century (a 'New Jerusalem' in the 'New World'), which has become such a key part of the cultural DNA of the USA since then and remains so today. What's not to like about a turkey dinner at Thanksgiving, which was originally celebrated by Puritan Europeans and Native Americans sitting down at the same table in 1621? Millions of school kids, dressed up in Puritan garb at their school pageants, can't be wrong, can they?

On top of this, the Puritan brand has left more than just a taste for turkey and cranberry sauce in the modern USA. The Pilgrim settlers at Plymouth Colony (in 1620) and even more so at Massachusetts Bay (in 1630) believed that they were founding, as the latter explicitly put it, 'a city on a hill'; a beacon of godliness, Bible Commonwealths in which all life would be lived in accordance with the Christian scriptures. It is not hard to see how this has morphed over four centuries into a belief in 'American exceptionalism' and even into strident calls to 'Make America Great Again'.

This formative experience in the seventeenth century has been one of the major factors in making the USA stand out from all comparable Western democracies. While a lot of water has flowed under the bridge since the 1620s and 1630s, something crucial and distinctive has fed into the national identity of what is now the USA as a result of its early history. This has led to a situation where a particular form of Christianity ('evangelical') remains highly influential as a confident, energetic, committed and active force within modern US culture and voting. The evangelical population has a significant political effect since its turnout is fairly reliable. This is especially the case if the electoral contest is tight. In 2016, about 81 per cent of white evangelicals supported Donald Trump.[5] Trump's victory illustrates how there is an unbroken stream of politically influential and biblically conservative Protestantism that flows from the seventeenth century to today, despite all the inflowing streams of other forms of Christianity (e.g. Roman Catholicism and Eastern Orthodox), not to mention other hugely influential faiths, such as Judaism and, more recently, Islam. As a result of this seventeenth-century formative experience, there is something very distinctive indeed about the modern USA. It points to the power of history in shaping a national identity. And in America's long run of history, the Puritans played and play an influential part.

In order to explore the importance of this legacy, it is necessary to examine who these Puritans were and why they ended up in North America; the kind of society they created; the mindset they embodied; and their importance for the future trajectory of what would become the United States of America. In other words, to analyse their contribution to the historic and cultural DNA of the USA. We will then (in Chapter Two) see how this Puritan past was celebrated, as well as adapted, and how it contributed to the character of the communities emerging in the British colonies in the eighteenth century, in a way that was out of proportion to the numbers of people originally involved. We will also explore the state of the Puritan legacy as the newly formed United States ended the eighteenth century, and how this legacy was highly influential in the moulding of the young country. Then (in Chapter Three) we will see how this heritage was adapted, celebrated and manipulated in the maturing United States as the westward drive turned it into a continental power, before (in Chapter Four) examining the way in which what is now often described as the evangelical religious right emerged as a recognisable group (with political influence) in the twentieth century. And we will assess how this significant group is indebted to the peculiar Puritan roots of the USA. From this foundation we will be better placed to explore how Donald Trump has tapped into this support base and why these voters see in him a politician who expresses their hopes and anxieties. This is the essence of *Trump and the Puritans*. But first, we begin with the arrival of the *Mayflower* Pilgrims. For, small as their numbers were, they were the start of a much larger influx of settlers who would create a distinct culture in New England.

1620: A YEAR THAT CHANGED NORTH AMERICA

In November 1620, an exhausted group of immigrants arrived at Cape Cod, now in Massachusetts, in New England. These were the *Mayflower* Pilgrims. They arrived on a ship that had never crossed the Atlantic before and had been delayed by a couple of months, so they landed just as the New England winter was starting. The *Mayflower* was grossly overcrowded and was carrying 102 passengers and about thirty crew. This was the same number of people they had set sail with; while one passenger had died on the voyage, a baby had been born while at sea. That single death was a taster of much worse to come.

Their story started in the Netherlands, where they had been living in exile due to persecution at the hands of English royal authorities and the bishops of the Church of England. Although the persecutors and persecuted were all Protestant Christians, they differed in their worship and lifestyles. Those who had fled to the Netherlands believed that the ceremonies of the Church of England were 'catholic' and 'popish', whereas they regarded their own as biblical, holy and in line with the will of God. There was a culture war going on. Many in society would have regarded them as religious extremist members of divisive and contentious sects. And, as a result, they had fled to the relative freedom offered by the more tolerant Netherlands. However, while the Netherlands offered greater religious freedom, it too had its problems. The Dutch did not seem to be as holy in their lifestyles; jobs done by the English exiles were poorly paid; their children seemed to be assimilating and losing their English identity; and religious war was once more looming in continental Europe. So, the Puritans looked to move and to build their New Jerusalem in the New World of North America. This was why they self-consciously adopted the term 'Pilgrim' to describe themselves.

Having decided to emigrate to North America, the Pilgrims negotiated with London-based Merchant Adventurers who agreed to finance the expedition and secure royal approval. These backers also insisted on some other individuals (economic migrants) joining the group. After protracted negotiations (which left the Pilgrims owing their backers much unpaid work in order to clear the debt), they finally left the Netherlands and rendezvoused with the other passengers at Southampton. From there, they set out on two ships but, due to the unseaworthiness of one vessel, were forced to put in to south-coast ports for repairs on two occasions. Eventually abandoning one ship, they crowded onto the remaining vessel and the *Mayflower* finally left Plymouth, Devon, on its voyage across the Atlantic and into history.

The passengers on the *Mayflower* were the first wave of what are often simply referred to as 'Puritan' settlers who colonised New England. Most of these early colonists in New England were what are now often called 'non-separating Puritans'. This means that they had no wish to set up separate congregations distinct from the Church of England. However, they wished to enjoy a large degree of semi-autonomy within their individual church communities, while still maintaining nominal loyalty to an over-arching system. In contrast, a fairly small minority of the immigrants to New England were 'separating Puritans', or 'Separatists', who wished to establish congregations outside of any national church structure both in Britain and in North America. At the time such groups were known as 'Brownists', after an early seventeenth-century proponent of Separatism (Robert Browne, died in 1633).[6] In North America, 'Brownism' became a name for Separatists, especially for those who had emigrated from Holland (on the *Mayflower* and later ships) in the 1620s.[7] The Pilgrims were one of these Separatist groups, and it was these arrivals who established the Plymouth Colony in 1620. So, strictly speaking, 'the Pilgrims' is a term describing the particular individuals who arrived in 1620 (and were joined by others over the next few years of that decade), while 'Puritans' describes the much larger groups that followed them in the 1630s. However, we do not need to be too restrictive in the use of this latter term, as a 'Puritan mindset' united all of these groups in a fairly distinctive view of the Bible, the world around them and their special place within God's providential plans. This is shown by the fact that the first arrivals and those who came after them got on fairly well together, despite differences over church organisation. They visited each other's churches and communities and prayed for each other as kindred spirits. This friendly state of affairs frayed at times but generally persisted. These people were part of a broad Puritan community which soon transformed New England. However, it should be noted that a hard-line theocracy was more of a hallmark of those who arrived after 1630. Alongside this, it is worth recalling that these early Pilgrims usually called themselves the 'godly' and the 'saints'. They did this with no sense of irony or reluctance, since they genuinely believed that their communities were superior to the sinful societies around them.

It should be noted that, while these colonists were the first English settlers in New England, they were not the first English settlers in North America. In 1585, an English colony had been established at Roanoke, in what is now North Carolina, but it failed and was soon abandoned. In 1587 another attempt was made to revive the settlement but it too met with failure and the complete disappearance of all the colonists. Not surprisingly, this became known as the 'Lost Colony'. A similar failure occurred at a place named Cuttyhunk, in Massachusetts, in 1602, where the fort there was swiftly abandoned. However, despite the total disaster at Roanoke and the disappointment at Cuttyhunk, other attempts at North American colonisation were more successful. The most famous of these was the settlement established at Jamestown in 1607, in Virginia, by the London (or Virginia) Company. As a result, it became the first permanent English settlement in North America.

Consequently, it was to Virginia Colony that the *Mayflower* and its passengers were heading in 1620. But bad weather and treacherous seas prevented them from getting to the northernmost part of the colony (then stretching as far north as the Hudson River) and so they turned back to Cape Cod. It was to be a fateful (or providential) turn of events. Virginia Colony was a commercial enterprise, poorly run by (mostly male) economic migrants, who had poor relationships with local Native Americans. In contrast, the colony established at Plymouth in 1620 was based on families and was overwhelmingly a godly enterprise (despite including some economic migrants). Its aim was to build a New Jerusalem of holy communities living in the American wilderness.

In the first winter, half of those who had arrived in November 1620 died of illness and exposure. And yet the colony survived. The

Pilgrims carved a life out of the wilderness in a strange land; they raised their homesteads; they explored and traded; they faithfully prayed and worshipped in good times and in bad. Making friends with local Native Americans – who were looking for allies, in their own local rivalries with other tribes – the English newcomers learned how to plant corn and use the resources of the sea and the land. As a result, it was English and Native Americans who sat down together to enjoy a Harvest Home meal in the autumn of 1621: the first so-called 'Thanksgiving', the marking of which is now such an important part of November in the USA. All in all, it was the stuff of which myths are made.

AN EXPLOSION OF PURITAN SETTLEMENT

Despite the fame of the Pilgrims who arrived in 1620, most of the godly emigrants to North America travelled there between 1630 and 1640. Unlike the Separatists in Plymouth, these were 'non-separating Puritans'. This period has become known as 'the Great Migration'. During this time 'non-separating Puritans' established the Massachusetts Bay Colony in 1629 (which would soon have Boston as its chief town); New Hampshire in 1629; Connecticut Colony in 1636; and the New Haven Colony in 1638.

Among these godly Puritan colonists, the most important migration occurred in 1630. It was then that John Winthrop led the so-called 'Winthrop Fleet', made up of 700 colonists travelling on eleven ships. This great movement, which soon led to the founding of the town and port at Boston, was encouraged by the fact that the Plymouth Colony, further south, had survived its turbulent first years: a godly New England really was possible.

The 'Great Migration' ended in 1642 when Charles I put a stop to emigration. It had become clear that a rather lax royal oversight of the westward movement was allowing Puritan settlers (enemies of King Charles's form of High Church Anglicanism) to dominate the North American colonies. But by then it was rather too late, as between 1629 and 1642 approximately 21,000 Puritans had moved from England to New England. Of these, roughly 13,000 had settled in the Massachusetts Bay area. New England belonged to the Puritans, and this would have far-reaching consequences.

LIFE IN THE BIBLE COMMONWEALTHS OF NEW ENGLAND

There were things about life in the Puritan communities that stand out dramatically and which were to resonate down the years. The first was their sense of godly exceptionalism. The fundamental nature of the new colonies was made clear by Winthrop's manifesto, which was entitled 'A Model of Christian Charity'. It declared:

> We are a Company professing ourselves fellow members of Christ, in which respect only, though we were absent from each other many miles, and had our employments as far distant, yet we ought to account ourselves knit together by this bond of love, and live in the exercise of it … We must be knit together in this work as one man.[8]

It is abundantly clear from Winthrop's words that this was not going to be just another commercial venture. The word 'Model' in the title of the manifesto indicated the new settlement's nature as an archetype and an ideal. It was going to be spiritually distinct and an example to the world. For, as Winthrop explained to his companions on the sea voyage to North America, their colony should be a 'city upon a hill' (quoting Jesus in Matthew 5: 14–16). That phrase would run and run and we will come across it again and again as we trace the trajectory of Puritan influence on the USA. There are echoes of it in Donald Trump's speech in Pensacola, Florida, in November 2018, when he declared that 'pioneers and visionaries raised up gleaming cities by the sea'. This was more than just a passing reference to Florida real estate and condominiums. The imagery reached back into the past, hence the reference to 'pioneers and visionaries'. It also echoed more exact quotations of Winthrop's actual words, such as when Ronald Reagan famously borrowed the very same phrase ('a city upon a hill') when articulating his vision for the USA in 1980,[9] and again in 1989.[10] President John F. Kennedy had done this earlier, which is particularly ironic given the way that Puritans regarded Catholics. In such references these later politicians connected with the aims of the seventeenth-century Puritan settlers, who believed that, far from the control of the English bishops and the English king, a New Jerusalem really might be raised in the context of the New World. It was a powerful contribution to the concept of American exceptionalism. That it was originally expounded by immigrants and asylum seekers is an irony lost on many (including President Trump) who reference it today. Such is the complexity of history as it is mined and quarried by later generations.

This sense of being on the right side of history – or, as they would have described it, being in line with God's providence – inspired a supreme sense of confidence as the Pilgrims stamped their ownership on the land. The settlers at Plymouth in 1620–21 had survived partly because they inherited overgrown fields left by Native Americans who had died of European diseases brought by passing fishermen. But despite this, this group and especially the settlers up the coast in Massachusetts Bay Colony soon imposed a very distinct form of land management on New England. Fenced villages became the norm, rather than life in dispersed homesteads. This fencing-in of land became a key feature of their settlements. God-given ownership was being laid out for all to see. It was being stamped on the land itself. Puritans contrasted their fenced and 'productive' fields with what they considered to be the 'laziness' of Native Americans with their mixed economy of agriculture and hunter-gathering which left much of the land – as it appeared to the Europeans – as untouched and unused.

The early English Puritan settlements were relatively self-sufficient and they were less integrated into wider trading networks than other settler communities in the expanding English empire elsewhere around the world. Alongside this relative isolation, they were more socially homogeneous and, of course, deeply religious. They were highly distinctive and, consequently, more ordered and unified as a group than the other seventeenth-century European colonies in North America.[11] As we shall see, this was more than a geographical and economic characteristic; it also had ideological implications. The historian Michael Zuckerman has called them 'a totalitarianism of true believers'.[12] While the isolation would not last, the idea of a tight-knit and ideologically distinct community would.

This confidence also revealed itself in the Pilgrim attitude towards those who did not form part of their godly commonwealth. At first, the Pilgrims at Plymouth enjoyed generally good relations with Native Americans and kept no slaves. But this approach did not last; as the more numerous settlers further north in Massachusetts Bay expanded inland, conflicts with local tribes developed. In the second generation of settlers this drew in the once more tolerant colony at Plymouth too. And when it did, it assumed an almost exterminatory character, which was rooted in the settlers' selective use of the Bible (almost always the Old Testament). This attitude first revealed itself in their interpretation of the Native American mortality in the face of European diseases. In parts of New England this had resulted in mortality rates of 90 per cent. This was seen as a sign of God's providence. John Winthrop expressed it succinctly in a letter he wrote in 1634: 'God hath hereby cleared our title to this place'.[13] John White, who supported the settlements but never made it to America, referred to providential 'defoliation', which had left the eastern coast-lands 'void'.[14] The image was that of 'weeds' cleared to make room for 'better growth'. And, as we have seen, the godly colonists believed in private property. They expected the immediate and permanent vacation of any land purchased from local tribes. By way of contrast, Native Americans did not consider that selling a piece of land meant granting exclusive and permanent ownership to the purchaser. Two worlds were on a collision course. This was accelerated by a settler attitude which rapidly assumed prior rights to any land they desired. The New England Puritan writer Increase Mather wrote, in 1676, of 'the Heathen People amongst whom we live, and whose Land the Lord God of our Fathers has given to us for a rightful possession'.[15] Not a lot of ambiguity there.

Well before Mather wrote this, violence had already occurred. An early example was in 1623, when a military force from Plymouth went north to aid settlers at Wessagusset Colony in a pre-emptive strike which involved the killing of Native American leaders invited to a meal. A larger outbreak of violence occurred in 1636, when war broke out between the New England settlers and the Pequot tribe. In 1637 a Pequot settlement on the Mystic River was utterly destroyed in an action which saw no mercy extended to non-combatants. In 1638, in a publication entitled *Newes From America*, Captain John Underhill, who had witnessed the massacre, wrote that

> many were burnt in the Fort, both men, women, and children, others forced out, and came in troopes to the Indians [local allies of the English], twentie, and thirtie at a time, which our souldiers received and entertained with the point of the sword; downe fell men, women, and children.[16]

He then added, in a justification which characteristically drew on Old Testament rather than New Testament Christian parallels, 'sometimes the Scripture declareth women and children must perish with their parents … We had sufficient light from the word of God for our proceedings'.[17]

Estimates of the Native American casualties range from 400 to 700 men, women and children.[18] The Native American allies of the English were shocked; this was a new kind of war. They would soon experience much more of it.

In 1675 resentment at English behaviour and loss of land led a number of tribes to join together in what became known as King

Philip's War. It raged from 1675 to 1678, and saw approximately twelve frontier towns destroyed and large numbers of homesteads burnt.[19] The war rapidly spread across what is now Massachusetts, Rhode Island, Connecticut and as far north as Maine. Only Connecticut survived without the devastation of other areas, due to its alliance with local tribes holding firm. Large numbers of settlers were killed across New England; but these numbers were dwarfed by the number of Native Americans who were massacred and those survivors that were enslaved. It was an exterminatory policy. Even Native American Christian converts were rounded up and imprisoned on Deer Island in Boston harbour, where 50 per cent died.[20] It was an indication of things to come as the colonies later expanded westward. And this exterminatory expansion was accompanied by a sense of cultural and, indeed, spiritual superiority. This was not inevitable. In Pennsylvania, Quakers (themselves persecuted in New England) had a much better relationship with Native Americans. Extermination was not the only option on the table. But it would become the option of choice as the years unfolded, however it was disguised in official statements.

This fear of 'the other' and the intolerance of 'difference' became a feature of the semi-theocracy established at Massachusetts Bay (far more so than at Plymouth). Social control was maintained through 'fierce gossip, defamatory and often obscene billboards, and court suits. In one town, 20 per cent of the adults in each decade found themselves charged with an offense, usually a morals violation.'[21] Moral and social conformity was policed by mutual surveillance in a conscious effort to restrict the corrosive influence of sinful behaviour. Isolation from home communities in England left the settlers free to develop these trends. It 'insured that American Puritanism would remain more severe (and, frequently, more intellectually subtle and rigorous) than that which they had left behind'.[22] In the area administered by the authorities in Boston a number of Quakers were hanged (though it should be noted, not in Plymouth Colony). They were Christian versions of 'the other' and as such were not regarded as 'Christians' at all. Even Puritans who were too independent in their outlook (such as the preacher Roger Williams, in 1636) or who exhibited a tendency to receive revelations from God alongside their study of scripture (such as Anne Hutchinson, in 1638) could find themselves expelled. In this way, the breakaway colonies at what became Portsmouth, Rhode Island, and Rhode Island and Providence Plantations came into existence where relative freedom of religion was practised. Something deeply intolerant was being worked into the identity of the settlers, alongside the positive virtues of holiness, hard work and American grit. Even among the godly congregations, those who tried but could not quite achieve the appropriate level of spiritual holiness would be excluded. Membership of the local church was restricted to those who had publicly confessed their experience of conversion and were able to persuade church authorities that this was genuine. And in such situations it was not long before a sense of the existence of 'spiritual outsiders' exploded into violence, as in the Salem witch hunt in 1692–93.

In January 1692, a group of young girls in Salem Village, north of Boston, claimed to be possessed by the devil and exhibited fits and bouts of screaming. They accused several local women of witchcraft: a Caribbean slave named Tituba; and two other women: an unpopular beggar named Sarah Good and the poor and elderly Sarah Osborne. Good and Osborne protested their innocence but Tituba 'confessed' and named other 'witches' in the community. The situation escalated and other individuals were dragged into the conspiracy. Unspoken spiritual anxieties, long dormant in the repressive community, burst out in vocal accusations. In June, the first 'witch' was hanged, and between then and September she was followed by eighteen others, with many more accused and awaiting trial. Then, from October, the hysteria began to subside. The calming of the situation was accelerated when so-called 'spectral evidence' (testimony involving dreams and visions) was no longer deemed admissible in court. In May 1693, those still held in prison were pardoned and released. The hysteria was finally over. In January 1697, the Massachusetts General Court declared a day of fasting for those who had been victims of the trials. It had been an ugly and shocking episode and all too deeply rooted in the intense fervour of the community. While it was not to be repeated in this extreme form, the tendency to exclude and condemn did not vanish and remained a potent force within the legacy bequeathed from these formative years.

Social control in the settler communities revealed itself in many other ways. Within the home, male headship was the clear model, and this was reflected in the names carried by women, such as 'Be-Fruitful', 'Fear', 'Patience', 'Prudence' and 'Silence'. It is not hard to see what lessons some individuals in modern-day America have drawn from this patriarchal model. At the same time, while the Puritans had a positive view of the place of sex within marriage, there was an assumption that childbirth and home-making were the key female roles. Giving birth to between seven and ten children was the norm and these were usually born at two-year intervals.[23] Evidence suggests that one in ten children died during the colonial era.[24] By the 1630s, death in childbirth led to a situation whereby men outnumbered women by a ratio of three to two. The female role centred on running the household under the authority of her husband; and this was summed up in the Puritan descriptor of 'goodwife', which was often abbreviated to 'goody'. Overall, women were regarded as 'weaker vessels' with a greater tendency to sin. The social control of women was accompanied by strong condemnation of fornication (as committed by both sexes) and homosexuality (which was punishable by death). There was also opposition to gambling, excessive drinking and working on the Sabbath. Social control was very much within the cultural DNA of the Puritans.

The Puritan communities also exhibited a strident millenarian focus on the imminent second coming of Christ, which still reverberates in the modern Protestant evangelical churches in the US, more so than it does in churches in the UK. It is a legacy that can be seen today in climate change denial; opposition to gun control; Christian conspiracy theory; and the political agenda regarding the Middle East (where conflict may simply be seen as part of 'End Time' events) and where the movement of the US embassy to Jerusalem, regardless of its consequences, is very much in line with this outlook. But more on this as our story unfolds.

With regard to government, a strange situation developed whereby, while church and state were separate, it was clear which was meant to influence which. A document entitled 'The Cambridge Platform' (1648) expressed the Puritan position concerning church government. It laid down that the civil magistrates had no power to intervene in church affairs, unless a congregation was considered to have seriously sinned. In practice a semi-theocracy was established in Massachusetts Bay, in which church ministers enjoyed huge political influence. This characteristic of a separate church and state – but one in which the churches expect a place at the table when it comes to political decision-making – continues to be a marked characteristic of the USA, to which we will return.

This system was accompanied by an emphasis on 'choice' and 'contract', whereby people both chose freely to be part of a community and had rights and obligations as members. This had its roots in the so-called 'Mayflower Compact', signed in November 1620, which drew together all the (male) signatories in a joint enterprise. They were, they stated, carrying out the venture 'for the Glory of God and advancement of the Christian faith'. They promised to 'Covenant and Combine ourselves together into a Civil Body Politic, for our better ordering and preservation'; setting up laws and public offices 'for the general good of the Colony, unto which we promise all due submission and obedience'.[25] These were powerful sentiments, which would later see their most potent expression in the US Constitution.

These early developments in the organisation of the settler communities extolled the virtues of an educated, active and engaged citizenry, aware of its status as well as its obligations. It is revealing that, within just six years of the start of the Great Migration in 1630, Harvard College was founded (taking this name in 1638). The prominence of such virtues can also be linked to the Puritan ideal of believers studying the Bible and being able to understand

and express their own beliefs. Among such a precocious population, it was a short step to questioning, challenging and even distrusting centralised authority. A powerful cultural feature was being established.

What is clear from all of this is that the seventeenth-century Puritan legacy was distinct and striking. It was to continue to contribute to the developing North American colonies as the eighteenth century unfolded, and as these colonies eventually broke away from Britain. Far from ending, as the seventeenth century drew to its close and royal authority asserted itself in New England, the Puritan contribution to America was only just beginning.

CHAPTER TWO

THE PURITAN LEGACY IN THE EIGHTEENTH CENTURY

As the seventeenth century gave way to the eighteenth, the Bible Commonwealths of New England found themselves forming one stream, among a number of streams, flowing into the expanding colonies of North America. The Puritans, of whatever persuasion, were no longer calling the shots in New England. And as European expansion spread beyond the Puritan heartland on the east coast, the influence of Puritan politics and Puritan culture was challenged. In fact this had started in the last decades of the seventeenth century, following the restoration of the Stuart monarchy in Britain in 1660.

At first, the Stuart Restoration did not seriously challenge Puritan power in the New World. Continued religious stress in Britain after 1660 led to some Protestants emigrating from Ireland to North America. These were the Scotch-Irish, who had benefited from Cromwellian interventions in the troubled island of Ireland in the 1650s, and their emigration preceded the much larger Irish Catholic emigration by almost two centuries. Some also shifted from Bermuda to North America. It has been estimated that approximately 10,000 Bermudians – of a godly persuasion – had immigrated to the mainland before the American Declaration of Independence in 1776. The majority of godly Bermudians ended up in colonies south of Virginia but a few relocated to the Bahamas, where they ended up in the colony of Eleuthera, which had been founded there as early as 1648.

PURITANISM IN CHANGING TIMES

Back in New England, though, things were also changing. At first this benefited the theocratically inclined settlers around Boston. Within a couple of decades of the establishment of the port and its associated satellite settlements, non-separating Puritan settlers in the Massachusetts Bay area outnumbered Plymouth's Separatist population by somewhere in the region of ten to one. While the Pilgrims of Plymouth were to have a massive impact on the mythology of what would one day become the USA, it was the settlers up the coast who contributed most to the Puritan current. So much so that Massachusetts Bay finally absorbed Plymouth Colony in 1691.

But by then the heyday of Puritan political semi-independence was over. The godly experiment in semi-theocratic government was brought to heel by the British crown. As far back as 1684 the Massachusetts Bay charter had been annulled by royal decisions made back in London. Then, from 1686, the various colonies of New England were unified as the Dominion of New England. Theocracy was brought under royal authority and curtailed. In 1689 power was briefly wrested back to the colonies but, in 1691, King William III issued another charter which unequivocally unified the colonies under royal authority. This area was styled the Province of Massachu-setts Bay. More fundamental for Puritan politics than a name and boundary change was the decision imposed on the province which extended voting rights to non-Puritans. This was a game-changer. The move effectively put an end to the godly semi-theocracy. But it would not erase it from the cultural and mythological national memory of either those who regarded themselves as the godly or the eventual nation of the USA. The effect of the Puritan belief system was out of all proportion to the numbers of people involved in the original New England settlement. The Puritan legacy would help flavour the eventual rebellion against British rule and the US Constitution which accompanied it.

At the same time as the political map of New England was being rebranded and reorganised, other changes were occurring within the Puritan world. As we saw earlier, in the case of Salem in 1692 (see Chapter One), the godly semi-theocracies of New England were facing disconcerting social and cultural changes before the end of the seventeenth century. It was these changes that fed into the in-famous witch hunts there. The Puritan Bible Commonwealths were finding that their New Jerusalem was being assailed from within and from without. Export trading networks and increased connectivity with other communities meant they were no longer isolated bas-tions of godliness. But changes from within the community were equally unsettling as the entry standards for church membership were lowered due to the lack of sufficient male members. Women were outnumbering men and second- and third-generation New Englanders (whether male or female) did not always possess the righteous zeal of the 'First Comers'. As a result, so-called 'Halfway

Covenants' began to be introduced from the 1660s, whereby baptised but 'unconverted' parents could have their children baptised, while the parents were denied the other privileges of full church membership (such as voting rights and access to leadership positions). Such individuals were classed as 'unconverted' because, while they came from godly families, they could not point to a personal conversion experience. Just believing the correct things, and living godly lives, were not considered sufficient evidence of spiritual regeneration. The move diluted something of the exclusive sectarianism that had been such a characteristic of the early communities in New England and it drew more people into the life of the church. That, though, was not enough to satisfy the spiritual hard-liners who longed for clear blue water between the elect and the unregenerate. Churches split over the issue of greater accessibility (or 'the sell-out' as some would have regarded it) and dissatisfaction with the new status quo was one of the things that fed into the revivalism leading to the First Great Awakening (more on this later).

Other changes were also discernible: New England citizens began petitioning for divorce; some moved to other settlements and fragmented the godly communities; and a greater degree of religious diversity was forced on New England as increased royal control broke down the monopoly on power enjoyed by the Puritans.[1] In such a changing and fluid social and cultural environment it became increasingly difficult to rigidly police the standards of personal behaviour that had once been taken for granted among the saints. All in all, it meant that within perhaps two generations of the original settlers in the 1620s and 1630s, the New Jerusalem seemed as distant as ever, and the formative years became increasingly regarded as something of a lost 'golden age' to be returned to if that were possible. Such is the nature of perceived 'golden ages', but the sense of the need to restore that which had been lost became a major feature of the Puritan psyche from 1700 onwards. And it would be an exclusive and rather rearward-looking angst that would be bequeathed from it to the cultural DNA of the emerging USA. The past golden age of godliness has been lost, but can somehow be restored. Lost purity can be rediscovered. Donald Trump's 'Make America Great *Again*' is the inheritor of such a mythical view of history. As they say: 'Nostalgia isn't what it used to be.'

Sectarian strife and conflict was declining, but it was at the cost of Puritanism itself. By the late 1700s, the godly churches had become more open 'centers of worship that could maintain a measure of peacefulness simply because the discontented could leave and join, or form, another group [church] whenever they pleased'.[2] The loss of godly unity was the price paid for reduced social tension. But this itself led to more community anxiety. The changing, splitting and reforming churches were becoming 'Congregationalist' in a way that reflected developments that were also occurring in England. Once-dominant groups were becoming one denomination among many in an increasingly diverse society. No longer was there one definable theocratic community, and this only added to anxieties in certain quarters.

EIGHTEENTH-CENTURY PURITAN COMMUNITIES AND THE FIRST GREAT AWAKENING

Once the communities of New England were firmly under English royal control, cities such as Boston became noticeably more cosmopolitan. By the late 1740s, three groupings could be identified among the once-united Puritan communities. There were the 'Old Lights', the 'Old Calvinists' and the 'New Lights'.

The Old Lights referred to the large number of Congregational-ist churches in New England who moderated their strict Calvinism in attempts to win new members. They had adapted to survive but were accused of compromising with the world.

Those fellowships who stuck closely to the older Calvinist tra-ditions became known as Old Calvinists. They were the die-hards who had attempted to keep the older pattern of beliefs and church practices alive in a changing world.

Then, in the 1730s and 1740s, there occurred the first of a number of religious revivals that swept across the New England communi-ties. Known as the 'First Great Awakening', the leaders of the first revival included the American Jonathan Edwards and the English minister George Whitefield. It involved a deep personal sense of the need for God's forgiveness and often accompanied life-changing experiences, which resulted in transformed conduct, personal piety and enthusiasm (a word regarded with suspicion in the eighteenth century by more traditional believers). The followers of this more outward-looking and evangelical Calvinism became known as the New Lights. Not all, it should be noted, were Calvinists, since the emerging Methodist communities were largely Arminian (i.e. they did not accept the Calvinist doctrine of predestination).

The movement which flowed out of the Great Awakening en-sured that the Puritan legacy gained a new buoyancy and influence, and it revived many of the personal and cultural traits associated with the earlier period of settlement. It also flowed across the boundaries of individual church communities and created something of a common evangelical identity that would have a lasting effect on large areas of the church in the eventual USA (as in the UK). Its emphasis on 'New Birth', on the personal experience of the working of the Holy Spirit and on an assurance of salvation had a number of effects.

Firstly, the Great Awakening was personally deeply empowering for those who experienced it. It led to enhanced confidence and a sense of regeneration and spiritual status. For many, it created a great deal of self-belief. This was by no means inevitable but, for some, such a behavioural pattern was apparent.

Secondly, it established a boundary between those who had been (as they termed and defined it) 'Born Again' and those who had not (again as usually defined by those who laid claim to that status for themselves). As a result, it was both uniting and divisive as a cultural phenomenon.

In the North American colonies, the Great Awakening caused both the Congregational and Presbyterian churches to split over the acceptance or rejection of the movement. As such, it fragmented some communities, even as it also united Born Again believers across denominational boundaries. Consequently, it strengthened the emerging Methodist movement and the already established Baptist denominations. The Great Awakening had little impact on most Lutherans and on the Quakers, and it seems to have bypassed the small number of Catholic communities.[3]

The Great Awakening set a pattern for religious revival and for a particular outlook which would continue to influence later generations and remains a distinct feature of US evangelical Christian communities in the twenty-first century. These features included personal spiritual assurance, exclusivity and a sense of exceptionalism, but also a sense of mission to convert others and to bring society into line with what was defined as Christian holiness. The Puritans would have recognised many of these features, even if they would have been less convinced by experiences of personal revelation and the personal authority claimed as a result.

Consequently, even as its influence became diluted and contested, Puritanism continued to influence the American outlook. The Boston pastor and theologian Jonathan Edwards (1703–58) and his disciple Samuel Hopkins (1721–1803), played a major role in reviving Puritan thought and kept it active and influential until 1800. While some historians would point to the gradual decline in power of Congregationalism in the North American colonies, Presbyterians led by the New Jersey minister Jonathan Dickinson (1688–1747) and Baptists led by the Massachusetts pastor Isaac Backus (1724–1806) 'revitalized Puritan ideals in several denominational forms through the 18th century'.[4]

All of this had a number of cultural effects which can be traced from the eighteenth century onwards among a significant number of American Christians through various strands of Protestantism.

The first was rooted in the well-established tradition of the Puritan sermon, denouncing contemporary sin and calling for a future transformation. Such a style of proclamation is sometimes termed a 'jeremiad' and takes its name from the Old Testament prophet, Jeremiah. The jeremiad would become firmly part of the literary and rhetorical character of North America, as we shall see.

The second was a rebooting of the Puritan emphasis on sin and salvation, and also on a personal and individual calling and sense of conversion. It was the decline in this that had led to the controversial Halfway Covenants. As it did among the emigrating Puritans of the 1620s and 1630s, this rapidly became closely associated with a sense of exceptional national destiny. Firmly entrenched and built on Puritan foundations, this sense was buttressed by the eighteenth-century revolution against British rule. It was reinforced (if unconsciously) by the presence of the alien other, in the form of Native Americans, as well as those Americans who were classified as spiritually unregenerate.

Once a community felt assured of its exceptionalism – and that was clearly felt within the American colonies – it became relatively easy to read one's own experiences as being played out in the context of God's providence. This was derived from the belief that God's righteousness and his sovereignty directed all things; human affairs were ordered by the exercise of God's will. Studying the pattern of events, it was believed, would reveal how God guided things to a discernible end. For the Bible-believing Puritans and for their descendants, God revealed his providential will in many ways: principally through the Bible, but it was also discernible in natural forces and events.

Actively reading the Bible, listening to sermons given by experts in biblical matters, analysing natural signs and also unusual events (like earthquakes and storms) could reveal God's will. This was further enhanced by reflection on personal experiences of prosperity, or calamity. For anyone doing well out of life, it was easy to read this as a sign of God's approval. On the other hand it was also easy to interpret the defeat or sufferings of others as signs of divine disapproval. Such a mental framework had already been deployed in the seventeenth century in order to explain the demise of Native Americans through European diseases. In the eighteenth century it was reinforced by the successful territorial expansion of the North American colonies and their eventual victory over the British. In this, the shaping of what would eventually be termed 'manifest destiny' in the next century was readily apparent. And, in its boost to the moral self-confidence of the successful, it overflowed the boundaries of religious belief and was more than capable of being embraced in contexts that were more secular.

This framework influenced the non-religious outlook that increased within the eighteenth-century Enlightenment. Biblical study and also examination of the natural world for evidence of God's nature and actions continued to stimulate the growth of education, as was alluded to in Chapter One in relation to the early establishment of the university at Harvard. Given the deeply spiritual nature of the early Puritan communities, this contribution to the eighteenth-century emphasis on human beings as rational creatures, able to make sense of the world through reasoned examination, may seem surprising. However, on reflection, it is not contradictory. Since God was conceived as the rational creator of a rational universe, which bore the hallmarks of his nature to those who studied it, and since human beings were regarded as being made in the image of God, the Puritan world could encompass both the pursuit of supernatural signs and spiritual manifestations and the systematic study of the Bible and the natural order and the logical thought which accompanied it. This applied to the inner life of mental contemplation as much as to the community life of ordered holiness. This was underscored by a churchmanship that lacked central human hierarchical structures and, instead, emphasised the priesthood of all believers and a direct personal relationship with God.

By the eighteenth century, this Puritan rationalism had come to provide intellectual comfort to many who, otherwise, might have felt a sense of confusion and uncertainty in a world where predestination decided eternal issues, and where God was beyond understanding given the flawed state of the fallen human nature. The two trends (positive and negative) were always conflicting, but the former was beginning to outweigh the influence of the latter. This emphasis on personal responsibility to make sense of the world and to discipline one's thoughts and actions is an often-overlooked stream flowing into the Enlightenment of the eighteenth century and is too often labelled as a secular phenomenon divorced from its Christian roots. This was so, even if for some it took them outside the boundaries of traditional Christianity into Deism and beyond. What is clear is that the Puritan legacy included an energetic and focused mental outlook that could exist outside the framework of the religious beliefs of the godly. Such self-assured ideas had legs, and could run!

Such a sense of moral self-confidence – once conversion was assured – combined with individual dynamism and a strong work ethic, produced a culture of entrepreneurialism, colonial pride and competitiveness. It 'would be eventually identified by others as the spirit of what foreigners called "Yankees"'.[5] As such, it had deep roots. Its contribution to what one might loosely call an 'American national character' in the twenty-first century goes beyond simply stereotyping. It is in the cultural DNA, even if not in the real DNA, of Americans. It is a cultural construct, and it owes much to the Puritan experience which was then revived in the Great Awakening. For, while traditional Calvinists had rejected human works as a means to salvation, by the eighteenth century the concept of hard work as an outworking of being saved was well established. It could even become unofficially seen as evidence of salvation (indicating God's approval). Capitalist free enterprise would later benefit from this outlook.

THE PURITAN CONTRIBUTION TO THE AMERICAN REVOLUTION

Puritan heritage revealed itself in other formative experiences in colonial North America. When the British Parliament passed the Boston Port Act in 1774 (in response to the Boston Tea Party) and attempted to force the port to compensate the royal treasury and the East India Company for the losses incurred due to the actions of the rebellious colonists, the response in the colony was revealing.[6] A number of local ministers announced a traditional Puritan fast day and preached against the British crown as a tool of 'Satan' which had unleashed King George, 'the great Whore of Babylon', to ride her 'great red dragon' upon America.[7] The language was taken from the verbal toolbox of millenarianism which had been used by earlier saints to condemn their enemies in prophetic terms drawn from the Bible. It was the kind of outlook that had taken Puritan settlers to the New World in the first place, and now it was being deployed against King George III, rather than Charles I. The afterlife of the Puritan mindset and its language could not have been more vividly made apparent. As we shall see, this apocalyptic mindset and the use of millenarian language can still be discerned in evangelical churches in North America today; although in the twenty-first century the targets are different.[8] However, the mood music remains the same, as does the ready use of prophetic denunciations of those judged to be enemies of godliness. And those so judged and condemned can find themselves subject to personal prejudices and contemporary political ideologies as in the past. It is difficult to imagine that when John penned the Book of Revelation in the late first century on the island of Patmos, he had King George III in mind. But that did not stop the apocalyptic denunciation by the Puritans in 1774; nor does it today.

As the colonies and Britain came to blows in the later eighteenth century, the influence of the Puritans came to be seen in that most quintessential US document: the US Constitution. The act of coming together to establish a new political community had long roots. When the *Mayflower* Pilgrims formed what we now call the Mayflower Compact in November 1620, they were behaving in a way that was familiar to members of the Puritan gathered churches. For when such people broke free from existing religious orthodoxy it was common for them to 'covenant' in order to form a new community. This was based on the biblical evidence that God enters into covenants with his chosen people. Indeed, it was the existence of such covenants that constituted the basis of the identity of such chosen people of God. It was significant that the Christian Bible was, and is, divided into an Old Testament and a New Testament, in which the word 'testament' signifies a 'defining statement' or 'declaration of will'. In the biblical case it was used in the sense of 'a covenant or dispensation'.[9] The word conveyed the idea of an agreement, or a compact, between God and his people: the Jews of the Old Testament (Old Covenant), and the non-ethnic Christian community, the church of the New Testament (the New Covenant). In fact, the Greek word that lay behind the concept of the 'church' meant a community gathered for a common purpose. No wonder that the Pilgrims and the other Puritans used signed covenants and declarations to communicate the idea that they were willingly coming together to form a new community.

A longer-term legacy of this arose from the Puritan devotion to orderliness, to disciplined conduct, to rules of moral behaviour and to a fenced landscape. The concept of written rules and clearly established moral boundaries, designed to promote both the pursuit of personal godliness as well as community cohesion and social holiness, fed into the later determination to create written constitutions. As will be seen, what was to emerge in the American Revolution of the late eighteenth century was a lineal descendant of Bible study, guides to right living and the characteristic picket fences of the rigidly ordered seventeenth-century Puritan communities.

On top of this, the Mayflower Compact was signed by both 'saints' (Puritan members of the Separatist godly community) and 'strangers' (economic migrants and those unknown to the inner core of the godly). This was important because it was inclusive. It is going too far to describe it as democratic, but it was a big step towards that future ideal. It implied that everyone in the community (well, the men anyway) were members of the political community. They created self-government, a sovereign group in a civil society. It was, in effect, a social contract, which was established some thirty years before Thomas Hobbes explored social contract theory; and a generation earlier than John Locke did the same.[10] And it was well over a century before Jean-Jacques Rousseau also theorised about the ideal basis of a political community in similar terms.[11]

To cut a very long story short, social contract theory assumed that law and political order are not natural phenomena, but, instead, are human creations. The agreement, described as a social contract (whether based on a real event, a hypothetical past or an abstract assumption), led to benefits for the individuals involved. It then remained legitimate to the extent that those involved in the contract fulfilled their part in the agreement. As Hobbes saw it, citizens are not obligated to submit to the rule of government if it is too weak to act effectively and provide protection. Other social contract theorists argued that if government failed to protect what they termed 'natural rights' (this was Locke's take on it) or failed to meet the best interests of civil society (which Rousseau termed the 'general will'), then citizens were free to withdraw their obligation to obey their rulers. Then they were, in effect, free to change their government. Just such an event had, it was argued, occurred in the British 'Glorious Revolution' of 1688, when the political elite had ditched King James II and VII in favour of William and Mary; and it happened on the other side of the Atlantic when the North American colonists abandoned their loyalty to George III and established the republic of the United States of America.

This, of course, was a long way ahead of what the *Mayflower* Pilgrims did and was bound up in a lot of later political theory and reflection; whereas those individuals on the *Mayflower* on that chilly morning of 11 November 1620 were simply trying to get every male on board to accept a common authority and government. It was an expedient action to avoid chaos, rather than an example of ivory-tower political theorising. But the *Mayflower* political arrangement worked. And it endured. At the time it was made, the Pilgrims still considered themselves loyal servants of (what was then) the Stuart monarchy, but what they had created survived the challenges of settlement in North America and the upheavals of the 1640s, 1650s and 1660s, while in Britain the monarchy was replaced by a republic, then a protectorate, then a monarchy was restored. Being a long way from London clearly helped, but the point was made: a sovereign civil community had been formed in North America, through mutual free contract.

When more theocratically inclined settlers arrived up the coast at Boston in the 1630s, they were far less inclusive, but the principle was still in operation; a community was formed by those freely entering into a compact, a covenant, a political and civil agreement. When John Winthrop wrote his famous statement of principles (entitled 'A Model of Christian Charity') on board the ship *Arbella* in 1630, in order to guide the governing of the Colony of Massachusetts Bay, he reminded his listeners that 'it is by a mutual consent, through a special overvaluing providence and a more than an ordinary approbation of the churches of Christ, to seek out a place of cohabitation and consortship under a due form of government both civil and ecclesiastical'.[12]

It was a covenanted community, entered into 'by a mutual consent', which he described as constituting the famous 'city upon a hill' which would, by God's will, so prosper 'that men shall say of succeeding plantations, "may the Lord make it like that of New England"'.

Ideas like these are difficult to control, as George III was later to discover. Even when the governing authorities at Massachusetts Bay were forced to include the less-than-godly in their civil society in the 1690s, the legacy of civil societies, freely entered into, hung about it like smoke above a homestead in a New England clearing. It was not a coincidence that the formal designation of that early New England community was the Commonwealth of Massachusetts. The name may have been chosen by John Adams in the second draft of the Massachusetts Constitution, in 1779,[13] because the term 'commonwealth', at that time, had a whiff of republicanism about it. Virginia had earlier adopted the same designation in 1776, and in the same year Pennsylvania's first state constitution referred to it as both a 'Commonwealth' and a 'State'. Later, in 1786, the citizens of what was then called Kentucky County petitioned the legislature of Virginia for permission to become a 'free and independent state, to be known by the name of the Commonwealth of Kentucky'.[14] On 1 June 1792, Kentucky County officially became a state and today is the only state which was not one of the original Thirteen Colonies that uses the term 'commonwealth' in its name.

The word had assumed a republican characteristic during the republican commonwealth period between the execution of Charles I in 1649 and the Stuart Restoration in 1660. Once again, as with the idea of the compact or contract, it was rooted in a Puritan past that still had potency in the late 1770s. Despite being 'the oldest written organic law still in operation anywhere in the world',[15] the Massachusetts Constitution was not the first to be written among

those states that would soon form the USA. In fact, as relationships with the British crown broke down, eight states had earlier
drawn up constitutions in 1776 and two more followed them in
1777. But the Massachusetts Constitution was influential because
these other states simply revised earlier documents and its writing
inspired the combined revolutionary states as they later shaped the
US Constitution.

For all the echoes in these eighteenth-century American documents of English legal statements, such as Magna Carta (1215), the
Petition of Right (1628) and the Bill of Rights (1689), the simple
reality is that there was no British precedent for the concept of a
formally stated written constitution, as became established in the
Thirteen States in North America (regardless of fairly common
references today to a so-called 'British constitution'). When the
American Revolution occurred, only five of the thirteen colonies
possessed formal charters, although they all had 'memories' of
earlier charters and arrangements designed to establish acceptable
forms of government.[16] What was equally potent was what can be
described as the cultural memory of covenants and civil agreements
dating from the formative Puritan years, even when these were not
consciously referred to in the feverish revolutionary atmosphere of
the 1770s.

In Massachusetts, for example, leaders decided that the creation
of a constitution required the active involvement of a more representative group than those traditionally empowered to vote in
the colony. As a result, property qualifications were not imposed
and all free males who were aged over twenty-one were allowed
to vote for delegates to the convention which eventually framed

the commonwealth's constitution. In reality, Massachusetts did not create a democratic polity employing universal suffrage, in contrast to the much more radical arrangements agreed in Pennsylvania.[17] Nevertheless, the driving force was the idea that what was required was a compact that was freely entered into by all adult males; and with its terms clearly stated in writing. This was certainly in line with the principles enshrined in the Mayflower Compact, even more so than in the exclusive statements of John Winthrop.

Consequently, it was more than simple Enlightenment rationalism that drove the formation of the Declaration of Independence when it was approved by the Continental Congress on 4 July 1776. There was a local and Puritan-derived element to it too. This was despite the fact that, in keeping with the Enlightenment outlook prevalent in 1776, the founders of the American republic separated church and state. Indeed, the US Constitution, which was ratified in 1788, made no mention of religion except stating that no religious test would be used to decide the eligibility of office holders. The First Amendment to the US Constitution, which was adopted in 1791, defined the commitment of the federal government to the completely free exercise of religion. Furthermore, it prohibited the establishment of an official church. So far, so secular. And yet the unreferenced origins of the covenant concept embodied in the Declaration of Independence are very clear.

Governments are instituted among Men, deriving their just powers from the consent of the governed, That whenever any Form of Government becomes destructive of these ends, it is the Right of the People to alter or to abolish it, and to institute new

Government, laying its foundation on such principles and organizing its powers in such form, as to them shall seem most likely to effect their Safety and Happiness.[18]

There is a definite strand of unstated Puritanism within this feature of the United States of America. It can be compared to the brief content of the Mayflower Compact which – though explicitly Christian in its stated aim of acting 'for the Glory of God and advancement of the Christian faith' – was comparable in its intention to 'Covenant and Combine ourselves together into a Civil Body Politic, for our better ordering and preservation'. Thus empowered, the settlers could, therefore, establish laws in Plymouth Colony and institute public offices, 'for the general good of the Colony, unto which we promise all due submission and obedience'.[19]

This influence is seen again and again in the outlook of key Americans at this seminal time. Benjamin Franklin (1706–90) was born in Boston and came from a committed Puritan family. He was baptised at the Old South Church in the town. Although he combined rationalist beliefs with Puritan-derived concepts, in a form (for a time at least) of Deism, his ideas are shot through with concepts of God, morality and thrift that can be traced back to his Puritan heritage. His belief that the press played a crucial role in instructing Americans in moral virtue reflects much of the seventeenth-century Puritan ideal of the educated and informed believer, actively engaged with the world.

He was not alone in having key aspects of his thought-world shaped, in part at least, by the Puritan heritage of New England. However, this was by no means universal. George Washington himself was an Anglican. During the Revolutionary War he attended services at churches that were associated with a wide range of Christian thought, including: Presbyterians, Quakers, Roman Catholics, Congregationalists, Baptists and Dutch Reformed.[20] After the war he withdrew from the Protestant Episcopal Church of America, which has led some to suggest that his Christianity was not orthodox, or that he was increasingly influenced by Deists. He should probably just be described as a typical eighteenth-century Anglican in a church which had not yet experienced the effects of the evangelical movement until close to Washington's death. But while this founding father was no Puritan, the cultural influence of that earlier movement was not dependent on state support; for it had contributed to the culture of the USA to a remarkable degree.

What is important to remember is that, while in Britain the Stuart Restoration of 1660 meant that Puritans were shut out of political power for almost two centuries (during which time they morphed into a Nonconformity which was more geared to economic activity and social action than political power), things were different in North America. There the children of the seventeenth-century Puritans certainly faced the loss of their cultural dominance, but they were not shut out of political power. In the North American colonies they continued to be political 'insiders', rather than Nonconformist 'outsiders'. This was to have significant ramifications for the future history of the United States.

CHAPTER THREE

AN ENDURING PEOPLE – PURITAN INFLUENCE IN THE NINETEENTH CENTURY

By the nineteenth century the Puritan heritage lay well in the past of the nation that had become the United States of America in the late eighteenth century. However, it continued to influence the character of the USA and to inform both the mythical way that the historic origin of the nation was celebrated and in the way that it justified its dramatic expansion westward. The explicit Puritan brand may have faded somewhat, as other influences came to bear on the churches of North America and as the make-up of its population changed dramatically in the nineteenth century, but its implicit influence endured. In some ways it became more firmly pronounced than ever.

THE NON-RELIGIOUS CHARACTER OF THE NEWLY MINTED AMERICAN STATE: A CURIOUS EXAMPLE

Given the apparent tensions between the current US administration of President Donald Trump and Islam, it is a curious irony that one of the earliest examples of the secular nature of the American state comes from its interaction with a Muslim power. The Treaty of Tripoli was concluded between the USA and Tripolitania and took effect in 1797. Article 11 of this treaty made a statement that would cause shock and alarm among evangelical Christians in the twenty-first century. It unequivocally states:

> As the government of the United States of America is not in any sense founded on the Christian Religion, – as it has in itself no character of enmity against the laws, religion or tranquility of Musselmen [Muslims], – and as the said States never have entered into any war or act of hostility against any Mehomitan [Islamic] nation, it is declared by the parties that no pretext arising from religious opinions shall ever produce an interruption of the harmony existing between the two countries.[1]

The treaty is intriguing, and a little ironic, given the current mood music within US politics. But what this 200-year-old treaty goes to show – as if we had not already perceived this – is that the nature of American religious politics is complex. The USA is an officially secular country. Church and state are officially separate. And yet the impact of the Christian religion on US political discourse is profound. As we look at how this developed in the nineteenth century, we will see that the course of this developing character has had a number of surprising twists and turns. The first twist was one that seemed, on the face of it, capable of derailing the entire Puritan project.

THE SHIFTING THEOLOGY OF THE
NEW ENGLAND CHURCHES

Many of the churches that had been founded in the Puritan heyday of New England experienced a dramatic shift in theology in the later years of the eighteenth century and the early years of the nineteenth. Today this can be seen in many towns in Massachusetts, in that many of the churches bearing names such as 'First Church...' or 'First Parish...' (indicating that they were the first official church in that settlement) are 'Unitarian' or 'Unitarian Universalists'. These churches do not subscribe to belief in the Trinity (God being the Father, Son and Holy Spirit), which has been Christian orthodoxy since the earliest creeds of the church, formulated in the Late Roman Empire.

While the way in which this non-Trinitarian faith in modern Unitarianism varies, the basic premise is that there is one God, but that – although he is inspired by God and acts as saviour of the world – Jesus is not God incarnate (God and Man combined in one person). In short, he is not God. Unitarians differ in how they understand the nature and status of the Holy Spirit, but none subscribe to the Trinitarian concept found in historic Christianity.

This non-Trinitarian monotheism is, arguably, closer to Judaism and Islam than to mainline Christianity as it has explicitly characterised itself since the fourth century. As a result, many mainstream Christian denominations would not describe Unitarians as being 'Christians', as is usually defined.

Unitarianism is also distinctive in that it does not subscribe to a number of other historic Christian doctrines that have featured large in mainstream Christianity over the years, such as original sin, predestination and the infallibility of the Bible. Similarly, few 21st-century Unitarians accept the doctrine of eternal punishment in hell.[2] This makes for a liberal theology that, while similar to that held by some liberal Christians, is still distinctive due to its comprehensive rejection of the Trinity doctrine.

Some (the 'Universalists') have such an open and permissive approach to personal spirituality and belief that their congregations include atheists, agnostics, theists and those who draw inspiration from a wide range of world religions, alongside those who would describe themselves as 'Christians' but who have a very liberal approach to beliefs.[3]

Although modern Unitarianism emerged during the sixteenth- and seventeenth-century Reformation period in Poland, Transylvania and England, from what had once been mainstream Protestant congregations, in North America it developed in many of the Puritan-derived churches to a remarkable degree. The first American congregation to officially move from orthodoxy and accept Unitarianism was King's Chapel in Boston, Massachusetts.[4] It was there that James Freeman (who later became rector) began teaching Unitarian beliefs in 1784, and eventually revised the church's prayer book, so that it reflected Unitarian doctrines, in 1786. A large number of other churches in Massachusetts went the same way.

This was an astonishing shift for believers whose roots lay in an uncompromisingly biblical orthodoxy, expressed in extremely strong Calvinistic beliefs, and adherence to all the historic beliefs of the Universal Church as pertaining to the nature of God.[5] Later conflicts with supporters of more traditional Puritan beliefs led to the election of the Unitarian Henry Ware to the post of Hollis Professor of Divinity at Harvard College in 1805. A number of US Presidents – including John Adams (President 1797–1801), Thomas Jefferson (President 1801–09), James Madison (President 1809–17) and John Quincy Adams (President 1825–29) – were sympathetic to liberal Unitarian beliefs.

As we have seen, the theocrats in Massachusetts Bay vigorously persecuted Quakers for their deeply personal and non-creedal ideas and practices. The road to more liberal (and unorthodox) Christianity was resolutely shut. So, how could such a dramatic change occur just over a century later? It happened for a number of reasons.

There was a reaction against the strict church controls that had been a hallmark of New England Puritanism in the seventeenth century. This was assisted, unintentionally, by the fact that the crown had intervened in the 1690s to bring the colony's government more firmly under its control, which severely restricted the political power of the Puritan preachers. It also meant that more liberal (even heretical) beliefs were harder to control. When the Boston-based theologian Increase Mather died in 1723, the golden age of Puritan control was coming to an end – appropriately, the biography of this New England preacher was entitled *The Last American Puritan*.[6]

Puritanism did not end in New England in 1723, but it was certainly on the defensive. In 1741 Mather's grandson, Samuel, was dismissed from his post as pastor of Old North Church in Boston for being too liberal. But by 1802 this church had formally become Unitarian. Things were certainly in a state of flux.

The congregational nature of the New England Puritan churches made it easier for groups to take control since there was no higher church authority to intervene. A majority could be persuaded by a new preacher, or influenced by a recently published theological tract. Once this happened, the process of change could snowball and rapidly spread from church to church – and it did.

The expanding nature of the trading population of New England (especially in Boston) meant that it became a crossroads of new ideas. Some of these were influenced by the European Enlightenment, which challenged traditional beliefs.

With the American Revolution of the 1770s, a number of (loyalist) ministers in key parishes in the Boston area were forced to leave the emerging United States, which meant that there were multiple churches looking for new leadership.

Unintentionally – having rejected traditional church authority in favour of the personal study of the Bible – some Puritans found that some of the key creeds of the church were not (it seemed) fully developed and expressed there. They began to debate, anew, things that had been officially settled in the church in the fourth century. As a result, the late Roman heresies arose once more. The rest, as they say, is history.[7]

In addition to this, there was the Calvinist emphasis on the unknowable nature of God and, in its most extreme form, on salvation being so dependent on the sovereign power of God that no human contribution was significant. This could have the unintended consequence of undermining specific human statements about the nature of God and could even raise the idea that everyone could be saved.

THE IMPACT OF THESE CHANGES ON US CHRISTIANITY

Why does all this matter? For two main reasons. The most obvious is that it reminds us that the Puritan legacy in the USA is not due to the direct transmission of ideology through an established church. If it was, it would have broken down when this great shift occurred in these historic churches. Instead, it is more a massive contribution to the idea of 'American-ness'. It is ideas – and myth and 'flavour' – that are more widespread, mutable and fluid. That does not rob the legacy of its power. In some ways it adds to its potency.

In the nineteenth century, aspects of this legacy would be developed for political reasons in a changing United States, without even giving a formal nod to the origins of the ideas being promoted. Other uses of the myth, though, would certainly reference the original Puritans (particularly the *Mayflower* Pilgrims), but would tease apart their historic actions from their theology.

Then, in the twentieth and twenty-first century (as we shall see in Chapter Four), the themes of Puritan-inspired renewal, moral probity, American exceptionalism and a peculiarly American evangelical domination of political debates would be advanced by an 'evangelical religious right', which had no claims to being formal descendants of the original Puritan congregations but were certainly their spiritual and cultural heirs.

So, today, the old Puritan heartland of New England is decidedly liberal (both in terms of religion and politics), but the mantle of Puritan heritage has shifted geographically to the southern states and the Midwest ('flyover') states. The 'geography of faith' has changed because ideas can shift, when historic buildings (and their communities) remain rooted in the same old spots. Puritan ideology has legs!

The other reason these changes matter is that the drift into Unitarianism by the early nineteenth century was not without a backlash. In 1834 a new Divinity School was established at Yale, in Connecticut, in order to counter the Unitarian influence at Harvard Divinity School. Other congregations split and founded more orthodox churches in opposition to the Unitarian ones. Some of these specifically included references to 'Puritans' and 'Pilgrims' in their names. Tellingly, at Plymouth, Massachusetts, the 'Church of the Pilgrimage' was built in 1840 after a split from the 'First Parish Plymouth', which had become Unitarian. The old Puritan heritage was not forgotten. And, indeed, the loss of ground in the years around 1800 only strengthened a resolve to defend this heritage which appeared under threat; and burnished the gloss on a perceived 'Puritan Golden Age' which seemed assailed by liberalism and heresy. This sense of being 'under siege' has continued to be apparent among modern Christian groups who look back to their cultural heritage which they consider to be under threat from modern rival ideologies.

A RATHER RELIGIOUS SECULAR STATE

The nineteenth century witnessed huge changes in the character of what had once been a predominantly Protestant nation. Eventually, mass migration from Ireland in the 1840s and 1850s, and then from eastern and southern Europe in the last decades of the century, saw vast numbers of Catholics and Orthodox Christians arrive in the USA, alongside very large numbers of Jewish immigrants. The

apparently secular nature of the USA helped facilitate this movement and their integration as US citizens. Nevertheless, by the
end of the century the Christian nature of the nation was perhaps
more firmly entrenched than in 1800. Indeed, for many of the 'Old
Comers' (descended from the first waves of Anglo settlers), this was
very much a Protestant (once Puritan) heritage, which separated
them from the new arrivals who, it was feared, might challenge
their cultural dominance; in the same way as Catholic arrivals from
Mexico and Central and Southern America are feared in sections of
the modern USA. The unspoken nature of the White Anglo-Saxon
Protestant (WASP) ascendancy was thus ingrained in the outlook
and the discourse of dominant sections of US society. And into that
Protestant character, the Puritan contribution had been significant.

The distinctive religious nature of the USA in the nineteenth
century can be seen in two key court rulings. In 1892, the US
Supreme Court made an intriguing ruling in the Church of the
Holy Trinity *v.* United States, as part of an employment case. The
nub of the issue was over whether the employment of an English
clergyman by a New York church constituted an illegal importation
of foreign labour. The court decided it was not illegal because 'this
is a religious people. This is historically true. From the discovery of
this continent to the present hour, there is a single voice making this
affirmation.'[8] The court went on to list all the Christian-orientated
commissions, grants and charters that had led to colonisation
and a wish to establish Christian religion in North America. This
included 'The celebrated compact made by the pilgrims in the
Mayflower.'[9] Mr Justice Brewer went on to approvingly quote another
ruling (that of the Chief Justice of the Supreme Court of New York,

Chancellor James Kent, in a conviction for blasphemy in People *v.* Ruggles in 1811) to illustrate the point that Christ and Christianity enjoyed a legal protection unlike that extended to 'Mahomet or of the Grand Lama', who were described in that earlier ruling as 'those impostors'.[10]

The significance of the 1811 conviction lay in 'the position that this was a common law crime, transposed to this country [USA] from England, despite a provision in the New York state constitution, similar to that of the First Amendment, disestablishing religion'.[11] The 1892 ruling also spoke to this curiously ambiguous situation whereby, although the USA had no state church, and although freedom of thought and expression was enshrined in the US Constitution and its First Amendment, nevertheless there was something peculiarly Christian about the United States.

This religious ambivalence had deep roots. As far back as 1802, Thomas Jefferson had spoken of 'a wall of separation between Church and State'.[12] This clear principle, as we have seen (in Chapter Two), is contained in the First Amendment to the Constitution of the United States of 1791. Article Six of the US Constitution also specifies that 'no religious Test shall ever be required as a Qualification to any Office or public Trust under the United States'. In fact, Jefferson's words echo those of the seventeenth-century American Baptist Roger Williams, who in 1644 wrote of a 'hedge or wall of separation between the garden of the church and the wilderness of the world'.[13] The theocrats of Massachusetts Bay Colony would not have recognised Williams as one of the godly, but, despite being a Baptist, he clearly was cut from the same Puritan cloth. And in that formative era, church and state were separated, yet church was to have an unofficial input into the actions of the state. It was – and the comparison is not meant to be provocative – analogous to the role of the Communist Party within the USSR. In that situation, the electoral system was theoretically independent and yet the party had the leading role and, behind the scenes, a controlling hand. In the same way, church and state in New England were separate and independent, yet the leaders of the latter were always assumed to be members of the former, and were guided by the ideology of their ministers.

This broke down as theocracy was undermined in the late seventeenth century, but a curious situation survived whereby Christian ideology remained remarkably influential – despite the Enlightenment and the rise of Deism, despite the decline of the Puritan-derived Congregationalist churches, despite the rise of other denominations and despite the influx of different faiths. It was this that the judgments in the legal cases of People *v.* Ruggles and Church of the Holy Trinity *v.* United States revealed. The USA is, to all intents and purposes, a secular republic; and yet Christianity has had a huge input into political conversations and decision-making. It continues to do so. As a result, today few nations 'do God' as openly as the USA, and even the most unlikely of US Presidents and presidential candidates feels the need to share a 'God-moment', no matter how unfamiliar they may seem on religious terrain or how far their values and lifestyles may be from Christian norms. The contribution of New England to the political DNA of the USA lives on.

THE SECOND GREAT AWAKENING

This Christian nature of the USA was greatly enhanced by the 'Second Great Awakening', which influenced large areas of US society between 1800 and the 1830s. It made evangelical outreach and enthusiasm a major part of what it meant to be an American Christian. This added a key ingredient to the cultural contributions already made by the early Puritans. As one historian of the American evangelical tradition has put it:

> Evangelicalism itself, I believe, is a quintessentially North American phenomenon, deriving as it did from the confluence of Pietism, Presbyterianism, and the vestiges of Puritanism. Evangelicalism picked up peculiar characteristics from each strain – warmhearted spirituality from the Pietists (for instance), doctrinal precisionism from the Presbyterians, and individualistic introspection from the Puritans – even as the North American context itself has profoundly shaped the various manifestations of evangelicalism: fundamentalism, neo-evangelicalism, the holiness movement, pentecostalism, the charismatic movement, and various forms of African-American and Hispanic evangelicalism.[14]

In 1800, major revivals began that spread from New England to Kentucky, Tennessee and southern Ohio. The long-lasting religious innovation, produced by the revivals which occurred in Kentucky, was the camp meeting. Camp meetings were, at first, organised by Presbyterians. Historically (in Britain at least) Presbyterians were members of the broad Puritan movement. Prior to this, this influential group had been less influential in North America than the Congregationalists who were the direct descendants of the original Puritan settlers. The idea was then taken up by the Baptists (who had historically been rejected by the Puritan mainstream). When the camp meetings became intensely emotional, the Presbyterians and Baptists began to distance themselves from the phenomenon. However, the idea was then adopted by the Methodists, who injected increased discipline into what had seemed to be getting out of control. By the late 1850s, the idea of the revivalist camp meeting had become ingrained across America and was also well known on the expanding frontier. While this greatly benefited the Methodists, whose system of travelling preachers – the circuit riders – helped them forge strong links with frontier communities, the concept of the 'Awakening' was deeply indebted to the first such Awakening which had swept New England under direct Puritan Congregationalist influence in the eighteenth century.

What this goes to show is that there was great fluidity in the movement of ideas and influences regardless of strict denominational boundaries and doctrinal differences. This fluidity of ideas that, nevertheless, had deep roots can be seen particularly clearly in the case of the so-called manifest destiny.

AMERICAN EXCEPTIONALISM AND MANIFEST DESTINY: THE UNACKNOWLEDGED PURITAN LEGACY

In 1845, a newspaper editor named John L. O'Sullivan coined the term 'manifest destiny' to justify the phenomenon of continental expansion. The phrase first appeared in an editorial published in the July/August 1845 issue of a publication entitled the *United States Magazine and Democratic Review*. Facing up to opposition, which was still being articulated, over the seizing of Texas from Mexico, the piece stated a belief in 'the fulfilment of our manifest destiny to overspread the continent allotted by Providence for the free development of our yearly multiplying millions'. The phrase also appeared, in a comparable context, in the *New York Morning News* of July 1845 (O'Sullivan edited both the *Democratic Review* and the *New York Morning News*). Later that year the same phrase was used with regard to the north-western frontier and settlement in Oregon.

The message was clear: Providence (i.e. God) had given over the North American continent to European-derived settlement and, as seventeenth-century Puritans would have phrased it, God's Providence had 'cleared their title to the land' (see Chapter One). Indeed, a seventeenth-century New England Puritan might almost have written the piece in the *Democratic Review*. What soon became well-known as manifest destiny owed much to both the individualistic personal self-confidence, and the sense of providentially approved community purpose, that was inherited from the Puritan national myth. Something very significant had worked its way into the national DNA; largely because it satisfyingly justified the precocious confidence of a newly minted and assertive state. And it also worked well, for those who articulated it, because it offered a profound justification for economic and cultural self-interest when it came to territorial expansion and the removal of inconveniently placed Native Americans. As far as those who subscribed to it were concerned, manifest destiny held the moral high ground, even as it rode rough shod over the lives and cultures of Native Americans. For a technically non-imperial state, it provided a manifesto for internal imperial expansion. In a similar way, imperial Russia grew its empire 'at home' in the nineteenth century.

In the same way that American exceptionalism and a divinely

sanctioned mission had justified land seizure from Native Americans in the later history of New England, so it was now deployed once more (albeit minus the explicit God references but with a nod to Providence) to justify an expansionist answer to a US population which had risen from around 5 million people in 1800 to more than 23 million by 1850. The need was accelerated by an economic depression which started in 1839. The drive westward to gain new land seemed a pressing matter, and it became explicitly buttressed by a sense of being at the cutting edge of history and inevitability.

The phenomenon of expansion was not a new one in the 1840s. As early as 1803, President Thomas Jefferson had sanctioned the Louisiana Purchase, which almost doubled the size of the United States, by adding c.828,000 square miles to it. At the same time, the Lewis and Clark Expedition (1804–06) explored the previously uncharted West, and Jefferson began a process of acquiring Florida from Spain, which was completed in 1819, under President James Monroe.

Under President James Polk (1845–49), the idea of manifest destiny gained increased traction. Victory over Mexico in the Mexican–American War of 1848 led to the transfer of almost the whole of the modern-day US Southwest, from Mexico to the United States (a total of 525,000 square miles). All, or significant parts, of Arizona, California, Colorado, New Mexico, Nevada, Utah and Wyoming joined the USA. Following a dispute with Britain, the USA also gained Idaho, Oregon and Washington, along with parts of both Montana and Wyoming. This truly was manifest destiny in operation.

In all of these huge territorial expansions, no regard was paid to the rights of Native Americans. Or, if they were involved in any arrangements, these would soon be abrogated. This was the backdrop for the second half of the nineteenth century. It was a long way from that first Pilgrims' Thanksgiving meal in 1621, but very reminiscent of the Puritan-led King Philip's War of the 1670s. Ultimately, Native Americans were in the way. Manifest destiny (as also in the earlier sense of 'cleared title') was a justification for pacifying or removing them.

The westward expansions also raised the question of whether these new territories should be slave or free states. It was to prove a major contribution to the Civil War that would soon engulf the United States. When the Civil War ended in 1865, manifest destiny provided the ideological justification for the renewed expansion westward, leading to the Plains Indian Wars of the 1860s and 1870s; and the eventual US domination of the continent, from east to west. What had started in King Philip's War, in New England in the 1670s, came to its brutal and predictable conclusion in the 1870s (even if it took another decade to finally complete the task). This was made easier to justify by framing it as a clash of civilisations between confident, officially Christian, settlers and non-Christian Native Americans. By the time that the Native American religious resistance, known as the 'Ghost Dance', was ended in the violent massacre of Miniconjou and Hunkpapa, of the Lakota (Sioux) people, at Wounded Knee (on the Pine Ridge Indian Reservation, South Dakota) in December 1890, two centuries of cultural domination had led to the victory of the Europeans. Those Native Americans who converted to Christianity were not shielded from this destruction of a way of life, in the same way that the so-called

'Praying Indians' of Massachusetts had not been spared during the suppression of native communities in King Philip's War 200 years earlier. Manifest destiny had certainly made its implication clear; title to the land had been taken by a new people.

CREATING THE PURITAN MYTH: THE INVENTION OF THANKSGIVING

What is intriguing is that, even as Native American culture was on its way to destruction, the myth of a cross-cultural day of harmony and sharing became increasingly emphasised in the USA. As we have already seen, a major contribution of Puritan heritage to the USA was the concept of the Thanksgiving.

These early Thanksgivings were practised by a number of New England settlements. The original events were days of prayer, fasting and thanksgiving to God for his mercies and were very different to how Thanksgiving is now celebrated. During the seminal events of the American Revolution, the Continental Congress had designated one or more days of Thanksgiving a year; the first occurred in 1777. Then, in 1789, George Washington issued the very first Thanksgiving proclamation in the name of the newly formed government of the United States. This was to give thanks for victory and the historic ratification of the US Constitution. Other days of Thanksgiving were announced during the presidencies of John Adams and James Madison. These were unambiguous legacy events that arose from the Puritan past and from the national myth of North American origins. They were things that 'Americans' did and they were derived from their Christian roots. Illustrative of this is the fact that Thomas Jefferson – who was a Deist and was sceptical about the subject of divine intervention – did not declare any Thanksgivings during his presidency.

In 1817, New York State was the first to announce an annual Thanksgiving holiday. Other states followed, although there was no unanimity regarding the day or days chosen. Interestingly, it was largely an unknown tradition in the southern states; but they, of course, lacked the Puritan heritage. The exception rather proved the rule. What all of these Thanksgivings were doing was moving away from the formal and solemn events that seventeenth-century New Englanders would have recognised as a 'Thanksgiving' and more towards one of community and family celebration and festivities. This was assisted by a re-focusing on the event of the famous Harvest Home celebrated by the Pilgrims at Plymouth in the autumn of 1621, despite it never actually being called a Thanksgiving. But it offered a more congenial model for a community celebration which had Puritan roots, but which was slowly losing its religious character.

Echoes of the Puritan roots of Thanksgiving remained, though, and this is hardly surprising in a nation that still possessed a strong Christian identity, even if constitutionally shorn of a national church and denominational orthodoxy. When President Lincoln called for a Thanksgiving at the height of the Civil War, in 1863, it was for more than community feasting and celebration. God's provisions were to be 'solemnly, reverently and gratefully acknowledged', and

> With humble penitence for our national perverseness and diso-
> bedience, commend to His tender care all those who have become
> widows, orphans, mourners or sufferers in the lamentable civil

strife in which we are unavoidably engaged, and fervently im-
plore the interposition of the Almighty Hand to heal the wounds
of the nation and to restore it as soon as may be consistent with
the Divine purposes to the full enjoyment of peace, harmony,
tranquillity and Union.[15]

After the Civil War ended in 1865, traditions of how to mark
Thanksgivings varied from region to region, but largely continued the trend of being community festivities seen before the Civil
War (and harking back to 1621), rather than taking on the fasts
and prayers of alternative customs. Consequently, Thanksgivings
became marked by community events, sports and feasts, as well as
family meals. People in fancy dress spilled into the streets of New
York in the 1890s; in the twentieth century this would transfer to
the peculiarly US way of celebrating Halloween (also autumnal in
its setting).

In 1863 Lincoln had fixed Thanksgiving on the final Thursday in
November. In this position it replaced an earlier celebration (held
in many places before the Civil War, on 25 November) that had
celebrated the evacuation of British troops from the USA after the
American Revolution. Once established there, Thanksgiving was
celebrated on that day every year until 1939. In that year President
Franklin D. Roosevelt moved it by a week in an attempt to encourage retail sales during the Great Depression. The plan was to give
a longer gap between Thanksgiving and Christmas. The move was
widely criticised and dismissed as 'Franksgiving'. As a result, in 1941
the President reluctantly relented and Thanksgiving returned to the
fourth (usually the last) Thursday in November.[16]

As Thanksgiving developed post-Civil War it consciously emphasised its putative 1621 roots, with an emphasis on food native to North America and allegedly eaten during that Harvest Home celebrated in Plymouth a year after the arrival of the *Mayflower*. Hence the turkey, the cranberry sauce, the mashed potato, etc. Echoes of its Puritan roots lie in traditions in some families of recounting blessings and saying grace before eating; in many 21st-century homes, however, it is simply now a family meal. In school and community events the presence of buckle-hatted Puritan boys and demurely coiffed girls recalls aspects from the seventeenth-century myth. The shift of fancy dress to Halloween since the late 1950s has allowed Puritan costumes to once again re-colonise the event. The presence of Native Americans at the first event provides an opportunity to celebrate apparent multicultural harmony over a century after manifest destiny finally brought down independent Native American resistance and rendered Native Americans no longer a threat.

THE PURITAN LEGACY IN THE CIVIL WAR AND ITS AFTERMATH

We have explored how in the War of Independence, American patriots co-opted the Puritan concept of a peculiar destiny for the colonists of North America. This same outlook – and the genre of the 'jeremiad', which denounced national sins while calling the nation to repentance – was again apparent in preaching during the Civil War in the 1860s. So influential is this Puritan-derived outlook and literary form that, 'in every war in which the United States has been involved, sermons and speeches about America's manifest destiny and sacred errand and heritage have been central to the discourses of the war'.[17]

Churches were divided by the Civil War, although the fact that New England lay in the federal zone meant that much that was culturally derived from Puritan and Revolutionary roots ended up on the winning side. The Methodists, Baptists in the north and Congregationalists strongly supported the war and the Union. Catholics, Episcopalians, Lutherans and Presbyterians seem to have avoided clear commitments. The Methodists, in particular, strongly supported Lincoln and saw Union victory as being in line with the advancement of the Kingdom of God, especially due to their support for the abolition of slavery. There were also, of course, many Catholics in the north by the 1860s.

On the other side, the Confederate States were overwhelmingly Protestant. Revivalist meetings, of the kind associated with the Second Awakening, were common in Confederate army camps during the war. The Protestant Episcopal Church in the Confederate States split off from the Episcopal Church in 1861 as a result of the war. Presbyterians experienced similar divisions.

After the end of the war, African-American Baptists set up a number of state Baptist Conventions. In 1866, the African-American Baptists of the southern and western states formed the Consolidated American Baptist Convention, which, in 1895, merged into the National Baptist Convention, and this is now the largest black religious organisation in the USA.

The dynamic nature of US Christianity was then influenced by the so-called 'Third Great Awakening' in the second half of the nineteenth century, which was closely associated with what is termed 'postmillennial theology', which teaches that the second coming of Christ will occur after mankind has reformed the entire earth. New Christian groups emerged from this time, such as the Holiness Movement and the Nazarenes, and some that would not be regarded as Christians in the traditional sense of adherence to the historic creeds, such as the Christian Scientists. At the same time, mainstream Protestant churches continued to expand and this led to the establishment of faith-based colleges and universities (the latter still sharply differentiate the higher education sector in the US compared to the UK). Many remained highly engaged with efforts to, as they saw it, reform society, and this would later be very influential in campaigns against prostitution and then in the establishment of Prohibition following the First World War. The attempt to create a godly society and establish 'a city on a hill' had long since overflowed its Congregationalist Puritan denominational boundaries. In the early twentieth century this was often associated with support for the Republican Party.

What all this goes to show is that the highly Christianised nature of North American society survived the polarising effects of the Civil War and ensured that the influence of Christianity would continue to be incredibly important in the United States as it entered the twentieth century. The old Puritan congregations had long since moved off centre-stage and been replaced by new groupings. However, their input into the cultural DNA of the USA was undeniable and, as the twentieth century progressed, Christian influence would increase to a remarkable degree. Within this there were features that clearly had seventeenth-century taproots. The Puritans certainly were an enduring people.

CHAPTER FOUR

THE EMERGENCE OF THE 'EVANGELICAL RELIGIOUS RIGHT'

The premise of this book is that US evangelical Christians constitute a crucial part of the Trump base; those who did once vote Democrat shifted Republican in significant numbers in 2016 (mostly in opposition to the candidature of Hillary Clinton);[1] and that the uniquely influential nature of Christian evangelicals in modern US politics owes more to the seventeenth-century Puritan heritage than to any other single factor.[2] Given this argument, it is about time that we examined the way in which the 'evangelical religious right' emerged as a recognisable group (with political influence) in the twentieth century.

THE APPEARANCE OF A RECOGNISABLE EVANGELICAL GROUP WITHIN US SOCIETY

Technically, there is no such group as the evangelical religious right. It is not a denomination and no groups formally gather under such a collective label. But it exists. Today, a number of terms are used to describe the phenomenon that we are about to explore: the

'Christian right', the 'new Christian right', the 'religious right'[3] and 'socially conservative evangelicals'.[4] The label used in this book emphasises that most within this group are self-identified 'evangelicals' (but not all evangelicals are in the group); some are not evangelicals (e.g. there are Catholics in the core base too), but are religiously committed Christians; despite this complexity, all subscribe to politically conservative responses in order to defend or promote socially conservative outlooks.[5] This differentiates them from theologically conservative groups such as the Amish and Mennonites who are not evangelical in outlook, nor are they recognisably right-wing in their political activism. And political activism, in support of a socially and theologically conservative agenda, is very much a feature of the group we have termed the evangelical religious right.

By the 1890s, as a result of the Great Awakenings of the nineteenth century, most American Protestants were part of what one can describe as 'evangelical' denominations. The main exceptions were the High Church Episcopalians and the German Lutherans. The evangelicals – Baptists, Methodists and others – represented denominations that had risen to prominence as the influence of those churches directly descended from the original Puritans – most notably the Congregationalists – declined in influence. Despite this, they were spiritual heirs of what had come before; cultural heirs to the seventeenth-century 'city on a hill' godly, the eighteenth-century American-exceptionalist patriots and the nineteenth-century believers in manifest destiny and the enthusiasm of the camp meetings. Like them, the evangelicals were devoted to the Bible, to godly living and traditional family values and to the personal pursuit of holiness. They also represented a rugged American individualism.

These were all values that would have been recognised by the saints of Massachusetts almost three centuries earlier, even if they would have fallen out over some church practices (such as infant versus adult baptism). From 1906, the rise of Pentecostalism (stemming from the Azusa Street Revival) added to and dynamically energised areas of the American church.

However, in the early twentieth century the evangelical block divided over the matter of 'fundamentalism'; that is, belief in the literal historical accuracy of every word of the Bible. In many ways this was a culture war between those wishing to maintain what they considered rigid adherence to scripture versus scientific modernity. The litmus test became attitudes to Darwinian evolution. Set against this was 'seven-day Creationism' and a literal reading of the creation story in the first chapters of Genesis. From 1910, the evangelical movement was dominated by fundamentalists. This and the opposition to the teaching of evolution showed itself in the Scopes Trial of 1925 (formally The State of Tennessee *v.* John Thomas Scopes and sometimes colloquially referred to as the Scopes Monkey Trial). In the case, a substitute high school teacher, named John T. Scopes, was accused of violating Tennessee's Butler Act, which prohibited the teaching of human evolution in state-funded schools. Scopes was found guilty (after just nine minutes of deliberation by the jury) and fined $100; but the verdict was later overturned by the Supreme Court of Tennessee on a technicality. It was not until 1968 that the US Supreme Court finally ruled that such bans contravened the First Amendment to the US Constitution because their primary purpose was religious. Incidentally, the State of Tennessee had repealed the Butler Act just the previous year. The significance of the

1925 trial lay in the way that it symbolised a widening gap between fundamentalist evangelical Christians and what they saw as secular liberalism. This division would have long-term ramifications.

It is significant that an attempt to promote the teaching of Creationism in state schools resumed in the 1980s and accompanied another stage in the culture war between those referring to themselves as Bible-believing evangelicals and a modern society that they felt was increasingly at odds with their values. But by that time theological concerns had become deeply intertwined with political activism.

THE GROWTH OF A REPUBLICAN PARTY ALLIANCE: THE 1940S AND 1950S

Right-leaning evangelical Protestants have been involved in politics for much of the twentieth century, and their political activities are not simply a modern phenomenon, although it is during the past thirty-five years that they have come to increasing prominence.[6] As far back as the 1940s, 1950s and 1960s, anxieties about the perceived threat of communism and changing patterns of social behaviour caused many with this outlook to gravitate towards the Republican Party as a way of defending what they would have described as the 'Protestant-based moral order'.[7]

In this period of development, opposition to Catholic influence also drove the movement to a significant extent. As far back as 1928, Protestant voters had sided against Alfred Emanuel Smith (aka Al Smith), the Democratic presidential candidate. While he managed to gain some support in the Deep South, it was noted that his Catholicism lost him support among a large number of conservative Protestant southern voters who might otherwise have

been expected to vote Democrat at this time.[8] This was particularly noticeable among Southern Baptists who would, by the end of
the twentieth century, be regarded as solid members of the 'Bible
Belt' evangelical right. In the end, Smith lost the electoral college
votes of six southern states. The incumbent Republican Secretary of
Commerce, Herbert Hoover, became President in a landslide.

Similarly, in the 1960 presidential election, sizeable numbers
of Protestant voters lined up in support of the incumbent Vice-
President Richard Nixon, who was the Republican Party candidate.
They did this in opposition to the Catholic, John F. Kennedy, who
was, of course, the candidate of the Democratic Party.[9] A notable
example of this was provided by the Southern Baptist Convention of
May 1960, which – while recognising the separation of church
and state and the fact that a candidate's religious faith should not
be a test for public office – passed a carefully worded resolution
that managed to target Kennedy without actually naming him.
The resolution, entitled 'Christian Citizenship', made it clear
that a candidate's church membership was of very real interest to
voters. The wording did not actually mention Catholicism, but it
was clear that Catholics were being referred to, and negatively.[10]
Although Kennedy won, it was a closely contested election and
he is generally considered to have won the popular vote by just
112,827 votes – a margin of only 0.17 per cent. Although Nixon lost,
the result revealed that it mattered a great deal where Protestants
(and especially committed evangelical ones, such as the Southern
Baptists) cast their votes. In a tight election, their loyalty mattered.
And if they moved as a block then they could be significant. This
time they lost, but in the future they would win.

THE DECISIVE SHIFT AWAY FROM THE DEMOCRATS: THE LEGACY OF THE 1960S AND 1970S

During the 1960s, the mood music of the USA changed (literally and figuratively), as it did across much of the Western world. In this period of change the threat of secularisation came to be seen by US evangelical Protestants as a bigger threat to their understanding of Christian values than that posed by Catholicism. Freedom of sexual expression and pressure for liberalising abortion laws presented a greater challenge than anxieties over the influence of the Pope and Catholic priests on the American (WASP) way of life. Things had moved on since the elections of 1928 and 1960. Now there were bigger issues to face than the Catholicism of candidates such as Smith and Kennedy. As a result of this shift in concern, by the 1980s US Roman Catholic bishops and evangelicals of a range of persuasions were cooperating on social issues, such as abortion. The Supreme Court decision to make abortion a constitutionally protected right in the 1973 Roe *v.* Wade ruling was a major accelerator in the rise of the evangelical right in the 1970s and created a common platform across the Protestant/Catholic divide. Catholics were no longer the high-profile target; instead, the target was modern US society.

At the same time, a long-term change occurred within the Democratic Party. For generations, so-called 'Dixiecrats' in the southern states (especially in the Deep South) had combined both Protestant ideology and socially conservative agendas, including on the subject of African-American civil rights. During the 1960s, this southern Democratic section of voters shifted ground. Fear of the counter-culture emerging across the USA, as well as opposition to the Civil Rights Movement, caused the Dixiecrats to move towards the Republican Party. This had been likely for some time. The so-called 'States' Rights Democrats' had already emerged as a recognisable right-wing Democratic Party splinter group during the 1948 presidential election. These southerners objected to the civil rights programme which was becoming associated with the Democratic Party national leadership. The Dixiecrats also opposed federal regulations which they considered as unwarranted interference with states' rights and individual liberties. During the 1960s, this intra-Democrat division deepened, and was exacerbated by the Democratic Party's increasing identification with a pro-choice position on the subject of abortion. As a result, socially conservative Dixiecrats (and other more conservative Democrats too) joined the Republican Party in increasing numbers as the 1960s progressed. Many of these would also have self-identified as 'evangelicals', including many Southern Baptists, but also members of other evangelical church congregations. A seismic shift was occurring within US politics. The boundaries of the plate tectonics behind these changes can clearly be traced in the US political scene of the twenty-first century.

To those unhappy with the trajectory of American society, the government was seen to be a major source of these problems. It was, after all, the US Supreme Court that had banned official (although not private) prayer and Bible readings in state schools (Engel *v.* Vitale, 1962), had legalised first-trimester abortions (Roe *v.* Wade, 1973) and had gone on to regulate government involvement in private Christian academies (Lemon *v.* Kurtzman, 1971). The situation seemed clear: the government had to be brought into line with the ideas of evangelical Americans.

At the same time – ever since the late 1960s and especially through the 1970s – evangelical Christians felt that they were under siege. They believed that 'traditional Christians are overlooked, if not caricatured, in network newscasts, situation comedies, and mass circulation periodicals'. Furthermore, they felt that the school system 'leads children and teenagers to believe that their parents' ideals are ephemeral constructions of time and place, and thus replaceable at will. Finally and perhaps most importantly, the traditional family finds itself besieged on all fronts.'[11] In short, a culture war had begun, and the Christian Right prepared to fight to defend its values as never before.

Such changes were leading to a growing sense of polarisation, which meant that evangelical Christians increasingly began identifying with a raft of political issues (e.g. opposition to abortion, non-traditional sexual behaviour and federal 'interference') that were associated with the Republican Party. Many – though not all – of these evangelicals were white, especially in the southern states. On the other hand, a more complex group of Christians (including both those who were more socially liberal and those who were more politically interventionist, such as some African-American evangelicals) lined up behind the Democratic Party. The Democrats were becoming increasingly associated with a pro-choice position on abortion, equal rights for minorities (including the LGBT community) and non-traditional social values. The religious and party-political battle lines, familiar in 2016 and today, were being drawn.

In the mid-1970s, there was a slight aberration in this development when Democrat Jimmy Carter received the support of the evangelicals as a result of his well-known religious conversion. Despite this, Carter's Christian credentials were soon considered as being heavily outweighed by his liberal policies. This lost him the support of Christian conservatives. Pastor Jerry Falwell Sr voiced strident criticism and declared that 'Americans have literally stood by and watched as godless, spineless leaders have brought our nation floundering to the brink of death'.[12] That he stated this in his introduction to Richard Viguerie's 1980 book, *The New Right: We're Ready to Lead*,[13] clearly indicated the way that the trend was flowing. The title of the book also revealed the increasing confidence and ambitions among evangelicals to influence political discourse and government policies. The evangelical right switched support to Republican Ronald Reagan. In response, the 1980 Republican Party platform adopted a number of policies that were in line with demands from right-leaning evangelicals. These included dropping support for the Equal Rights Amendment (designed to guarantee equal legal rights for all US citizens regardless of gender) and supporting the restoration of school prayer (largely banned from the public elementary, middle and high-school system by a number of Supreme Court decisions since 1962 and still in force). In 1980, Reagan won the presidential election.

THE EVANGELICAL RIGHT GAINS TRACTION

Since the late 1970s, what we have termed the evangelical religious right has clearly developed into a significant force within the Republican Party and across US politics generally. The shift to support Reagan in 1980 marked a key point in the development of this political force. While the journey to political influence had started long before this, 1980 was a crucial milestone. This accompanied calls by evangelical leaders, such as by the Southern Baptist pastor, televangelist and conservative activist Jerry Falwell, to conservative evangelical Christians to get more involved in politics. Falwell himself was the founding pastor of the Thomas Road Baptist Church, a so-called 'megachurch' in Lynchburg, Virginia, with over 20,000 members. He was highly influential in the propagation of socially and politically conservative beliefs. This included founding Lynchburg Christian Academy (now Liberty Christian Academy) in 1967, and Liberty University, a fundamentalist university, in 1971. Together these institutions ensured that a young person's entire education was conducted within an evangelical environment. He also co-founded the Moral Majority movement in 1979. The election of Ronald Reagan to the presidency in 1980, along with a large number of Republicans to Congress, was, at the time, credited partially to the influence of this organisation.

The term 'moral majority' soon became a general label for the campaigns of a range of conservative political activists, televange-lists and fundamentalist preachers. These included Pat Robertson (media proprietor, televangelist and former Southern Baptist minister) and James Robison (pastor and televangelist), as well as Jerry Falwell. Falwell disbanded the Moral Majority movement in 1989, but its influence continues. By 1980, his weekly TV programme, called *Old-Time Gospel Hour*, had 21 million viewers. It has since been replaced by *Thomas Road Live*, hosted by his son, Jonathan Falwell, which still continues to be broadcast.[14]

Jerry Falwell's career encapsulates much that is now associated with the evangelical religious right in the USA. He opposed homosexuality and stated that 'AIDS is not just God's punishment for homosexuals, it is God's punishment for the society that tolerates homosexuals'.[15] He argued strongly for Christian involvement in US politics and his official website stated that its goal was to defend traditional family values and battle the liberals who opposed 'those godly principles'.[16]

In a conversation with the Reverend Pat Robertson, on Robertson's evangelical TV channel three days after the 9/11 terrorist attacks, Falwell linked the attacks to abortion, stating:

> The abortionists have got to bear some burden for this because God will not be mocked. And when we destroy 40 million little innocent babies, we make God mad. I really believe that the pagans, and the abortionists, and the feminists, and the gays, and the lesbians who are actively trying to make that an alternative lifestyle, the ACLU [American Civil Liberties Union], People for the American Way – all of them who have tried to secularise America – I point the finger in their face and say: 'You helped this happen.'[17]

Later, on CNN, Falwell issued an apology for this statement.

With regard to Middle Eastern politics, Falwell was consistent with the stance of many in the evangelical wing of the US Protestant churches in offering robust support for the State of Israel. This support was so clearly articulated that some commentators have described it as 'Christian Zionism'. It is alleged that, following the Israeli bombing of Iraq's nuclear plant (Operation Opera, or Operation Babylon, in June 1981), the first telephone call that Israeli

Prime Minister Menachem Begin made to the USA (in order to explain the reasons for this action) was to Jerry Falwell, rather than to President Ronald Reagan. In the late 1990s, it was again alleged that the Israeli Prime Minister, Benjamin Netanyahu, asked Falwell to mobilise evangelical Christian supporters to put pressure on President Clinton to prevent him from urging Israel to accept the Oslo Accords.[18]

In addition to these fairly representative examples of policies and attitudes found among the evangelical religious right, and represented by Falwell, the Christian right has also engaged in rigorous action designed to: prevent the further extension of abortion rights; oppose euthanasia; criticise the promotion of contraception among young people and sex education (other than abstinence) in schools; oppose pornography and obscenity; and encourage revising school textbook contents (concerning the teaching of Creationism alongside evolution).

The power and influence of the religious right increased considerably during the presidency of George Bush Sr between 1989 and 1993. The relationship did not start well, though. Bush was regarded as being too socially liberal and too associated with family planning (his family had helped found Planned Parenthood). The evangelicals had already been disappointed during the eight years of the Reagan presidency (1981–89) as he had not delivered as much progress on 'evangelical issues' as had been hoped for when the evangelical weight had been thrown behind him back in 1980. And, despite Bush having reversed his attitude to abortion while Vice-President in 1984 (he had announced he would oppose federal funding for abortion except to protect a mother's life, and promised to back a constitutional amendment to overturn Roe *v.* Wade), he was still not considered sufficiently on-message when he became President.

The evangelicals had reluctantly backed Bush in preference to Pat Robertson, the televangelist, in the Republican primaries because they thought Bush was more electable. In 1989, in order to ensure that any future Republican President was more in line with the evangelical agenda, leading church leaders founded the Christian Coalition, which spent the early 1990s building a widespread grassroots organisation that eventually claimed over 1 million members. From this base, they launched a massive infiltration of the Republican Party, such that by 1992 some 40 per cent of the delegates to the Republican National Convention were evangelical Christians.[19] The resulting Republican stance against abortion and gay rights came about as a result of this, as was Bush's choice of evangelical Dan Quayle as Vice-President and his nomination of a conservative who was acceptable to evangelicals to the Supreme Court. While these actions were aimed at satisfying the evangelical right, they failed to stem its drive to take over the Republican Party from within.

The determination of the evangelicals to dominate the party was exacerbated during the years of the Clinton presidency (1993–2001) as he enraged the right with his perceived liberalism and as a result of the charges of sexual improprieties levelled against him. The latter, it should be noted, was something that they set aside with ease in 2016 when it came to supporting the Trump campaign. But then things had changed since the late 1990s and the evangelical resurgence was in full swing by 2016, with a more aggressive and determined tone than ever before. To return to what we might call the seizure of power within Republicanism, by 1994 the representation of members of the Christian Coalition at the Republican National Convention stood at over 50 per cent of delegates. This was a position from which to dictate the direction of the party. The result of this activism was the election of George W. Bush in 2000.[20] By that time, while the committed inner core of the religious right may have numbered no more than 200,000 US adults, those who explicitly identified themselves as broadly in line with their policies ranged from 10 to 15 million, while a broader group of sympathetic voters 'who might be mobilized over a specific issue such as abortion or gun control may have enlisted thirty-five million'.[21]

THE APPEARANCE OF THE MATURE EVANGELICAL RELIGIOUS RIGHT: CONSERVATIVE CHRISTIAN POLITICS AT THE START OF THE THIRD MILLENNIUM

George W. Bush's electoral success owed much to the widespread support he received from white evangelical voters. It has been estimated that, in 2000, he secured 68 per cent of the white evangelical vote. By 2004 that percentage had increased to 78 per cent. Bush was, in contrast to his moderate Republican father, an evangelical and a conservative who was very acceptable to the transformed Republican Party and its evangelical supporters.

In his victory over Senator John McCain for the Republican nomination in 2000, the evangelicals played a major role. Public policy specialist Mark J. Rozell described how 'The Republican nomination race quickly became a bitter contest between Bush and McCain, with the Christian Right taking central stage in the drama and ultimately delivering victory to Bush. Amid predictions of the movement's political irrelevancy, Christian Right activists became the kingmakers in the GOP contest' – the GOP (Grand Old Party) being an alternative name for the Republican Party.[22]

Following this decisive intervention, the same movement then mobilised its base to ensure Bush's re-election in 2004.

Despite this, the extent to which Bush Jr fulfilled the expectations of the evangelical religious right has, at times, caused pundits to exaggerate their power in the White House during his presidency:

> The Christian Right has infiltrated and taken over the White House – in the person of the President of the United States. If Jerry Falwell and Pat Robertson had sat down some fifteen years ago and created the profile of their perfect President – a born-again Christian from the Bible Belt, flagrantly open about his faith – George W. Bush would fit it almost to a T.[23]

In fact, the evangelicals had not 'taken over the White House', although this may well be conventional wisdom when charting the progress of evangelical influence against George Bush Jr's rise to power and his re-election. For, while Bush was certainly a close friend to the movement (perhaps the most complete embodiment of the movement's ideal President until Trump), he was, in fact, not a puppet of the evangelical right. This reflected the reality that, although the evangelicals had played a major part in his success, Bush's triumph was due to the usual coalition of reasons that combine to ensure electoral victory. As a result, he was indebted to more than just the televangelists and the energised evangelical base, and this meant that they did not call the shots during his tenure in the top job. They were highly influential, but they had not 'taken over the White House'. His presidency pleased them in many ways and frustrated social conservatives in other ways.[24] In his inaugural speech in 2005, Bush's words 'brimmed with religious imagery, but abortion was the only top priority of the Christian right that he mentioned, in a fleeting and oblique reference near the end'.[25] Prior to that, he had commented on the difficulty of banning gay marriage, only to have to re-state his opposition to it when his nuanced approach attracted harsh criticism from evangelicals. This mixing of pragmatism with evangelical idealism was a characteristic of Bush's presidency and reminds us that even the most focused special interest group cannot entirely control the political process. Life is complex. But, despite this, the evangelical right was in a position of power and influence that surpassed anything achieved in its previous history.[26]

Then, in 2008, Barack Obama happened. The election of a young, intelligent, telegenic and highly articulate social progressive (committed to proactive federal government initiatives on a number of fronts) was a sharp reversal of all that the evangelical right had been working on for over twenty years. The Obama presidency (2009–17) was regarded as an existential threat to the evangelicals, and it was no coincidence that in February 2009 – just one month after his inaugural speech – the right-wing, populist Tea Party was formed. Over the years of the Obama administration, the Tea Party played a major role in articulating right-wing opposition to both the Democratic administration and those within the Republican Party who were deemed lacking in sufficient rigour in the increasingly and viscerally polarised US political system.

The movement's commitment to limiting the size and activity of federal government, reducing government spending, and opposing tax increases appear to reveal it primarily as a movement of libertarian small-state economics. However, that is misleading, because many Tea Party members were drawn from the same evangelical base from which earlier activists had been drawn in the battle to infiltrate the Republican Party. This was revealed in a survey conducted in 2013, which indicated that 61 per cent of self-identified 'libertarians' in the US did not consider themselves part of the Tea Party movement.[27] That year, the annual American Values Survey, conducted by the non-partisan Public Religion Research Institute, revealed 'a libertarian constituency in America that is distinct both from the Tea Party and from the Christian right'.[28] These self-identified libertarians were half as likely to consider themselves part of the evangelical right when compared with Tea Party members. As such, they differed over key issues central to the Christian right's platform, such as abortion and euthanasia.

What this indicates is the extent to which the Tea Party should be considered part of the broad right-wing movement that has swept through the USA since the millennium and which has roots within the evangelical religious right. As this has occurred, those who would once have been regarded as 'moderate Republicans' (à la George Bush Sr) have been marginalised, silenced, or have adopted the new-right stance in order to avoid being outflanked on the right. US politics have been transformed, and much of this is due to the impact of the right-leaning evangelicals and their allies.

The extent to which the Tea Party vote had captured the imaginations and loyalties of Louisianan Republicans, well before the rise to prominence of Donald Trump, has been sensitively documented in Arlie Russell Hochschild's 2018 study, entitled *Strangers in Their Own Land: Anger and Mourning on the American Right*.[29] These voters included a large number of evangelical Christians, who supported the Tea Party's small-state, anti-federal government, anti-National Environment Agency-intervention stance – this, despite the poverty, pollution and poor health affecting the state, its dependence on federal assistance and its apparent need of federal protection to safeguard its natural resources. This Tea Party support morphed into support for Donald Trump in 2016. This was because both the Tea Party and Trump appeared to speak to the 'deep story' of these voters as they lived in a bewildering USA that was changing around them and in which they increasingly felt marginalised and cut-in-on by others as they queued for access to the American Dream.

That the policies of the radical right, arguably, were not inclined to assist such people – who were often damaged by the actions of the oil industry and inadequately served by private sector health provision – was as nothing compared to the right's ability to (apparently) speak to their deep story and to articulate their anxieties. And in this, the appeal to Christian and traditional values played a major part. Both the Tea Party and Trump showed themselves highly sensitive to, and influenced by, the evangelical right within the Republican Party and outside it. It is this ability to speak to

Americans who feel increasingly anxious and angry about aspects of the modern USA that has been the key to the success of the evangelical religious right and its allies since 1980.

SUMMING UP THE US EVANGELICAL RELIGIOUS RIGHT

As this brief analysis has shown, although often associated with Republican politics since the late 1970s, the movement we have termed the 'evangelical religious right' actually emerged earlier in the century and became increasingly allied with the Republicans in the 1940s and 1950s, arriving as a distinct force in the 1960s as the Democrats were becoming associated with more liberal policies and as the counter-culture (from hippies to anti-Vietnam protests) challenged traditional US values and culture. From the 1970s, issues such as abortion increased the movement of socially conservative Christians from supporting the Democrats to voting Republican. This gained increased traction from the 1980s onwards over issues such as textbook content (i.e. calls for the inclusion of Creationist ideas), LGBT rights and sex education. From the 1990s, the size and influence of this grouping made it a formidable force within US politics, and this accelerated in the twenty-first century with intense opposition to the actions of the Obama administration (having its epicentre in the visceral opposition to federally led 'Obamacare'), challenges to traditional family structures such as same-sex marriage and the 'sexual and gender politics' associated with Hillary Clinton (focusing on alleged plans to extend abortion rights and LGBT rights). Latterly, the evangelical influence has been highly noticeable in its large-scale support for Donald Trump in 2016 and during his presidency. Much of its power within the US political system is due to the extraordinary turnout rate at the polls of highly motivated evangelicals.

In 2016, as Donald Trump sought the job of President, he became the unlikely recipient of support from one of the most remarkable phenomena in modern US politics. The evangelical religious right – operating in a secular state – has come to wield extraordinary power on behalf of a religious group. However, although its contemporary impact is due to particular issues peculiar to the USA in the late twentieth and early twenty-first century, the foundations of the movement are buried deep in the history of North America. They are part of a national and religious culture 'that stressed individual self-reliance, voluntary association, and resisting authority and hierarchy', which was originally buttressed by the Puritan religious ideology of choice and contract but which has outlived Puritanism and now follows 'more the preaching than the practices of the early Pilgrims and Puritans'.[30] This accompanies a distinct emphasis on personal religious beliefs, on freedom of expression and on vigorous opposition to the perceived censorship of Christian ideology which has produced a modern political dialogue that is extremely confrontational and combative and which is ultimately rooted in 'puritan rituals of national repentance, reawakening, and renewal'.[31]

This remarkable movement openly stresses the exceptionalism of the USA – in ways that Winthrop would have recognised in 1630 – while condemning the fallen state of US society,[32] in a way reminiscent of the Puritan jeremiad. These historic ambitions to promote godly personal and community conduct are combined with a peculiarly American antagonism to federal government, opposition to gun control and support for the State of Israel.[33] But even these have seventeenth-century roots, for they are ultimately derived from (and at times explicitly referenced to) millenarian beliefs in the imminent second coming of Christ which see Israel as God's chosen instrument in the Middle East and the necessity of an armed citizenry at home to resist anti-Christian 'feds' and to resist the antichrist himself. Even evangelical opposition to combating climate change can be linked to an assumption of its irrelevance in the face of an inevitable End Time apocalypse, as well as deriving from opposition to the feds and their interventions against the petroleum-based wealth of many US industries and individuals. These are modern issues – but with Puritan-derived roots.

It is this remarkable combination that often leaves fellow Christians in the UK puzzled and feeling: 'Now and then we hear a language that we understand … and then the person speaking it goes off and does something quite inexplicable. We are left asking: "Why ever did they do that? I thought they were just like me!"'[34]

And if it puzzles many fellow-believers, it is even more incomprehensible to those of other faiths, no religious faith and to secular commentators. For that is because the US and UK are divided by their common Puritan heritage. The Puritan legacy has taken different routes on either side of the Atlantic. But, while Puritan politics might seem a thing of the past in the UK, it is very much alive in the USA, and has become a part of the belief system of the evangelical religious right.

This brings us back to evangelical support for Donald Trump. In order to understand this, we will explore six key areas – race, immigration, gender and identity, life, law and Israel – and the parts these played in Trump's electoral success and future strategies; and the ways in which these areas intersect with the outlook and actions of US evangelicals who support him. And we will further identify the deep roots within American history that help explain this and set it in context.

CHAPTER FIVE

THE POLITICS OF RACE

To what extent does race play a role in support for, or opposition to, Donald Trump? This is a very important question; as is the way that this impacts on and is affected by evangelical outlooks and voting patterns.

The Civil Rights Act was signed into law on 2 July 1964 by Lyndon B. Johnson. The thirty-sixth President took up the cause from his predecessor John F. Kennedy, who had proposed the legislation in June 1963, five months before his assassination. Southern Democrats had staged a filibuster in the Senate that, at seventy-five days – with former Ku Klux Klan member Senator Robert Byrd of West Virginia putting in more than fourteen consecutive hours – was one of the longest in US history. Despite this, the Bill passed. It is a reminder of how the orientation of the US political parties has shifted over time. In the mid-1960s, so-called 'Dixiecrats' represented views on racial politics that are now anathema to 21st-century Democrats.

The Bill, described by Martin Luther King Jr as a 'second emancipation', ended segregation in public places and banned employment discrimination on the basis of race, colour, religion, sex or national origin. After the Bill was signed, Johnson reportedly told an aide: 'It is an important gain, but I think we just delivered the South to the Republican Party for a long time to come.'[1]

The prediction proved accurate, but earlier that year Johnson had made another prediction, better known and equally prescient. The quote has acquired an apocryphal ring, but Ronald Kessler, in his book *Inside the White House*, traces it back to its source.[2] Kessler took the trouble to talk to the staff who catered to Presidents from JFK to Bill Clinton, and LBJ does not emerge well from the narrative. 'If presidents before Johnson had engaged in deceit on occasion, it was Johnson who turned fooling the public into a wholesale operation,' Kessler claimed.[3]

Kessler talked a lot to Air Force One steward Robert M. MacMillan. During one trip Johnson had been discussing his proposed civil rights Bill with two governors, and Macmillan was present during the conversation. LBJ explained to the governors why it was important to get the Bill passed: 'I'll have them n*****s voting Democratic for two hundred years' were the words that he overheard, Macmillan told Kessler in an interview on 28 March 1993.

'That was the reason he was pushing the Bill,' said MacMillan. 'Not because he wanted equality for everyone. It was strictly a political ploy for the Democratic Party. He was phony from the word go.'[4]

Macmillan's antipathy towards LBJ is evident, but he comes across in Kessler's pages as an astute judge of character, in the way that so many 'below-stairs' personnel prove to be in their assessments of the 'superiors' whom they serve.

The statement resonates today in the rhetoric of those Trump-supporting black voters who urge their fellow African-Americans to 'get off the Democrat plantation' and vote for those who truly have their interests at heart. That may not be the Democrats, they point out, asking to what degree the loyalty of black voters has been rewarded by the party's politicians over the past half century.

However, half-way through Trump's first term, those politicians, pastors and activists who raised such questions were very much in a minority. No Republican presidential nominee in the past eighty years has done better in gaining the support of African-Americans than Eisenhower did in 1956, when he won 39 per cent of the African-American vote. Trump's claim in the run-up to the 2016 election that he would win 95 per cent of the African-American vote in 2020 (made at a rally in Dimondale, Michigan, on 19 August 2016) looks a little optimistic.

THE VOTING PATTERNS OF AMERICAN PEOPLE OF COLOUR

In the 2016 election, according to the non-profit, non-partisan Public Religion Research Institute, Hillary Clinton took 90 per cent of the African-American vote, while 70 per cent of African-American evangelicals identified with the Democratic Party. In stark contrast, about 81 per cent of white evangelical Christians voted for Trump in 2016, and two years later, just before the mid-terms of 2018, 73 per cent of this group were still loyal.[5] But while holding on to this base is necessary for Trump's re-election, their backing is not sufficient. He has to reach out beyond them, and racial differences are a highly significant factor when it comes to the political allegiances of Christian evangelicals. As Janelle Wong, the author of the 2018 book *Immigrants, Evangelicals and Politics in an Era of Demographic Change*,[6] pointed out in an article in *American Prospect* on 6 June 2018, one out of every seven evangelicals in the US is of Asian or Latino origin, and, taken together with African-American evangelicals, non-white evangelicals make up nearly one third of the evangelical population.[7]

Asian-American, Latino and black evangelical politics look very different from those of their white counterparts, Wong pointed out. Despite similar theological beliefs, only a minority of these believers voted for Trump. Evangelicals are very widely regarded as more conservative than the general population, but ethnic minorities among the evangelicals are, according to Wong, much less conservative than either white evangelicals or whites more generally. Analysing data from more than 10,000 respondents, she found that on many issues, including voting for Trump, Asian-American, Latino and black evangelicals have more progressive, left-ward leanings than even non-evangelical white people.

She offered a telling explanation. White conservative political beliefs are often based on a perception that whites face levels of discrimination on a par with or even higher than discrimination against Muslims, African-Americans or Hispanics. For whites, these perceptions elide into conservative political attitudes. Such perceptions make up what Arlie Russell Hochschild, in her study of Louisiana's right-leaning voters, has called a 'deep story'. It is an outlook rooted in the particular history, society, traditions, values and perception of any given group; and it may or may not accord with hard facts.[8] Deep stories will prove to be crucial in explaining many of the phenomena explored in this book. And deep stories exist on both sides of the current US political divide. Different deep stories produce different outcomes. Consequently, perceptions of racial discrimination against their own groups do not lead to more conservative political attitudes among Asian-American, Latino and black evangelicals. Wong suggests that this is what lies behind the current political divides between white and non-white evangelicals. It is something that needs to be borne in mind when assessing the behaviour of evangelicals, for not all evangelicals view the world through the same prism.

Trump was obviously aware of the challenge. On 1 August 2018, he invited twenty inner-city pastors and faith leaders to the White House. He was seeking support for the First Step Act, a criminal justice reform, the passing of which he would later celebrate in his 2019 State of the Union address. As well as drawing attention to the considerable inroads on unemployment among African-Americans, he wanted to make it easier for former prisoners – among whom there are a disproportionate number of African-Americans – to reintegrate into society. 'This is probably the most pro-active administration regarding urban America and the faith-based community in my lifetime,' said African-American Pastor Darrell Scott, of New Spirit Revival Center in Cleveland Heights, Ohio.[9] Scott had been an unashamed supporter of Trump in 2016. His fellow African-American, celebrity pastor John Gray, also at the meeting, was more equivocal.

I can't speak for everyone in the room. I came in with my mouth closed and my ears open out of respect because as we know there has been a lot of great pain and turmoil in the first part of this administration from many different sides. So, my job was not to come in with my own mindset.

'That was not a partisan issue, but a human issue,' he told NBC News after the meeting.[10] At least Gray was equivocal. Bishop Paul S. Morton, founder of the Full Gospel Baptist Church Fellowship, an Atlanta-based network of predominantly African-American churches, tweeted after the meeting, which he had not attended:

> Devil is so slick 2invite a group of black preachers 2 a praise party 4 N unworthy underserving lying POTUS 2 divide the Body of Christ in trusting man instead of God [.] God Please don't allow the Very Elect 2b fooled by a man who is not concerned abt blacks or the poor but himself.[11]

CNN's Don Lemon later asked Gray if he believed that Trump was 'responsible for hate in the nation's discourse now'. Gray replied: 'I believe that our President has fostered a culture and climate that has allowed for what was there and has been there for years to bubble up. It has empowered people in a horrific way. Absolutely. I don't think there's any question about it.'[12]

It was Gray and Morton, rather than Scott, who at this stage set the tone for the black community. If Trump was in any doubt, a national event at the end of the month illustrated, as much as any poll could, the challenge he faced and still faces in winning over African-Americans.

THE CHARGE OF RACISM

On Friday 31 August 2018, 100 pink Cadillacs lined the street and forecourts outside the Greater Grace Temple, a 4,000-seater megachurch on the outskirts of Detroit where the eight-hour funeral service for Aretha Franklin was to take place. As a celebration of African-American culture, in particular its contribution to the popular music of the world, the service was gloriously unrestrained. Legendary singers paying homage included Stevie Wonder, Smokey Robinson, Faith Hill, who sang 'What a Friend We Have in Jesus', and gospel singers including Yolanda Adams and the Clark Sisters. Chaka Khan sang 'Going Up Yonder' and Jennifer Hudson received a standing ovation for her rendition of 'Amazing Grace'. Ariana Grande had the honour of performing Franklin's signature hit, '(You make me feel like a) Natural Woman'.

Pastor William J. Barber II described Franklin's voice as being both vital to the civil rights movement and evocative of the glory of God. 'Before Obama said "Yes we can", Aretha sang "We can conquer hate forever, yes we can,"' he declared, with reference to Franklin's song 'Wholy Holy'.[13]

But there was a spectre at the funeral: the ghost of Donald Trump. Civil rights stalwarts from Franklin's generation criticised Trump. From the podium emblazoned with the words 'One Lord, One Faith, One Baptism' (the name of Franklin's seminal 1987 gospel album), Reverend Al Sharpton declared: 'Now I want y'all to help me correct President Trump, to teach him what [respect] means.' The reference to Franklin's seminal hit song was pointed. Sharpton continued: 'I say that, because when word went out that Ms. Franklin passed, Trump said, "She used to work for me." No, she used to perform for you. She worked for us … Aretha took orders from no one but God.'[14]

Sharpton's outrage was directed at remarks Trump had made while speaking at a White House Cabinet meeting on 16 August, the day Franklin died. According to CBS News, he said:

> I want to begin today by expressing my condolences to the family of a person I knew well – she worked for me on numerous occasions; she was terrific – Aretha Franklin, on her passing. She's brought joy to millions of lives, and her extraordinary legacy will thrive and inspire many generations to come. She was given a great gift from God: her voice. And she used it well. People loved Aretha. She was a special woman. So I just want to pass on my warmest, best wishes and sympathies to her family.[15]

The damage was done. 'She worked for me' was all the ammunition Trump's opponents needed. Franklin had indeed performed a three-day engagement at Trump's Castle in Atlantic City in 1988. She also performed several different engagements at the Trump Taj Mahal, another casino in Atlantic City. But to call this 'working for me' betrayed an unfortunate blindness to divinity on the part of the business tycoon. In fact, Trump was not ungracious on this occasion. He was renowned for responding to rejection with ferocity, and Franklin had performed at the inauguration of three Democratic Presidents, including that of Barack Obama, but reportedly refused Trump's request to perform at his own in 2017. There was no evident ill will. But Sharpton received a standing ovation for his remarks at Franklin's funeral, and there was more to come.

Georgetown Professor Michael Eric Dyson, after welcoming 'President Clinton and her husband Bill' to the service and passionately extolling the 'blackness' of Detroit, took aim at President Trump: 'This orange aberration had the nerve to say Aretha worked for him. You lugubrious leach. You lethal liar. You dim-witted dictator. You foolish fascist. She didn't work for you. She worked above you. She worked beyond you. Get your composition right,' he said.[16] Resounding applause followed, from the live audience and no doubt from many across the nation who heard what Dyson had said. It was a vivid demonstration of how strong the opposition to Donald Trump was among key leading figures in the African-American community. It was grounded in an allegation that 'Trump is a racist'.

The 'Trump is a racist' narrative is well known, and Trump does not appear to want to help himself. On 11 August 2018, the front page of *The Guardian* newspaper carried an edited picture of President Donald Trump and his former aide Omarosa Manigault Newman looking past one another. The headline read: 'Omarosa says Trump is a racist who uses N-word – and claims there is tape to prove it: Former Apprentice contestant and ex-White House adviser writes in new memoir that she witnessed "truly appalling things"'.[17]

Manigault Newman claimed in her book *Unhinged: An Insider's Account of the Trump White House*, a copy of which *The Guardian* had obtained a week before its publication, that Trump was caught on mic 'multiple times' using the 'N-word' in the making of his reality TV show *The Apprentice*, which he presented on NBC between 2004 and 2015.[18] Manigault Newman did not claim to have heard Trump use the word herself, but said three sources from *The Apprentice* had contacted her to say a tape existed to corroborate her story.

Critics argued that Manigault Newman was motivated to seek revenge for having been fired from her highly paid job as director of communications, and pointed out that some supposed sources did not corroborate her stories. The alleged tapes did not emerge. But Trump, rather than taking cover and hoping the controversy would go away, raised the stakes.

On 14 August, he tweeted: 'When you give a crazed, crying low-life a break, and give her a job at the White House, I guess it just didn't work out. Good work by General [White House chief of staff John] Kelly for quickly firing that dog!'[19]

The word 'dog' unsurprisingly precipitated a mainstream media and social media firestorm. On MSNBC's *Morning Joe,* former GOP Congressman Joe Scarborough, who left the party in 2017 over disagreements with Trump, referred to the comments in the context of a book by David Livingstone Smith, entitled *Less Than Human: Why We Demean, Enslave and Exterminate Others.* Noting that 'tyrants and autocrats, and, yes, fascists, communists, others, have used the language of dehumanisation to justify a movement away from democracy and a movement away from decent stand-ards', and, citing a 2011 NPR story on the book, he said: 'During the Holocaust Nazis referred to Jews as rats. In Rwanda genocide was often justified calling Tutsis cockroaches. Slave owners throughout history considered slaves subhuman animals.' It was important to describe it as dehumanisation, he said, 'because it opens the door for cruelty and genocide'. 'Nobody is saying that Donald Trump is a Nazi,' he continued, 'nobody is saying that he's Adolf Hitler in 1938, 1939, 1940, but you can see time and time again … this is how dictators and tyrants open the door, and they do it by dehumanising their political opponents.'[20] Remarkably, Manigault Newman faded from the public sphere in due course, but the damage had been done, and it reminded onlookers that allegations (whether proved or otherwise) concerning race and Donald Trump were and are a major part of the bitterly contested nature of current US political discourse.

However, this was by no means the first time that President Trump had flirted with disaster. On 11 January 2018, at a behind-closed-doors meeting in the Oval Office, the topic was immigration. Illinois Democratic Senator Dick Durbin passed on an idea from the Congressional Black Caucus that beneficiaries of the visa lottery (a Democrat-sponsored programme introduced in 1990 that awarded immigration rights to 50,000 people a year from countries with low levels of immigration to the United States) should include less-represented African countries, and nations with temporary protected status (a status that allows people from countries affected by armed conflict or natural disaster to stay temporarily in the United States). Haiti was mentioned as one of these countries. Trump, it was alleged, responded by asking why the US wanted people from Haiti or more Africans in the country, and mentioned Norway as a preferable country of origin. 'Why are we having all these people from shithole countries come here?' the President reportedly asked, adding that he would be more open to immigrants from Asian countries because they would help the US economically.[21]

He learned that afternoon, as he was recording a message for Martin Luther King Day, that the story was breaking, and told aides that the media were blowing it out of proportion.

The *Washington Post* broke the story on 12 January, on the basis of leaks from the meeting. Cedric L. Richmond, the Democratic chairman of the Congressional Black Caucus, tweeted that Trump's remarks were 'further proof that his Make America Great Again Agenda is really a Make America White Again agenda'.[22] Republican Congresswoman Mia Love, whose family came from Haiti, said Trump's remarks were 'unkind, divisive, elitist and fly in the face of our nation's values. This behaviour is unacceptable from the leader of our nation.'[23] The *Post* story mentioned that Trump had praised Haitian Americans during a roundtable in Miami the previous September. 'Whether you vote for me or don't vote for me, I really want to be your greatest champion, and I will be your champion,' he had said at the meeting. But there were to be no more acts of journalistic balancing on this particular issue for a while. And it could be argued that the President's alleged remark had made that state of affairs unsurprising.

The following day his comments were reported with outrage around the world. '"There's no other word but racist": Trump's global rebuke for "shithole" remark', was the headline to *The Guardian* story on the fallout, on 13 January.

Late-night comedians weighed in. The *Daily Show* host Trevor Noah, a South African, said: 'I don't know how to break this to you but I think the President might be racist. Hear me out, I know I sound crazy.' 'Personally,' he went on, 'as someone from South Shithole, I'm offended ... It might take a few weeks, but once the news donkey reaches our village, we'll be so mad.'[24]

'What do Norwegians have that Haitians and Africans don't?' asked Jordan Klepper, host of Comedy Central's *The Opposition*. 'It's simple. They're all white-knuckle enthusiasts about making America great again.'[25]

African leaders expressed their shock, with Ghana's President saying Trump's remark constituted an unacceptable insult, and Senegal's leader pointing out that 'Africa and the black race' deserved 'the respect of all'. The African Union demanded a retraction of the comment and an apology 'not only to Africans but all people of African descent around the globe'.[26]

Trump delayed his response for several hours, weighing his options. Then he acted. On 12 January, at 1.28 p.m. he opted to deny he ever made the remark and offered no apology, tweeting: 'The language used by me at the DACA meeting was tough, but this was not the language used.'[27] Unfortunately, others in the room from both parties either testified to the accuracy of the initial report, or dodged the question.

Friends who rushed to Trump's aid were not necessarily the ones he would have wanted to do so. Steve King, who one year later would be disciplined by the House for comments seemingly endorsing white supremacy, tweeted: 'Hang in there Mr. President. If those countries aren't as you described, Democrats should be happy to deport criminal aliens back to them.'[28] Media coverage of the event continued to be dominated by denunciations and the White House continued to flounder. President Trump and his allies realised that the characterisation of the remark as racist was the most damaging part of the fallout, and so did Don Lemon, *CNN Tonight* host, who had already opened his show on the Thursday night with the words: 'The President of the United States is racist. A lot of us already knew that.'[29]

On 14 January, according to a press pool report, as he headed for dinner at his Florida golf club, Trump was asked if he was a racist and reportedly replied: 'No, I am the least racist person you have ever interviewed.'[30]

The next day, 15 January and Martin Luther King Day, Trump retweeted a video of his weekly address that included the words: 'Dr King's dream is our dream. It is the American Dream.'[31]

Unfortunately, the previous day Congressman John Lewis, who had marched with King for voting rights in Selma, Alabama, in 1965, told ABC: 'I think he is a racist ... It's unreal. It's unbelievable. It makes me sad. It makes me cry.'[32]

Then, on the night of 15 January, the *Washington Post* reported an intriguing twist. Republican Senators Tom Cotton (Arkansas) and David Perdue (Georgia) had apparently told the White House that the Trump phrase they remembered was 'shithouse countries' and not 'shithole countries'. Vox published a tweet from Scott Wong that offered his own explanation of the change of nuance. 'Some Rs [Republicans] say "shithouse countries" refers to poor countries w/ no plumbing – places where you have to walk out to the shithouse – and therefore the phrase is NOT racist.'[33] Regardless of whether the word used was 'shithole' or 'shithouse', the derogatory quality of the utterance was similar.

Kirstjen Nielsen, the then Secretary of Homeland Security, who had been in the room when the remark was uttered, said in sworn testimony before a Senate committee the following Tuesday: 'I did not hear that word used.' Pressed on what she did in fact recall, she said: 'The conversation was very impassioned. The President used tough language in general, as did other congressmen in the room.'[34]

Just one African leader of long standing was unfazed. President Yoweri Museveni of Uganda was addressing the East African Legislative Assembly in Kampala some days later. A video published by local media showed that he was not as ready to be outraged as might have been expected.

'America has got one of the best presidents ever. Mr Trump. I love Trump. I love Trump. I love Trump because he talks to Africans frankly. I don't know if he's misquoted or whatever, but when he speaks I like him because he speaks frankly.'

'It is the fault of Africans that we are weak,' he added. 'They have this huge continent. If you look at Africa, Africa is twelve times the size of India in terms of land area, lots of resources, and the population is growing now. Why can't we make Africa strong?'[35]

Clearly Museveni, rightly or wrongly, refused to follow the general consensus on the US President's alleged comments.

But where did the race issue sit with evangelicals?

RACE AND THE EVANGELICALS

John C. Richards, an African-American who was then managing director of the Billy Graham Center Institute, expressed deep concern in an article published by *Christianity Today* (18 October 2018). The article drew on research by his then colleagues Ed Stetzer and Andrew MacDonald, in partnership with LifeWay Research, and he described what he called 'nuanced issues' among evangelicals that led them to vote for Trump.[36] Given the nature of the racial allegations against him, support for Trump was clearly a phenomenon that required investigation. For, whatever the truth behind individual allegations, the overall impression of the claims against the President might have been expected to give evangelicals pause for thought – indeed, they might have dented the extraordinary levels of support recorded among white members of the evangelical religious right.

For many, Richards suggested, it was a question of 'holding their noses', and about casting a vote against Hillary Clinton rather than one for Trump. However, Richards was disturbed by attitudes on the part of some evangelicals with regard to Trump's alleged words and actions, that ranged from apathy to 'outright defence', attitudes that seemed 'ripe for critique from the Christian community'. He reflected: 'I'm talking about things that Christians should hold out as important matters – like honesty, character, and integrity ... is it so difficult for some to criticise the President when he says or does something that doesn't align with the evangelical worldview – or embodies common human decency?'

Richards was making a point that had been made in rather different circumstances by Trump's so-called 'deplorables' in his electoral base: economic advantage was no longer the final arbiter when it came to the casting of one's vote. Trump appealed to something deeper, to something that resonated with deep stories. And this appeal appeared capable of shrugging off repeated accusations of racism.

'African-Americans have seen the tweets and heard the statements. Low IQ. Crazy. Unhinged. Dog. Crime loving. Disrespectful. These are just a few of the descriptive terms President Trump has used to describe Black men and women throughout his presidency,' Richards stated.

When asked whether they agreed with the statement 'I am

disturbed by comments President Trump has made about minorities', 55 per cent of evangelicals agreed, Richards reported. However, when broken down by race, the numbers told a different story. According to the survey, 82 per cent of evangelical African-Americans were disturbed by Trump's comments about minorities, while only 42 per cent of white evangelicals were. Once again the internal divisions within the evangelical movement were apparent. But how could the difference be explained?

While white evangelicals had generally moved the bar downwards in terms of the importance of the personal life of political leaders, in a revising of their attitude towards the Cyrus Factor discussed earlier, African-American evangelicals continued to regard character as important. In other words, it seemed that honesty, character and integrity mattered more for African-Americans than it did for white Americans. Given statements from members of the evangelical religious right about the importance of 'godly character' and 'godly government', this is surprising. Clearly, Donald Trump had appealed to something within their own view of America that outweighed allegations of racism, or indeed allegations regarding personal morality generally.

It is not a big leap from this assessment to the characterisation of white evangelicals as racist, and this thesis was offered by Nancy D. Wadsworth, who spent fifteen years as a scholar studying American evangelicals and race. She argued in Vox on 30 April 2018 that those evangelicals who were disappointed in their faith brothers and sisters for overlooking 'Trump's racism and misogyny' for short-term political gains were failing to see what was staring them in the face.[37]

These sympathetic critics fail to grapple with the idea that Trump's racism and misogyny might actually resonate with the evangelical base, which happens to constitute about thirty-five per cent of the GOP coalition. In fact racism and intolerance are more woven into the fabric of evangelicalism than these Christian critics care to accept ... the failure to consider motivations rooted in anxieties about race and gender as an explanation of evangelical Trump support represents a striking omission. The history of American evangelicalism is intensely racially charged. The persistent approval for Trump among white evangelicals ought to prompt far more critical self-reflection within the evangelical community than we've seen so far. Evangelicals' tenacious affection for Donald Trump is not a bug driven by expediency. Instead, it reflects defining *features* of American evangelicalism that become clearer when we examine the historical record.

A test of this assumption offered itself in the aftermath of the event that earlier became known simply as 'Charlottesville'. On 12 August 2017, a car was driven into a group of demonstrators who were protesting against a Unite the Right rally in the Virginia town. James Alex Fields Jr, who was twenty years of age and had driven from Ohio to attend the rally, deliberately drove into a crowd of protesters, killing Heather Heyer, aged thirty-two, and injuring up to twenty-eight other people.

Hours after the violence erupted, President Trump said that he condemned 'in the strongest possible terms this egregious display of hatred, bigotry and violence on many sides'.[38]

Both Republicans and Democrats criticised his failure explicitly to condemn the white extremists at the rally. 'Mr President – we must call evil by its name. These were white supremacists and this was domestic terrorism,' tweeted the Republican Colorado Senator Cory Gardner. Ivanka Trump tweeted: 'There should be no place in society for racism, white supremacy and neo-nazis'.[39]

The following day, a White House spokesman issued a statement saying: 'The President said very strongly in his statement yesterday that he condemns all forms of violence, bigotry and hatred. Of course, that includes white supremacists, KKK, neo-Nazi and all extremist groups.'[40]

Statement or no statement, the initial condemnation of violence 'on many sides' – seemingly implying a spread of blame – would continue to fuel charges of racism throughout Trump's first term. In addition, surviving Charlottesville more or less intact, was Trump's religious evangelical advisory board, a mix of born-again preachers, televangelists and conservative Christians with political influence.

Jerry Falwell Jr, president of the evangelical Liberty University, was one of the best-known members, who had earlier said evangelicals had found their 'dream President' in Donald Trump. On the Wednesday following Charlottesville, Falwell tweeted: 'Finally, a leader in the White House. Jobs returning, North Korea backing down, bold truthful statement about Charlottesville tragedy. So proud of Donald Trump.' The next day, he added: 'The truth as stated by Donald Trump is that violent white supremacists, Nazi, KKK and similar hate groups are pure evil and un-American.'[41]

Council member, preacher and Fox News commentator Robert Jeffress told CBN news: 'Racism comes in all shapes, all sizes and, yes, all colors. If we're going to denounce some racism, we ought to denounce all racism.'[42] Again, to many, this appeared to imply a spreading of the blame for what had occurred at Charlottesville. The only casualty, in terms of resignations from the board, was A. R. Bernard, a senior pastor and chief executive of the Christian Cultural Center in Brooklyn, New York, who issued a statement on 18 August announcing he was quitting. He said he had agreed to serve on the board because 'it often takes a gathering of unlikely individuals to shape the future of our nation'. 'However,' he continued, 'it became obvious that there was a deepening conflict in values between myself and the administration. I quietly stepped away from my involvement with the board several months ago and submitted my formal letter of resignation as of Tues. Aug. 15, 2017.'[43]

Allegations that Trump was 'really all about white supremacy' did not stop. Nor did concerns that something about this stance perhaps resonated with sections of the white evangelical community. Critics of that community could point to alleged traits within its history, which had, from the earliest settlements in the New World, shown an alarming propensity towards insularity and defining 'self' in contrast to those regarded as 'the alien other'. Was there something that stressed 'white' as much as it stressed 'evangelical' in some quarters, whatever the official statements to the contrary? Some critics, as we have seen, have certainly suggested this deserves consideration.

TRUMP AND THE PURSUIT OF THE AFRICAN-AMERICAN VOTE

For many, the Charlottesville incident and the President's response underscored their concerns, which had been growing for some time. But, even so, it was a tide that did not carry everyone in the black community with it. Here it is worth returning briefly to Aretha Franklin's funeral in 2018, where Reverend Jasper Williams Jr, pastor of Salem Bible church in Atlanta, delivered a eulogy that offered a lesson, as he saw it, in old-fashioned personal responsibility.[44]

Reverend Williams had eulogised Franklin's father, minister and civil rights activist C. L. Franklin, thirty-four years before, and so his appointment was seen by the family as particularly fitting. But his words were not what many in the congregation wanted or expected to hear. He blamed integration and the civil rights movement for 'ripping the heart' out of black micro-economies that once relied on black-owned small businesses, such as grocery stores, hotels and banks. And he said the black community was suffering because so many black children had no father taking care of them. The idea of children being raised without a 'provider' father and a 'nurturer' mother was like 'abortion after birth', he declared, before suggesting that a household could become stronger with two parents rather than one.

In a phone interview with Jonathan Landrum Jr of Associated Press the following Sunday, he did not apologise – as he had been called on to do following an avalanche of hostile reactions – but he did try to explain.

'Here's the root of what I've been talking about: in order to change America, we must change black America's culture,' he said. 'We must do it through parenting. In order for the parenting to go forth, it has to be done in the home. The home.'[45]

Williams had also been strongly criticised for his thoughts about the Black Lives Matter movement, which claimed that black people were selectively targeted by the forces of law and order. 'No, black lives do not matter!' he said. There was uproar, and Stevie Wonder yelled out: 'Black Lives Matter!'

'I think Stevie Wonder did not understand what I said,' Williams told AP.

I said blacks do not matter, because black lives cannot matter, will not matter, should not matter, must not matter until black people begin to respect their own lives. Then and only then will black lives matter. That's what I said, and again, and again, and again. We need to have respect for each other. Once we start doing that, then we can begin to change.

On social media, Williams was accused of misogyny and bigotry. 'I'm sure much of the negativity is due to the fact that they don't understand what I'm talking about,' he said.

Anybody who thinks black America is all right as we are now is crazy. We're not all right. It's a lot of change that needs to occur. This change must come from within us. Nobody can give us things to eliminate where we are. We have to change from within ourselves. It is ludicrous for the church not to be involved. The church is the only viable institution we have in the African-American community. We must step up and turn our race around.

If that happened, he said, 'it would be the greatest and best immortalisation we could properly give to [Aretha Franklin] for what she did for black America and the world when she lived'.

The words were hardly an endorsement of Trump, but Williams

was challenging the dominant narrative in a way that would be echoed by the movements trying to persuade African-Americans away from what they provocatively called the 'Democratic plantation'.

A few months later, on 31 January 2019, Trump invited black leaders to the White House to mark National African-American History month. Gathered with him in the White House were more African-American leaders consciously 'swimming against the tide'. Trump's official script for the evening began with a tribute to the community that had emerged from slavery:

In the year 1619, a Dutch trading ship sailed into the Chesapeake Bay and dropped anchor at Point Comfort, Virginia. The vessel's arrival marked the beginning of the unscrupulous slave trade in the American colonies. It was from this immoral origin – and through inhuman conditions, discrimination, and prolonged hardship – that emerged the vibrant culture, singular accomplishments, and ground-breaking triumphs that we honour and celebrate during National African-American History Month.[46]

In his actual address, however, he did not keep to this script. And what followed is significant: 'African-American leaders, pioneers, and visionaries have uplifted and inspired our country in art, in science, literature, law, film, politics, business, and every arena of national life. The depth and glory of these contributions are beyond measure. You know it. I know it. And everybody knows it.'[47] He continued:

Every citizen alive today, and generations yet unborn, are forever in debt [to] the brave souls who stared down injustice and championed the eternal cause of civil rights. During the Revolutionary War, African-American soldiers fought at the battle of Yorktown and helped our nation gain independence. In the next century, Frederick Douglass, Sojourner Truth, Harriet Tubman, and countless others risked everything to end the evil of slavery and secure the sacred blessings of freedom. And here we are, all together in the White House. This is a great thing. Right? This is a great thing. And this is a very, very special place.

He went on to name Rosa Parks, Medgar Evers, 'the immortal Dr Martin Luther King Jr', who 'challenged our nation to fulfil its founding promise that we are all created equal by God', as well as the trailblazing baseball great Jackie Robinson, born exactly 100 years before.

Those called to the podium included Pastor Darrell Scott, who received a noteworthy accolade: 'If you want somebody to defend you, this is about as good as you can get – he is brutal. Sometimes I say, "You're a pastor? You're the toughest pastor I've ever met … thank you, Darrell."'

He then called up Bob Woodson, the legendary civil rights leader 'who met Dr King, and was jailed for leading a very peaceful protest'. Trump quoted Woodson: '"Even when defeat was all around us, it was not in us." That's beautiful, right?'

Woodson replied:

I just want to thank God and also President Trump for turning the tables over in the temples – and attacking the status quo that is hostile to the interest of poor people. And I also want to bless you for your administration and the policies of Opportunity Zones and to giving low-income people an opportunity to help themselves. That's all they want; they want an opportunity to achieve. And your administration is working with us to make that happen.

Clearly, the Cyrus Factor was again in operation, but this time from an African-American evangelical perspective.

A comparison between Trump and Jesus might have been controversial on a less good-natured evening, but in the event, it was a reference by Clarence Henderson that drew on the biblical roots of the civil rights movement in an even more controversial manner. Clarence Henderson was among the first students to begin the Greensboro sit-in, Trump recalled.

In 1960, on the second day of the sit-in, Clarence was one of four students who sat at the long-segregated Woolworth's lunch counter – very, very famous event – in Greensboro, North Carolina. He helped spark a national movement. In cities and towns all across America, students joined in the protest, and really, it was an incredible moment in the history of our country. The grave injustice of segregation was really spelled out loud and clear. After more than 170 days of protest, the Woolworth lunch counter finally integrated … As Clarence has said, 'It doesn't take many people to make a change. It just takes courage.' And, Clarence, you have incredible courage, and I want to thank you very much for being here.

Trump knew what he was saying. All black leaders who supported him paid a price in terms of ostracism or worse. But Henderson made a particularly controversial reference. 'I am delighted to be here with the President. You know, Nehemiah was told by God to build a wall. And that's what you're doing. Amen.' It was, to put it mildly, a rather surprising parallel between the Old Testament rebuilding of the walls of a ruined Jerusalem and Trump's core election promise from 2016 of building a border wall between the USA and Mexico.

The battle with the Democratic opposition for funding to build the wall on the Mexican border, which Trump had promised repeatedly during his presidential campaign, had at that point plumbed depths of bitterness that still dominated the national conversation. Trump knew what he was doing when he praised Henderson's courage. For, if he is to increase his share of the African-American vote in 2020, it is crucial that he gains more African-American endorsements. This is regardless of whether white evangelicals appear unconcerned at the charges of racism levelled against him. Trump needs to win all evangelical votes: black as well as white.

However, whether Trump appreciated the full resonance of Henderson's reference to Nehemiah on this occasion was less certain, but resonant the reference certainly was. The biography of John Winthrop written by the New England Puritan Cotton Mather (son of theologian Increase Mather discussed earlier in Chapter One), published in 1702, was entitled *Nehemias Americanus* (American Nehemiah). Just as Nehemiah led the Israelites out of Babylonian captivity to the promised land, so Winthrop (as Mather argued) had led his flock from the deprivations of Europe to New England. In the mid-Atlantic, Winthrop had preached, 'the eyes of the world are upon us'. From the start, the Puritans were imbued with a sense of manifest destiny, and a sacralised vision of America. It was a mantle Trump sometimes seemed to reach for.

'As we commemorate African-American History Month, we remember the words of Dr King,' Trump said. 'In 1964, Dr King said, "When years have rolled past … children will be taught that we have a finer land, a better people, a more noble civilization – because these humble children of God were willing to suffer [for] righteousness' sake."'

With this under his belt, Trump launched out on his concluding paean to America:

> So we pledge, in the honour of our great African-American com-
> munity, to build a future when every American child can live in
> safety, dignity, liberty, and peace. As Americans, we all share the
> same dreams, the same hopes, and the same magnificent destiny.
> We are now, and will forever be, one people, one family, and one
> glorious nation under God.

The claim to a destiny that could be traced back to the Puritans was becoming more evident. But this time it was being referenced in an attempt to woo a crucial section of the US electorate that had hitherto resisted the appeal of the Trump phenomenon. Whatever Trump's personal views on matters of race, the very heritage that some felt was at the root of the willingness of many white supporters to back him was then deployed in an attempt to win votes from the black community. Only time will tell if the same complex heritage will appeal to both black and white US citizens.

CHAPTER SIX

IMMIGRATION AND THE WALL

On 8 January 2019, in the midst of what would prove to be the longest government shutdown in US history, Diane Rehm, on her podcast on American University Radio, asked Robert P. Jones, the chief executive of the Public Religion Research Institute, why white evangelical Christians so fervently supported the building of Trump's wall on the border with Mexico.

Jones offered some helpful insights, based on research into the question by his organisation. But first it is necessary to explain how the stand-off came about.

The building of a wall on the southern border of the United States, providing a barrier with Mexico, was an oft-repeated Trump campaign promise in 2016. At rally after rally, the Republican candidate stoked an image of undocumented migrants ('illegals') crossing the open border in their thousands, bossed by hardened criminals, human traffickers and drug traffickers, who were bringing with them the fentanyl and other drugs that were claiming hundreds of thousands of American lives. Even those not complicit in crime, it was alleged, were people whose contribution to the economy would be minimal, while their welfare dependency and cost to the taxpayer would be great.

During the first two years of his presidency, when he had a Republican majority in both the House of Representatives and the Senate, the building of the wall was not a top priority for Trump. He did, though, pride himself on delivering what he promised – and he could point to a long, if little publicised, list of goals previously met.[1]

He may well have intended to keep the building of the wall until the second part of his term, when it would be a likely vote winner that secured the loyalty of his support base in the 2020 election year. But if this was his plan, losing control of the House in the November 2018 mid-terms made the task much more complicated.

THE IMPORTANCE OF THE WALL

As he sat in the Oval Office mulling over the 2020 campaign, or turned on the TV to check on the few voices supporting him and the many going after him, it is easy to imagine the cries from the campaign rallies of 2016 – 'Build the wall! Build the wall!' – echoing around Trump's head. The author of *The Art of the Deal* may well have been speculating on what kind of face-saving accommodation might be reached with the Democrats in the House.[2] If so, he was about to receive a rude awakening.

Trump might be adept in the art of negotiation, and it might be true that – as Richard Cohen concluded in his 19 February 2018 article in the *Washington Post* – 'a lifetime in real estate has taught him an invaluable lesson: Everyone has a price', but it is one thing to negotiate with business or political rivals, and quite another to think you can negotiate with your political base, when you have given them absolute undertakings. Trump's enemies repeatedly portrayed him as a liar, and this narrative was beginning to drown out his portrayal of himself as a promise keeper. He needed to consolidate on the latter narrative, and hope that the 'pro' of 'promise-keeping' outweighed the 'con' of 'not always honest' when the voters go to the ballot box for the 2020 election.

He could modify his promise to 'make Mexico pay for the Wall': it might be possible to argue that lower illegal immigrant numbers would mean lower US dollar remittances to Mexico, as did the author and historian Victor Davis Hanson.[3] Hanson suggested Mexico and Latin America together receive $50 billion in annual remittances, with the majority of such transfers likely being sent by illegal aliens. Some of this is subsidised by welfare entitlements funded by American taxpayers. The system, Hanson asserted, helps the Democratic Party, in that it has already 'turned California blue. It soon will do the same to Colorado, Nevada, and New Mexico, and someday may flip Arizona and Texas.' While from the point of view of employers, 'open borders have ensured the hiring of industrious workers at cheap wages while passing on the accruing health, educational, legal, and criminal justice costs to the taxpayer'.[4] These are, of course, controversial claims.

In any case, perhaps many of Trump's supporters saw the promise of a wall as typically Trumpian rhetorical exaggeration. So that promise could be circumnavigated. But a wall was solid and visible; you can see it and touch it. Its absence, or its presence, in 2020 would speak louder than any words on the campaign trail. Without the wall, no matter how potent his words might be on paper, they would have a hollow ring at the rallies.

The appropriations Bill to fund federal government operations for the 2019 fiscal year had to be agreed by the President and Congress. But the Democrat-controlled House refused to agree to a sum of $5.7 billion that Trump demanded for the building of the wall. They knew that his political life depended on it, and he came to see this too. Any negotiation or accommodation that he might have been inclined towards quickly disappeared when he was reminded by supporters on the right, such as Fox News broadcaster Judge Jeanine Pirro, that any compromise, let alone capitulation, could lose him his base.

So, President Trump embarked on a narrative of 'keeping America safe', while the Democrats resorted to a narrative of 'compassion'. Then Leader of the House Nancy Pelosi said the wall was 'immoral' because of the suffering it brought to innocent, persecuted people from Central America seeking refuge in the United States. In response, Republicans might claim that hundreds of thousands of illegal immigrants today meant hundreds of thousands of Democratic votes tomorrow and that this was hidden under a moral cloak. President Trump pointed to drugs gangs, drugs deaths and the number of American families who had lost loved ones through the actions of illegal aliens; and likewise, albeit for different reasons, he held back from references to demographic transformation. He did not want to alienate those Latin-American voters who were starting to support him.

So, both sides dug in, with the result that the government was shut down for a total of thirty-five days, from 22 December 2018 to 25 January 2019. But why was the matter of immigration so important to evangelical voters in the first place? It is an important question that connects 2016 with 2019; and presages issues relevant in 2020.

It was in the middle of this shutdown that on her radio show Diane Rehm asked Robert Jones 'why [do] evangelical Christians support Trump's wall?'

First of all, Jones confirmed that this assumption was not just correct, but more than correct. While a sizeable 58 per cent of this group had supported the building of the wall in the election year of 2016, this figure had risen to a whopping 67 per cent in the Public Religion Research Institute poll of September 2018.

'So, do we need walls just to satisfy the evangelicals, or is there more to it?' Rehm asked.[5]

The promise to build a wall, Jones explained, was more than anything a 'symbolic winner'. Jones emphasised that even conservative organisations opposed to immigration admitted that a wall was not the most effective way of controlling immigrant numbers and that 'walls work as political messaging' more than they do as 'policy'. They are a visible 'bulwark against change', holding back the 'barbarians at the gates'. This symbolism worked so powerfully in the 2016 election because the white evangelicals really did feel 'anxiety, vertigo and fear', as they saw the sun setting on the world they grew up in, and once thought they owned.

This was why the key word in Trump's slogan 'Make America Great Again' was the last one, 'Again', because it signalled a return to a world where the white evangelical Protestants actually owned America's 'cultural table', rather than struggling to find a seat at it, as had been the case (they believed) under President Barack Obama. 'Again' possessed the same potency as the word 'Back' in the Brexit slogan of 'Take Back Control' in the EU referendum in the UK in the same fateful year of 2016. Many of those who voted Leave voted for the same reasons as those American voters who elected Trump as President. Leave promised the return of something that was perceived as having been lost, regardless of the contentious nature of such assertions. Such words have power.

From Trump's point of view, while his support group was declining and ageing as a demographic, and now made up only 15 per cent of the US adult population (some analysis suggests 17 per cent), they still constituted 26 per cent of voters.[6] And this population would vote for someone who would assist their rear-guard action against what they perceived to be their loss of influence over America. They needed the kind of leader who could not only stand his ground when their values were under attack, but make forays into enemy territory.

THE EVANGELICAL PERSPECTIVE: AN AMERICAN CYRUS?

In an interview with Julie Lyons conducted in March 2016, well before Trump sealed the Republican nomination in July, Robert Jeffress, the then sixty-year-old pastor of the 12,000-member Dallas First Baptist church explained why he supported Trump:

A couple weeks ago, Max Lucado,[7] a very respected Christian, wrote an op-ed denouncing Trump because of his tone and because of his vocabulary. When I'm looking for a leader who's gonna sit across the negotiating table from a nuclear Iran, or who's gonna be intent on destroying ISIS, I couldn't care less about that leader's temperament or his tone or his vocabulary. Frankly, I want the meanest, toughest son of a gun I can find. And I think that's the feeling of a lot of evangelicals. They don't want a Casper Milquetoast as the leader of the free world.[8]

It seems that 'Blessed are the meek' (Jesus's words in Matthew 5: 5) did not appear to be a pressing matter in the context of this particular analysis of evangelical responses to global political issues.

Two years into the Trump presidency on 23 January 2018, Tony Perkins of the Family Research Council spoke with Edward-Isaac Dovere for Politico's *Off Message* podcast.[9] 'Evangelical Christians', Perkins said, 'were tired of being kicked around by Barack Obama and his leftists. And I think they are finally glad that there's somebody on the playground that is willing to punch the bully.'

'What happened to turning the other cheek?' Dovere asked. 'You know, you only have two cheeks,' Perkins replied. 'Look, Christianity is not all about being a welcome mat which people can just stomp their feet on.'

We have referred to the King Cyrus theory of why evangelicals support Trump, and on 31 December 2018 Katherine Stewart elaborated on this idea in considerable detail in the *New York Times*.[10] 'The month before the 2018 mid-terms, a thousand theatres screened *The Trump Prophecy*, a film that tells the story of Mark Taylor, a former firefighter who claims that God told him in 2011 that Donald Trump would be elected President,' Stewart wrote.

In the film, the actor playing Taylor, in the midst of a vision, picks up a Bible and points to Isaiah 45. 'I will strengthen you though you have not acknowledged me,' the Lord says to Cyrus in this chapter, 'so that from the rising of the sun to the place of its setting men may know there is none besides me.'" 'I will raise up Cyrus in my righteousness: I will make all his ways straight. He will rebuild my city and set my exiles free.'¹²

Stewart quoted Lance Wallnau, an evangelical author and speaker who appears in the film, who once said: "'I believe the 45th President is meant to be an Isaiah 45 Cyrus", who will "restore the crumbling walls that separate us from cultural collapse"'.

In fact, Wallnau said rather more than this, and he merits quoting at greater length:

> Figures like Margaret Thatcher, George Patton, Winston Churchill and Abraham Lincoln do not step out of cathedrals onto the stage of history, yet we canonize them later as the instruments raised up by God to meet a singular crisis. Curiously many of these leaders were not the darling or favorite of contemporary Christians. Preachers thought Lincoln to be a godless skeptic; they stumbled over Winston's cigars and scotch; and they balked at Reagan's divorce and children from two marriages. Likewise, today's leading evangelicals have made their rejection of Trump public! Strangely ... *each* of them ended up as a defender of Christian values ... The question a Christian needs to ask, especially when their favorite candidate fails to get the nomination, is not, 'Who is the most Christian?' Instead ask, 'Who is the one anointed for the task?'¹³

Wallnau referred back to the presidential nomination process in 1860. 'God ... disrupts nomination processes,' he wrote. 'In 1860, the pious evangelical Salmon P. Chase was a better Christian than the men he ran against, but the wily Lincoln got the nomination on the third ballot. Chase could not understand why God had denied him, but in the end the Springfield lawyer proved to be the most suitable vessel for the coming chaos.'

'From my perspective, there is a Cyrus anointing on Trump,' said Wallnau, before paying tribute to even his character. 'Donald Trump may be shrewd but in matters regarding his faith he possesses the self-conscious candor of a man who knows he falls short but who fundamentally shares the same beliefs.' Wallnau would later say: 'Trump is like a child when it comes to the kingdom. He's open.'[14]

Wallnau provided an unusual insight into the Donald Trump that emerged in a two-and-a-half-hour meeting with 100 African-American pastors in Trump Tower in New York on 30 November 2015.[15]

'He [Trump] did a remarkable thing and challenged the room,' Wallnau revealed. '"I think you've gotten weak in speaking up and making your own voice heard. You, me included, as Christians have been spoiled by a long period when Christianity was acceptable."' 'It was a delightful jab in true Trump fashion,' said Wallnau. 'Marco Rubio is weak on immigration and Christians are weak on, well, being Christians.'

Wallnau had been invited to that meeting by Pastor Darrell C. Scott, co-founder of the New Spirit Revival Center in Cleveland Heights, Ohio, and co-founder and board member of the National Diversity Coalition for Trump.

'Trump wanted to meet and hear feedback from a variety of ministries assembled by Darrell. It was intense and interesting,' said Wallnau, before relating how Darrell Scott spoke out across the room to him. 'Dr Lance, share with Mr Trump what you told me on the phone yesterday.' Scott was referring to Wallnau's prophecies about a Trump presidency, that he would write about in his book *God's Chaos Candidate*.[16]

'I was shocked,' said Wallnau. 'He [Scott] could see as much but repeated, "Tell Mr Trump."' 'I was going to skip parts but when I did he insisted I explain it. So I shared it all and Trump took it in, telling me afterward with a hand on his chest, "What you said really, uh, it…"' He was trying to say it "ministered" to him or "touched" him but he's Presbyterian, not Pentecostal so he finally settled on, "that meant a lot. Really. I mean it."'

Stewart had her own take on this comparison between Trump and Cyrus, the sixth-century king of Persia, and it is not a flattering one: 'A lot of attention has been paid to the supposed paradox of evangelicals backing such an imperfect man, but the real problem is that our idea of Christian nationalism hasn't caught up with the reality,' she wrote. We are not dealing, in her view, with a pragmatic ends-justifies-the-means compromise – mere hypocrisy – but something even more sinister. Stewart argued that the evangelicals constitute what she described as a 'Christian nationalist' movement that is 'authoritarian, paranoid and patriarchal at its core. They aren't fighting a culture war. They're making a direct attack on democracy itself.'

Stewart quoted Trump telling evangelical leaders that they had 'gotten soft' and offered this as proof that Trump 'well understands this longing for the hard hand of the despot'.

From this she concluded that Trump supporters are longing, not just for a President, but for a 'king'. For them, kings like Cyrus, who don't have to follow rules but 'are [themselves] the law', are 'ideal leaders in paranoid times'.

It might be asserted by the defenders of US evangelicals that it was not only Christian evangelicals who were affected by the paranoia of the times, and that their opponents were not impervious to the condition either, but Stewart was not alone. It is clear that alarm at the perceived negative potential of the Trump phenomena can give rise to very strong feelings indeed.

REFLECTING ON EVANGELICAL MOTIVES

Tara Isabella Burton interviewed John Fea, a historian of American religion at Messiah College in Mechanicsburg, Pennsylvania,[17] for Vox in November 2018 about what motivates white evangelicals.[18] They are driven, Fea claimed, by 'religious fear':

> If you look closely at American evangelical history, you see fear everywhere. During the early 19th century, white evangelicals in the South constructed a 'way of life' built around slavery and white supremacy. When Northern abolitionists threatened this way of life by calling for the end of slavery, white evangelicals in the South responded by turning to the Bible and constructing a theological and biblical defense of slavery and racism. After the Civil War, the fear of integrating blacks into white society led to Jim Crow laws and desegregation.

However, the Trump era also marks a significant change said Fea, a self-described evangelical:

> Some believe that Trump, like King Cyrus, is delivering them from the 'captivity' of the Obama administration. Bible verses calling for obedience to government are used to justify immigration

policies that seem to contradict the teachings of the Scriptures in relation to refugees and 'strangers'. They find some verses useful and ignore others. They all read pseudo-historians ... who argue that the United States was founded as a Christian nation but has lost its way in the last 75 years. They are all in the business of 'reclaiming' and 'restoring' what they believe has been lost.

In this context the Trump wall offers a two-fold attraction. Literally, it promises to safeguard a threatened demographic, which feels the USA is changing beyond recognition as a result of real and feared immigration – this being especially important if those entering the nation are perceived as Democrat-inclined future voters. Figuratively, the wall emphasises a psychologically satisfying sense of an American fortress with its US exceptionalism protected against future change.

In a 24 June 2018 article in *The Atlantic*, Fea put these arguments into a deeper historical context.[19] 'White conservative evangelicals in America are anxious people. I know because I am one. Our sense of fear, perhaps more than any other factor, explains why evangelicals voted in such large numbers for Donald Trump in 2016 and continue to support his presidency,' he wrote, before reminding his readers of the assurance in John's Gospel that 'perfect love casts out fear'. He then traced the evangelical failure to overcome this fear back to the Puritans. 'A history of evangelical fear might begin with the 17th-century Puritans in Salem, Massachusetts, who feared that there were witches in their midst threatening their "city upon a hill" and their status as God's new Israel,' he described. 'They responded to this fear by hanging 19 people.'

'Our history of evangelical fear might also include a chapter on the early 19th-century Protestants who feared the arrival of massive numbers of Catholic immigrants to American shores,' he said. 'But other evangelical options were available. Biblical faith requires evangelicals to welcome strangers in their midst as a sign of Christian hospitality.'

Other Christians were more strident in their opposition to Trump. Zack Hunt, a self-described progressive Christian blogger, took issue (on Patheos on 7 January 2019) with Robert Jeffress on the question of whether there is a wall in heaven. Jeffress said there is, which in his view gave divine approval to Trump's wall. The text at the heart of the dispute is Revelation 21: 9–27, which includes the following lines:

And he carried me away in the Spirit to a mountain great and high, and showed me the Holy City, Jerusalem, coming down out of heaven from God. It shone with the glory of God, and its brilliance was like that of a very precious jewel, like a jasper, clear as crystal. It had a great, high wall with twelve gates, and with twelve angels at the gates...[20]

As this is apocalyptic writing, argued Hunt, it is not meant to be taken literally, and therefore there is no biblical support for Jeffress's 'bigotry'. Yes, there is a metaphorical wall in the Book of Revelation, admitted Hunt, 'but it's not there to sanctify Trump's monument to racism, bigotry, and fear. It's there as a subversive message of hope. A promise that one day the walls of exclusion and oppression and fear will be torn down. And the gates of heaven will be thrown open to welcome everyone regardless of race, language, or place of birth.'

Which is why, Hunt asserted, Trump's wall 'isn't just immoral. It's anti-Christ.' Whatever others may make of this heated argument, a more pressing issue for many readers will be trying to work out how the heavenly wall mentioned in Revelation has anything whatsoever to do with a steel, wire and concrete barrier to be erected on the US–Mexico border in the first place. The matter seems far beyond biblical exegesis. But it provides a fascinating insight into a particular evangelical mindset that is determined to find justification in the Bible for contentious contemporary US domestic policies.

Jim Wallis, of the progressive Christian social justice organisation the Sojourners, used the same device in an article in the organisation's newsletter, and came as close as possible to calling Trump the antichrist. He argued that a coming together of Trump's policies and evangelical concerns over issues, such as the appointment of federal judges, abortion rights, same-sex marriage and anxiety over Muslims, acts to assuage any concerns regarding the moral tone and strident nationalism of the Trump 'regime'.

I believe the Faustian bargain for power, undertaken by the white evangelical religious right, must be exposed and opposed on the basis of Donald Trump's support for white nationalism, which is in direct disobedience to the reconciling gospel and person of Jesus Christ. Even some political and media leaders, both Republican and Democrat, are now saying that Donald Trump's life and behavior is a direct contrast to the Beatitudes, Sermon on the Mount, and Matthew 25. I am asking why the white evangelical leaders of the religious right haven't drawn a moral line in the sand on the racial idolatry of white nationalism and supremacy that is directly and distinctively anti-Christ…

Its rhetorical overreach notwithstanding, this view of Trump and his supporters is developed in a lengthy paper by Robert Kagan published in the *Washington Post* on 14 March 2019.[21] Kagan argued that a resurgence of authoritarianism around the world – with its typically anti-immigrant agenda – represented the greatest threat to the liberal democratic order since the 1930s, and that white Christians were among the main culprits.

The premise underlying liberal convictions, according to Kagan, was that 'all humans, at all times, sought, above all, the recognition of their intrinsic worth as individuals and protection against all the traditional threats to their freedom, their lives and their dignity that came from state, church or community'.

However, this view of human nature did not account for the fact that 'humans do not yearn only for freedom. They also seek security – not only physical security against attack but also the security that comes from family, tribe, race and culture.' This was where white Christians came in.

In Europe and the United States, Kagan suggested that liberalism 'has progressively recognized the rights of people of color; of Jews and Muslims; of gays and others with sexual orientations frowned upon, if not forbidden, by the major religions; and, more recently, of refugees and migrants.' And this in turn precipitated 'the breakdown of white, Christian cultural ascendancy'.

MODERN ANXIETIES WITH DEEP ROOTS

Kagan argued that from at least the nineteenth century, American Protestants have felt anxiety regarding what they considered threats to themselves and their society. These ranged from emancipation to the immigration of large numbers of people whose culture was not Protestant, and for many was not European. This was only accelerated in the past century. These anxieties are a lot older than this. They can be seen in the foundational attempt by seventeenth-century Puritans to set up Bible Commonwealths and then to see their autonomy – from their perspective – being undermined by political and cultural changes from the 1690s onwards. This anxiety had deep roots. The Salem witch hunts were one very early manifestation of such anxiety, but by no means the only one. In Kagan's analysis the latest attempt to defend 'deeply rooted folkways and mores' from perceived threats, regarding gender roles, sexual definitions, gay rights and immigration, 'certainly played a part in the election of Donald Trump'.

Kagan was particularly disturbed by the nationalist tendency of Trump and his supporters. Trump told a rally in Texas on 22 October 2018:

A globalist is a person that wants the globe to do well, frankly, not caring about our country so much. And you know what? We can't have that. You know, they have a word – it sort of became old-fashioned – it's called a 'nationalist'. And I say, really, we're not supposed to use that word. You know what I am? I'm a nationalist, okay? I'm a nationalist. Nationalist. Nothing wrong. Use that word. Use that word.

An alarmed Kagan noted that these remarks were echoed by US Secretary of State Mike Pompeo when he addressed the German Marshall Fund in Brussels on 4 December 2018. Pompeo said that President Trump 'knows that nothing can replace the nation-state as the guarantor of democratic freedoms and national interests'. Pompeo could hardly have chosen a more potent venue to voice these opinions than the city that forms the engine room of the supranational European Union.

What must be remembered, though, when analysing Trump's focus on nationhood is that in the USA it is deeply intermingled with both the concept of liberty and the deep story of US Christianity that has seventeenth-century roots. The liberty to practice religion freely was exactly what the *Mayflower* Pilgrims were seeking in 1620 as they crossed the vast Atlantic ocean. And it was part of their Christian legacy that Americans 150 years later, on 4 July 1776, were able to declare that 'all men are created equal' and 'are endowed by their Creator with certain unalienable Rights', and that governments only derive their powers from the consent of the governed. The Declaration of Independence is often read as embodying Enlightenment principles (for all its ignoring of the rights of slaves, Native Americans or women), but its origins are, arguably, deeper still. For this remarkable document, that would come to be interpreted in ways far different from those envisaged by its original authors, was embedded in a concept of American exceptionalism and covenanting to form a community that can be traced back to the Winthrop Fleet of 1630 and the Mayflower Compact of 1620.

Nation, liberty and exclusion are thus all deeply intertwined in the cultural DNA of the USA. Not all politicians have attempted to exploit all three strands at the same time. But Donald Trump certainly has, and this has resonated with members of the US right; and particularly the evangelical right. He has tapped into their deep story.

By 25 January 2019, Trump could see from the polls that he was leaking support, and endorsed a stop-gap measure to allow the government to reopen for three weeks.

On 15 February, with the Democrats still refusing to budge, Trump elected not to shut the government down again, but to declare a national emergency. This allowed him to bypass Congress in pursuit of funding the wall. He could have done this earlier, he admitted, but he had wanted to find a bipartisan way through the impasse if that was possible.

In the event, it turned out he would be able to access significantly more than the $5.7 billion he had initially requested, using a combination of the $1.38 billion that Congress did agree, and other government sources.

Both the House and the Republican-controlled Senate passed a resolution rejecting Trump's emergency declaration, to which he responded by issuing his first veto. Overturning the veto would need a two-thirds majority in the House, and in the end the 248 to 181 vote on 26 March 2019 did not clear that threshold, with just fourteen Republicans voting with the Democrats.

Meanwhile, the national emergency allowed Trump to divert $3.6 billion, which was earmarked for some military construction projects, towards building the wall. On top of this, it transpired, the White House would be able to access $2.5 billion from the Defense Department's anti-illegal drugs fund. Acting Defense Secretary Pat Shanahan said in March 2019 that the first instalment of this –

$1 billion – would be used for fences, roads and lighting at the border. An additional $600 million would be available for the wall project from the Treasury Forfeiture Fund.[22]

After the House failure to overturn his veto, Donald Trump still faced fierce resistance from outside Congress, from a group of twenty states that were also seeking to block his emergency declaration. However, after the 26 March 2019 vote, it looked like the President would be able to take some pride of ownership in what his opponents had disparagingly called 'Trump's wall'.

CHAPTER SEVEN

SEXUALITY AND GENDER IDENTITY

Bernie Sanders is white, like Trump; in his seventies, like Trump (seventy-eight in September 2019 to Trump's seventy-three in June 2019); and like Trump was a presidential contender in 2016 and has declared his candidacy again for 2020. He lost to Hillary Clinton in the battle for the 2016 Democratic nomination, but has maintained his presidential ambitions since then.

He duly appeared at Al Sharpton's National Action Network (NAN) 'audition' for Democratic candidates in April 2019, bidding for the African-American vote that Hillary held on to, at his expense, in 2016. But, while it was an easy calculation to try to put that right, it was not so easy to understand his attack strategy, which was closely reminiscent of Clinton's attack on the 'deplorables' in September 2016.

Addressing the NAN convention on 5 April, Sanders declared:

It gives me no pleasure to tell you that we have a President today who is a racist, who is a sexist, who is a homophobe, who is a xenophobe, and who is a religious bigot ... I wish I didn't have to say that, but that is the damn truth and we gotta say it.[1]

It was not the first time Sanders had used the formula. On 30 October 2018 during a campaign event for Maryland Democratic candidate Ben Jealous, he said mid-term campaign staffers across the country 'are working to make sure that the agenda of the most racist, sexist, homophobic, bigoted President in history will go nowhere because Democrats will control the House and the Senate'.[2]

And on 5 April 2019, before he repeated the words at the NAN conference, at 8.16 a.m., he tweeted: 'We have a President who is a racist, a sexist, a bigot and a homophobe. I wish I didn't have to say that, but it is the damn truth. And we have to say it.'[3] It was clear that he was making the issue of identity politics one in which there was clear blue water between himself and Trump in the run-up to 2020.

Not all commentators thought this was a winning formula. 'Democrats seem to be doubling down on the "deplorables" attack,' wrote Tyler O'Neil on PJ Media on 5 April 2019, 'and that is good news for the President'.[4] But clearly Sanders and other Democrats had decided that identity was the issue to press.

THE ISSUE IN CONTEXT

In examining the part played by the white evangelicals and the continuing influence of their Puritan forebears in the rise of President Donald Trump, the key phrase used by Sanders in his accusation is 'religious bigot'. Many opponents of Trump have felt it is not difficult to find material that could help support allegations of racism, as we have seen. Allegations of sexism, albeit primarily historical in nature, were also well-rehearsed during the 2016 campaign, and we will return to these later in this chapter. If 'religious bigotry' was meant to suggest 'Islamophobia', this allegation had been made with regard to what became known as Trump's 'Muslim travel ban' early on in his presidency that singled out would-be immigrants or visitors from certain Muslim countries of origin. However, his 'ban' did not cover the majority of Muslim countries, and Trump argued that he was concerned not about the religion of people coming to America, but the fact that they might be arriving from countries where the government – if there was one – was unable to keep would-be terrorists in check. The case was litigated in the Supreme Court, and the President's policy was upheld.

Where the phrase 'bigot' did come into play, however, in the fevered national conversation, was as a code targeting evangelical Christians, and their beliefs regarding human sexuality. However, it was not easy to give Trump the label of 'bigot' in this regard. Given the weight of research that had gone into Trump's alleged racism, it is likely that, if he had made homophobic remarks, these would have been discovered and widely reported. But if searches for presidential homophobia were fruitless, much more promising, in this respect, were the professed personal beliefs and proven political positions of Trump's Vice-President, the evangelical Christian Mike Pence. A notable assault in this regard was mounted by South Bend mayor and presidential candidate Pete Buttigieg.

At the NAN convention, Mayor Buttigieg showed that he was alive to the importance of identity politics in his bid for the highest office. He began by apologising for his use of the phrase 'all lives matter', made in a state of the city address on 11 March 2015.[5] He later explained to reporters:

At that time [11 March] I was talking about a lot of issues around racial reconciliation in our community. What I did not understand at that time, was that phrase, just early into mid-2015, was coming to be viewed as a sort of counter-slogan to Black Lives Matter. And so, this statement, that seems very anodyne and something that nobody could be against, actually wound up being used to devalue what the Black Lives Matter movement was telling us.[6]

Having corrected himself on racial identity politics, Buttigieg would prove implacable – perhaps newly implacable, as it turned out – on the moral positions of evangelical Christians. In an interview with Kirsten Powers for *USA Today*, conducted on 29 March 2019 and published on 4 April, Powers asked Buttigieg, who is a gay man married in the Episcopalian Church, whether he thought Trump was a Christian. Buttigieg replied:

I'm reluctant to comment on another person's faith, but I would say it is hard to look at this President's actions and believe that they're the actions of somebody who believes in God. I just don't understand how you can be as worshipful of your own self as he is and be prepared to humble yourself before God. I've never seen him humble himself before anyone. And the exaltation of yourself, especially a self that's about wealth and power, could not be more at odds with at least my understanding of the teachings of the Christian faith.[7]

On NBC's *Meet the Press*, on 7 April, Chuck Todd tossed this quote back to Buttigieg. 'How do you square that assessment with the fact that the evangelical Christian community is so devoted to his candidacy?' Todd asked.

Buttigieg explained that, from his understanding, scripture and the church were about caring for strangers ('another word for immigrants', he stated) and 'humbling yourself before others'. He contrasted 'footwashing … one of the central images in the New Testament', with what he saw as the 'chest thumping look-at-me-ism' of the President of the United States. On the politics of abortion, meanwhile, in his view Trump had been cynical. To 'pretend' to be pro-life, said Buttigieg, was 'good enough to bring many evangelicals over to his [Trump's] side'.[8]

LGBT RIGHTS AND SAME-SEX MARRIAGE

Buttigieg was hardly the first public figure to view Trump in this way, as we have seen. But on the same day that he made these comments on *Meet the Press*, Buttigieg issued a challenge to Vice-President Pence. The grounds for Buttigieg's attack on Mike Pence were not the cynicism and lack of humility that he attributed to Pence's boss, but a charge of religious bigotry that was laid squarely at the feet of Pence himself.

Speaking at the LGBTQ Victory Fund National Champagne Brunch in Washington on 7 April, Buttigieg reflected on his personal struggles with his sexuality. 'If me being gay was a choice, it was a choice that was made far, far above my pay grade,' Buttigieg said. 'And that's the thing I wish the Mike Pences of the world would understand. That if you got a problem with who I am, your problem is not with me – your quarrel, sir, is with my creator.'[9]

Pence has personally opposed same-sex marriage. He responded to Buttigieg, whom he knew from his time as governor of Indiana, while Buttigieg was South Bend mayor, in an interview with Joe Kernen on CNBC's *Squawk Box* on 11 April. Kernen put it to Pence that Buttigieg was invoking Pence's name to 'highlight a conservative pushback to certain LGBT ideas on marriage equality'. 'Is that fair to use you as the bogeyman?' Kernen asked.

Pence was unfazed. He replied that he worked closely with 'Mayor Pete' when he was governor of the state, and their working relationship was 'great'. 'But I get it. You know, it's look … nineteen people running for president on that side … In a party that's sliding off to the left. And they're all … they're all competing with one another for … how much more liberal they can be. And so, I get that.'

Kernen did not leave the matter there, but asked Pence whether his views had 'evolved' on marriage equality and gay rights.

Pence pointed out that the Supreme Court had made its decision, and stressed that when he was governor of Indiana 'we fully implemented that decision into law'. But far from apologising for a view of marriage that informed the faith of the Pence family, he affirmed his stance by saying 'we stand by that'. That did not mean that the Pence family were critical of those who thought differently. On the contrary, in his view, freedom of religion and of consciences were among the blessings of the United States of America. So, the Pence family was free to continue to 'cherish our values, cherish our views'. He was part of an administration that wanted to be 'an administration for every American', so his views could live side-by-side with those who viewed marriage differently.[10] But it was clear that LGBT rights were becoming presented as a point of difference between the pro- and anti-Trump groups.

If Pence was starting to feel somewhat isolated, a week later he found, if not the cavalry, at least a senior diplomat with a big stick, arriving from an unexpected direction. Richard Grenell, the gay US ambassador to Germany, came to his support, and castigated Buttigieg in an interview on Fox News with Martha MacCallum on 18 April. Grenell compared Buttigieg's attempt to portray Pence as homophobic to a Jussie Smollett-style 'hate hoax'. He claimed that

> Mayor Pete has been pushing this hate hoax along the lines of Jussie Smollett for a very long time now, several weeks, and I find it really ironic that Mayor Pete stayed silent about this so-called hate hoax on him and others during 2015, 2016, 2017 when Mike Pence was governor [of Indiana]. There was total silence. It's ironic that right about now when he's starting his fund-raising apparatus to run for President that he comes up with this idea and this attack.[11]

Smollett, the gay African-American actor from the Fox TV drama *Empire*, had hit the headlines a couple of months before by allegedly staging a 'hate attack' on himself by Trump supporters, whom he claimed had tried to lynch him. The Chicago police department allocated considerable resources to the case, before coming to suspect that the 'attack' on the night of 29 January was a hoax. Initial attempts to prosecute Smollett for filing a false police report were dropped.[12]

After making this unflattering comparison, Grenell then gave his personal support to Pence and his wife, Karen, whom he vouched for as 'great' and 'godly' people. 'One of the things that really bothers me about this attack [by Buttigieg] is that Mike Pence is a friend of mine. Mike and Karen are great people. They are godly people. They're followers of Christ. They don't have hate in their heart for anyone. They know my partner, they have accepted us.'

Grenell said that, of course, he and the Pences did not agree philosophically on every issue, but for that matter, he didn't agree with his 'hero Dietrich Bonhoeffer' on everything; neither did he 'agree with [his] partner on everything'.

The ambassador said it was regrettable that the gay community, which 'used to be the community pushing tolerance and diversity … everyone should be able to accept and love each other … now suddenly there's a whole community of people that are demanding that we all think alike'. When Buttigieg came out as gay – which he did in 2015 – Grenell vouched for the fact that Pence 'complimented him' and 'said he holds him in high regard'. Grenell concluded: 'The Vice-President or then-governor has said nothing but positive things about Mayor Pete. I think this is a total hate hoax and I think it's outrageous.'[13]

The US Supreme Court ruling Pence was earlier referring to in his *Squawk Box* conversation with Joe Kernen was delivered on 26 June 2015. The court ruled 5 to 4 that same-sex marriage was a legal right across the United States. At that time fourteen states still had bans in place on gay marriage, and this ruling meant that they were no longer enforceable. President Barack Obama called the ruling a 'victory for America'. 'When all Americans are treated as equal, we are all more free,' he said.[14]

However, not all Americans shared this view. The ruling found particular disfavour among evangelical Christians, traditional

Catholics and other conservatives. Former Arkansas governor and then presidential candidate Mike Huckabee called the decision 'an out-of-control act of unconstitutional judicial tyranny'. Texas Republican governor Greg Abbott tweeted: 'Marriage was defined by God. No man can redefine it.' Archbishop Joseph Kurtz of Louisville, Kentucky, president of the US Conference of Catholic Bishops, called the decision 'profoundly immoral and unjust'.[15]

Such views were very much in the tradition of the jeremiad, made popular by Puritan preachers, but certainly not confined to Protestant thought, as exemplified in this case by the Catholic Archbishop Kurtz.

What was celebrated as being progressive by some, was condemned as an attack on traditional definitions of marriage by others and as undermining of the fabric of society. In a dissenting opinion, Justice Antonin Scalia claimed the decision showed the court was a 'threat to American democracy' because it said that 'my ruler and the ruler of 320 million Americans coast-to-coast is a majority of the nine lawyers on the Supreme Court'.[16]

Same-sex marriage was legalised in the UK since 13 March 2014, so this was an area where Brits could claim that the Americans were only just catching up with them, rather than vice versa. But while in the UK the battles around issues of abortion and gay marriage equality were long since over, in America, Christians of an evangelical persuasion were, and are, highly resistant to such changes. Trump's choice of Pence as a running-mate in 2016 had secured evangelical support on an issue where Trump himself appeared to offer little to the evangelicals.

Consequently, those evangelicals who believe that marriage is a permanent union of one man and one woman knew after 2016 that they had a like-minded fellow believer in the administration. The thrice-married President has kept his counsel on the matter. But the Vice-President was consistent in maintaining his personal views on marriage, which are well established.

MIKE PENCE ON LGBT ISSUES AND HIS CHRISTIAN CONTRIBUTION TO THE TRUMP PRESIDENCY

In 2006, as head of the Republican Study Committee, a group of 100 conservative House members, Pence supported a constitutional amendment that would have defined marriage as being between a man and a woman. Citing a Harvard researcher, Pence claimed: 'societal collapse was always brought about following an advent of the deterioration of marriage and family'. He further claimed that being gay was a 'choice' and said that preventing gay people from marrying was not discrimination but an enforcement of 'God's idea'.[17]

In his speech, Pence was declaring for traditional Christian views on sexuality, sexual identity and marriage that would be recognised by many traditional believers (including Jews and Muslims) and which was fully in line with the Puritan heritage.

Ten years later, on 20 July 2016 and as governor of Indiana, Pence addressed the Republican National Convention in Cleveland, Ohio, following his acceptance of the party's vice-presidential nomination. 'I'm a Christian, a conservative, and a Republican, in that order,' he said. His grandfather was an immigrant. He was raised in southern Indiana with a cornfield in his backyard, and the heroes of his youth were John F. Kennedy and Dr Martin Luther King Jr.

'We were raised to believe in hard work, in faith, and in family,' he said, introducing his three children and his wife Karen, to whom he had been married for thirty-one years. Pence's views may not have 'evolved', but they had perhaps become more coded.

Moreover, Pence knew well, as the whole country knew, that the man he would be campaigning with – and who was standing next to him on the stage – had allegedly not lived a life of marital faithfulness. It was an intriguing political alliance, and an equally intriguing chemistry that was displayed as Trump shook his hand. The men with such wildly contrasting personal histories appeared to like each other.

Pence would give implicit support to Trump's Christian credentials: if someone this devout could work with Trump, then perhaps the President's faith claims were not entirely hypocritical. And the longer the relationship endured, as Trump's White House appointees fell away with some regularity after he took office in 2016, then the more substance this thesis acquired. From the opposing point of view, accusations regarding Trump's amoral and immoral behaviour would offset the perception that Pence was thoroughly wedded to a theocratic Christian fundamentalism – a perception that shaded in the public imagination into the folk memory of the Salem witch hunts of the 1690s. It seemed a win–win combination.

Of course, the bond was not necessarily a stable one, and a misstep on either side could bring both men down in 2020 or before. But in an administration whose wayward shifts on personnel and – less so – on policy were much storied, Pence's role as an anchor of stability has been under-appreciated.

Arguably, Pence also drew some hostile fire away from Trump. In the UK, the term 'Project Fear' became part of the currency of the Brexit debate, and pointed to an alleged conspiracy on the part of politicians and the media to paint a picture of Britain outside the EU in apocalyptic terms. In the US, a different type of Project Fear developed, which generated fear of what might happen if, say, the successful impeachment, assassination or medical collapse of President Trump brought Mike Pence to the White House. *The Shadow President: The Truth About Mike Pence* by Michael D'Antonio and Peter Eisner was a widely reviewed bestseller. Frank Bruni of the *New York Times* was given an advance copy, and wrote an opinion piece on 28 July 2018, a month before publication date, entitled 'Mike Pence, Holy Terror: Are you sure you want to get rid of Donald Trump?'

'There are problems with impeaching Donald Trump,' Bruni wrote. 'A big one is the holy terror waiting in the wings. That would be Mike Pence, who mirrors the boss more than you realize. He's also self-infatuated. Also a bigot. Also a liar. Also cruel.' Bruni went on to contrast Trump – who at least had the virtue, according to Bruni, of not believing he was on a mission from God to shape America according to 'a regressive, repressive version of Christianity' – with Mike Pence. 'Trade Trump for Pence and you go from kleptocracy to theocracy. That's the takeaway from [this] forthcoming book,' Bruni told the *New York Times*' readers.[18]

The evangelical leader Franklin Graham (son of Billy) rushed to Mike Pence's defence and defended the faith the two individuals shared. '@NYTimes published a slanderous vile op-ed piece about @VP, specifically attacking his faith, which really is an attack on all of us who believe in God. I'm disappointed they'll stoop so low. I've never seen such hatred poured out against such a good man,'

Graham tweeted, adding a prayer for God to put a 'hedge of protection' around Pence and all his family.[19]

Others on the right echoed Graham's sentiments. Glenn T. Stanton in *The Federalist* described the attack on Pence by the *New York Times* and Bruni as 'anti-Christian Bigotry, Plain and Simple'.[20] The Christian Broadcasting Network, a conservative evangelical television station, founded by televangelist Pat Robertson, gave Pence a chance to respond to the allegation made in the book that he was a 'Christian supremacist'. 'The Bible says count it all joy when you endure trials of many kinds,' Pence told CBN's David Brody and Jenna Browder. 'Any time I'm criticized for my belief in Jesus Christ, I just breathe a prayer of praise.'[21] Faith battle lines had clearly been drawn on the LGBT issue.

WOMEN AND PERSONAL BEHAVIOUR

For Pence, however, a delicate balancing act has proved necessary with regard to his alliance with a man whose moral compass spins as wildly as Donald Trump's appears to do, at least with regard to his personal behaviour. Trump's chequered personal history, in particular with regard to women, is well-reported. However, so long as he is seen to have put such behaviour behind him and avoids embarrassing those evangelical supporters and allies who have defended him on the grounds that he is a changed man, then his defence of values that he shares with them outweighs reservations they might have about his character flaws.

Female supporters, however, are less sanguine than male supporters in this respect, as the loss of many women voters in the 2018 mid-terms showed. For this reason, the misogynist line of attack is a weapon that all the 2020 contenders have kept in their armoury. From their point of view, the President's personal history leaves a lot to be desired.

A history of Trump's marriages and alleged affairs was attempted in an article by Kate Taylor on Business Insider on 25 August 2018. In 'Porn star Stormy Daniels is taking a victory lap after Michael Cohen's guilty plea. Here's a timeline of Trump's many marriages and rumoured affairs', Taylor lists Trump's three marriages and his alleged affairs. The article is pegged to the deal Michael Cohen, Trump's long-time lawyer, struck with prosecutors on 21 August 2018 to plead guilty to eight federal crimes. While Stormy Daniels, whose real name is Stephanie Clifford, was not mentioned by name, Cohen pleaded guilty to making illegal contributions to the Trump campaign and to facilitating a $130,000 hush money payment to Daniels's lawyers, with regard to an alleged sexual encounter with Trump in 2006. 'There is no allegation of any wrongdoing against the President in the government's charges against Mr Cohen,' Trump's attorney Rudolph Giuliani said in a statement on the same day. However, the event put the alleged liaisons between a porn star and the President back on the news agenda.

Earlier, similar revelations and accusations could have wounded Trump's political ambitions fatally but did not. There are three in particular that deserve looking at. The so-called '*Access Hollywood* tapes' were published by the *Washington Post* a month before the November 2016 election. The tapes recorded Trump in September 2005 telling *Access Hollywood* host Billy Bush that he was able to 'grab' women 'by the pussy', stating that 'when you're a star they let you do it'.[22]

Reactions were immediate. Republican National Committee Chair Reince Priebus said in a statement: 'No woman should ever be described in these terms or talked about in this manner. Ever.'[23]

'This is horrific,' Hillary Clinton tweeted from her account. 'We cannot allow this man to become President.' Clinton's running-mate, Senator Tim Kaine, told reporters in Las Vegas, where he was campaigning: 'It makes me sick to my stomach.'[24]

The Action Fund of Planned Parenthood, which had endorsed Clinton, issued a statement by Executive Vice-President Dawn Laguens, which stated: 'What Trump described in these tapes amounts to sexual assault.'[25]

The prominent conservative Trump supporter Tony Perkins of the Family Research Council told BuzzFeed's Rosie Gray: 'My personal support for Donald Trump has never been based upon shared values.'[26]

Trump's running-mate, Mike Pence, said on Twitter that he could not defend Trump's words. 'As a husband and father, I was offended by the words and actions described by Donald Trump,' said Pence, although he ignored calls from several Republicans for Trump to step aside and let Pence himself be the nominee.[27]

The recording was made in September 2005, eight months after Donald married Melania, his third wife, in January 2005. 'The words my husband used are unacceptable and offensive to me,' Melania said in a statement after the national – and international – release of the tapes. 'This does not represent the man that I know. He has the heart and mind of a leader. I hope people will accept his apology, as I have, and focus on the important issues facing our nation and the world.'[28]

When asked about the tapes, Trump said: 'This was locker room banter, a private conversation that took place many years ago. Bill Clinton has said far worse to me on the golf course – not even close. I apologise if anyone was offended.'[29]

A further incident from 1997 came back to haunt Trump on the campaign trail in 2016. In the first year that Trump took ownership of the Miss Universe beauty pageant, he had been disappointed to discover that the reigning Miss Universe, Alicia Machado of Venezuela, had gained weight. Joined by reporters with cameras, he followed Machado into a gym to watch her work out. 'This is somebody that likes to eat,' Trump told the reporters. Hillary Clinton used this story in the first presidential debate in 2016. 'He called this woman "Miss Piggy",' said Clinton. 'Then he called her "Miss Housekeeping", because she was Latin-American. Donald, she has a name: Her name is Alicia Machado.'[30] Trump did not deny making the remarks, but made no apology, telling Fox News: 'She gained a massive amount of weight, and it was a real problem.'[31]

Although different to the Stormy Daniels accusation, this incident put Trump's attitude towards women firmly under the spotlight. Similar issues dogged other parts of the 2016 Trump campaign.

In 2016 Trump tweeted an unflattering photo of the wife of his leading primary rival Ted Cruz. An anti-Trump super-political action committee had used Facebook to post photos of Melania Trump's nude appearance in a *GQ* magazine spread some years before. Trump suspected that the Texan senator was behind the ruse, and tweeted on 22 March: 'Lyin' Ted Cruz just used a picture of Melania from a *GQ* shoot in his ad. Be careful, Lyin' Ted, or I will spill the beans on your wife!'[32] Cruz responded: 'Pic of your wife not from us. Donald, if you try to attack Heidi, you're more of a coward than I thought. #classless'.[33]

The next day Trump retweeted a tweet by @Don_Vito_08 with the caption: 'A picture is worth a thousand words'. An attractive photo of Melania was juxtaposed with an unflattering one of Heidi.

Cruz responded by tweet with the words: 'Donald, real men don't attack women. Your wife is lovely, and Heidi is the love of my life.'[34]

SEX, WOMEN AND VOTING PATTERNS

In facing such a rival, Clinton assumed that she had the votes of the female half of the American population in the bag. But she was wrong. Clinton won 54 per cent of the women's vote in 2016, with 42 per cent backing Trump. But when the figures were analysed to count how white women voted, a surprising 53 per cent voted for Trump.[35]

For Democrats, this figure was deeply alarming. It suggested that they did not know the electorate as well as they had assumed. Two years later the 2018 mid-terms registered a significant electoral shift away from Trump towards the Democrats on the part of women voters, but it was still not as substantial as the party's supporters felt they had a right to expect.

The Guardian's US columnist Moira Donegan searched for an explanation in an opinion piece on 9 November 2018, immediately after the elections. 'Half of white women continue to vote Republican. What's wrong with them?' was the headline. She noted that there was evidence that, while Republicans were slowly losing support among suburban white women, the situation was not as straightforward as it should have been.

She commented: 'No other race and gender group is so split. There is a battle on for the soul of America, between the peevish, racist cruelty of Trump and his supporters and a vision of inclusion, justice, and decency forwarded by an increasingly diverse coalition on the left.'

According to Donegan, this battle was being waged 'in white women's hearts'. The left was hoping that these women would abandon 'their historical loyalty to white supremacy' and instead embrace something 'kinder, more sustainable'.

But Donegan was not optimistic about the prospects for such an outcome. White women were not moving over to the Democrats in the numbers she had expected. 'What is wrong with white women?' Donegan asked.

Her highly controversial conclusion was that many women (and men for that matter) were attracted to a style of politics that many opponents simply considered racist and aggressive.[36]

The millions of women who have backed Trump would clearly reject this analysis. But Donegan recalled that the feminist writer Andrea Dworkin had long before suggested in her book *Right Wing Women*[37] that 'conservative women often conform to the dominant ideologies of the men around them as part of a subconscious survival strategy, hoping that their conservatism will spare them from male hatred and violence'.[38] The fact that this 'survival strategy' was 'subconscious' made it difficult to test. However, everyday experience, voiced via the independent and forthright conservative female figures heard daily in the media, or on a personal level among ordinary Americans, suggested that many members of this demographic were capable of thinking for themselves. Something more complex was going on.

In the same newspaper on 10 May 2019, Tom Perkins reported on a trip he made to Detroit to meet female Trump supporters in person. 'Women for Trump' was an offshoot of the Michigan Conservative Coalition and Michigan Trump Republicans, and was already inspiring similar initiatives in other states. Aware that among college-educated women in 2018 the Democrats held a 47 per cent advantage, Women for Trump was organising 'Trump-erware' parties designed to target that exact demographic. There were around sixty-five women at the party Perkins attended.

Anne Mutter, a Vietnam veteran who described herself to Perkins as 'an old-time conservative who believes in God and country', said she was alarmed by the number of young people drifting towards socialism, but thought this could work to Trump's advantage. 'He stands for what most of us really feel, especially those of us in flyover country,' she explained. The major concerns expressed by the attendees were immigration and abortion. Lenore Kurek told Perkins: 'The biggest questions I get are [about Trump's tweeting] and the way he says things, and I tell them: "You don't have to date him, you don't have to marry him, you just have to want to get the country going in the right direction."'[39] Perkins's interviews suggest that the matter of faith and traditional values was a clear driver of Trump's support among this group, not fear.

Cambridge University sociologist Kate Gaddini writing on The Conversation website in February 2019 provided a sober analysis of 'why white evangelical women support [Trump]'. The article drew on research conducted during visits to Bethel Church in Redding, California, a highly influential church in global evangelism and where Banning Liebscher launched the evangelical Jesus Culture (a youth outreach ministry) in 1999.

One reason women back Trump, Gaddini explained, is because of their 'prioritisation of racial and religious identity over their gender identity'. The sociologist pointed out: 'All of us manage and negotiate our various identities, emphasising some and suppressing others depending on the socio-political context we are in.' For white evangelical women, to be evangelical was 'firstly to be politically engaged with Republican partisanship, and secondly to focus this engagement around core issues – including abortion and immigration'. In other words, the women's evangelical identity, particularly in its white nationalist aspect, was the 'most valued aspect of their identity', while gender was secondary.

Clearly, for these women, being 'a woman' was not the most powerful factor when it came to personal identity and political activity. This can help explain why such evangelical women may be less offended by alleged misconduct by Trump and accusations of misogyny than female Democratic Party supporters and women generally. Such evangelical women, in effect, side-stepped the matter of women's identity politics as it is often understood. For them the future of the USA owed more to faith than to gender and sexuality.

Another factor that Gaddini observed in her study was that such women measured themselves 'against an "ideal" Christian woman, a figure of femininity many in the West may view as old-fashioned or outdated'. This ideal, as described to her by research participants, 'is strong but submissive, traditionally pretty but also outdoorsy, smart but not too smart, sexy but also chaste'. Ivanka Trump, Gaddini was told, was a favoured role model.

Such individuals might also have, perhaps, pointed to the pioneering Puritan women of seventeenth-century New England with names such as Mercy, Patience, Hopestill, Verity, Honour and Silence. Women whose strength and character were expressed within clear boundaries of behaviour, speech and sexual expression derived from a particular form of Christian faith. This is a model of femininity that is often forgotten but continues to affect the outlook and actions of many women within the US evangelical tradition.

'The fact that several scandals and allegations of sexual impropriety have failed to cost [Trump] their support reveals how some groups of people prioritise the different identities they hold – and how strongly ideas of femininity operate within tightly bound communities,' Gaddini concluded.[40] For Gaddini, then, there was a very specific form of identity politics at play in the evangelical support for Trump.

Moreover, a new breed of activists are urging members of their own nominal identity group to break away altogether from what they would regard as its 'straitjacket'. They argue that the fact that a person is black, or female, or gay, does not automatically mean that they should vote Democrat. And prominent among these activists are evangelical Christians.

Candace Owens is African-American, female and a Trump supporter. She has devoted her energies to 'Turning Point USA' (TPUSA), the pro-free-market, anti-big-government organisation set up to transmit these values to college students. She resigned as communications director of Turning Point USA in May 2019, having come under pressure over remarks she made earlier in the year in the UK on the compatibility (as she saw it) of nationalism and democratic freedom, which were construed by her opponents as defending elements of Hitler's programme. She frequently repeated her abhorrence of all that Hitler stood for, notably at a House of Representatives hearing on hate crimes and white nationalism on 9 April 2019, where Democratic Congressman Ted Lieu replayed a video of her UK remarks. As well as firing back at Lieu for taking the remarks 'out of context', she attempted to turn the agenda of the hearing back on itself, arguing it should really be addressing the issue of harassment of conservatives of colour.

By this time she was a widely known voice of the Christian right. In an address to a mainly white audience at Jerry Falwell's evangelical Christian Liberty University on 26 September 2018, she urged students to think and act as individuals, reject victimhood, and ask themselves 'why does the left mock God?' 'It's a weird thing – there's a lot of things you can make fun of, but it's very weird when you start making fun of Jesus Christ,' she said. 'Why would they do that?' The answer, she believed, was that 'the left wants to grow government, and it wants government in many ways to replace God in people's lives … it wants people to turn to government for every solution.'[41]

Owens has collected 10 million YouTube views, and gained more than 1 million Twitter followers, as well as an endorsement from President Trump. At a 10 April 2019 meeting with the press, when asked about the hate crimes hearing the day before, Trump said that he knew Owens, that she was 'a fine person, a fine young woman', and while he had not seen what happened in the House hearing, it sounded 'disgraceful'.[42]

Owens was not alone in demonstrating that support for Trump can be found among evangelical women and members of the African-American community, in a way that may surprise many observers. Lynette Hardaway (Diamond) and Rochelle Richardson (Silk), two African-American Christian sisters from an evangelical background, initially came to prominence, like Owens, through making YouTube videos and through other social media channels. Diamond and Silk have controversially called the Democratic Party a 'plantation' and Hillary Clinton a 'slave master'. Their counter-cultural backing of Trump brought them more than 1 million followers on both Facebook and on Twitter, and a visit to the White House on 24 March 2018. They insisted on *Fox and Friends* that 'Trump is not a racist, he is a realist'.[43]

Similarly surprising support can be identified in the LGBT community. Brandon Straka, a gay initiator of the #WalkAway campaign, has not opened up about his faith in public but, like Owens, Diamond and Silk with regard to African-Americans and women, has urged the LGBT community to – as he would put it – think for themselves, rather than follow what activists tell them to think. Such a message would have only been helped by President Trump's tweet on 31 May 2019:

> As we celebrate LGBT Pride Month and recognize the outstand-
> ing contributions LGBT people have made to our great Nation,
> let us also stand in solidarity with the many LGBT people who
> live in dozens of countries worldwide that punish, imprison, or
> even execute individuals … on the basis of their sexual orien-
> tation. My Administration has launched a global campaign to

decriminalize homosexuality and invite all nations to join us in this effort![44]

'BEST.PRESIDENT.EVER' wrote Straka, retweeting the President's tweet to his own 178,000 followers.[45]

In the run-up to the 2020 election in the USA these evangelical women, African-Americans and members of the LGBT community who depart from the conventional – what they see as the 'approved' – narrative on identity and gender often encounter opposition from fellow members of their apparent identity group. But this has not stopped such departures from happening. Understanding this helps make sense of the support that Donald Trump gets from some surprising gender and identity quarters. When combined with the Cyrus Factor explored earlier, it helps explain why these particular evangelical voters – and others – prioritise support for Trump ahead of factors relating to their demographic.

CHAPTER EIGHT

THE POLITICS OF LIFE

In 1969, Norma Leah Nelson McCorvey, aged twenty-one and born in Louisiana but by now living in Texas, fell pregnant for the third time. Her father had left the family when she was thirteen, leaving her in the care of her alcoholic mother. She married Woody McCorvey at the age of sixteen in 1963, but left him two years later alleging that he assaulted her. Her first child, Melissa, was born in 1965. Norma was drinking heavily and using drugs, and Melissa was adopted by McCorvey's mother. She gave birth to another child the following year who was also adopted.[1]

Abortion was legal in Texas in 1969, but only in circumstances where it was necessary in order to save the mother's life. After failing to procure an illegal abortion, McCorvey was referred to lawyers Linda Coffee and Sarah Weddington, who filed a lawsuit against the district attorney of Dallas County, Henry Wade. Five years earlier Wade had prosecuted Jack Ruby, who had killed Lee Harvey Oswald live on national television on 24 November 1963, two days after the assassination of President John F. Kennedy. But it was the McCorvey case, not the Ruby prosecution, that would write Wade into the annals of American history.

Despite a Texas district ruling in 1970 that the state anti-abortion law was illegal on the grounds that it violated the constitutional right to privacy, Wade determined to continue prosecuting doctors who performed abortions. In challenging him, Coffee and Weddington stated they were acting not just on behalf of McCorvey but of all women 'who were or might become pregnant and want to consider all options'.[2]

ROE *V.* WADE

The case worked its way up to the Supreme Court, and on 22 January 1973, with McCorvey accorded privacy as 'Jane Roe', and the child in question now adopted, the court ruled seven to two in favour of Roe, on the grounds that the right to an abortion was rooted in the right to privacy that was protected by the US Constitution's Fourteenth Amendment. On the same day of the judgment, former President Lyndon Johnson died, so the momentous ruling took second place in most newspaper headlines the following day.

The Fourteenth Amendment, which was ratified in 1868, granted citizenship to all persons born or naturalised in the United States – including former slaves – and guaranteed all citizens 'equal protection of the laws'. The amendment was bitterly contested by the recently defeated Confederacy and read:

> No State shall make or enforce any law which shall abridge the
> privileges or immunities of citizens of the United States; nor shall
> any State deprive any person of life, liberty, or property without

due process of law; nor deny to any person within its jurisdiction the equal protection of the laws.[3]

The Texas abortion ban was struck down as unconstitutional, and the federal reach of the Fourteenth Amendment meant that – like the Civil Rights Act before it in 1964, and the Obergefell *v.* Hodges same-sex marriage ruling in 2015 – the Roe *v.* Wade ruling applied to the whole of the United States.

The court divided pregnancy into three trimesters, and ruled that ending a pregnancy in the first trimester was solely up to the mother; in the second, the question of the mother's health came into play with some scrutiny by the state allowed; in the third trimester, the state could prohibit the abortion of a baby as at this point in pregnancy a foetus could survive outside the womb, provided that the mother's health was not in danger.[4]

America has been divided over the ruling ever since and, along with the Catholic Church, Christian evangelicals have been most fervent in their opposition to abortion, and even more determined than the Catholic Church in their attempts to bring down the Roe *v.* Wade decision since the 1970s.

Defenders of abortion rights, including leading abortion providers, have maintained that thousands of women died every year from botched abortions in pre-Roe *v.* Wade America.[5] Complex as the matter is, the official statistics tell a different, though still tragic, story, which only adds to the intensity of this debate, in which pro-life and women's rights arguments clash with increasing intensity.

By 1972, when the Centers for Disease Control and Prevention started keeping track of abortion-related mortality rates, the official record stated that there were twenty-four deaths from legally in-duced abortions and thirty-nine deaths from illegal abortions. The real number was almost certainly higher but it is unlikely to have reached the 'thousands' often alluded to.[6] Regardless of the figures, any such death is a tragedy.

In January 2018, the National Right to Life Committee (a pro-life advocacy group) published a far-reaching statistical analysis: 'The State of Abortion in the United States'. It estimated that since 1973 there had been 60,069,971 abortions in the country. This was based on data provided by the Guttmacher Institute, a pro-choice organisation producing some of the most reliable and complete estimates regarding the numbers of abortions performed.[7] The analysis also found that as a general trend, and despite significant demographic variations, the number of abortions and the abortion rate (per 1,000 women of childbearing age) were falling across the board: 'Nationally, abortions finally dipped below a million in 2013 for the first time since 1974, and the abortion rate is lower than it was when the Supreme Court decided Roe *v.* Wade.'[8]

Quoting an *American Journal of Public Health* article in which Guttmacher Institute researchers published their broader findings, the analysis revealed that abortion rates among women earning at or below the poverty level decreased by 26 per cent between 2008 and 2014, but still ended with the highest abortion rate of any demographic group studied (36.6 abortions per 1,000). This was against an overall 14.6 per 1,000 abortion rate for the population of women of childbearing age (aged fifteen to forty-four) as a whole.

The abortion rate among African-American and non-Hispanic women, which was above 60 per 1,000 women in 1991, fell by

27.1 per cent in 2014. However, the 2014 figure was still nearly three times the figure for white women, whose abortion rate in 2014 was ten per 1,000 women.[9]

These recent statistics remind us of the socio-economic complexity of abortion, alongside the moral, philosophical and political arguments that surround the issue, which we will now explore in more depth.

THE GROWTH OF THE PRO-LIFE MOVEMENT AND ITS POLITICAL IMPACT

The first anti-abortion March for Life, which called for Roe *v.* Wade to be overturned, was held on 22 January 1974 and attracted 20,000 people.

Through the 1990s, participation grew markedly. In 1998, on the twenty-fifth anniversary of Roe *v.* Wade, marchers were joined by Norma McCorvey herself, who had become a pro-life campaigner. In 2009, one year after the election of pro-choice President Barack Obama, hundreds of thousands took part in one of the biggest anti-abortion marches, according to the March for Life website. As with many large crowd estimates, the numbers reported differ among the sources.

For the 2019 event, organisers predicted 100,000 attendees but on the day itself some sources estimated that twice or three times that number walked up Constitution Avenue to the Supreme Court and Capitol Building. Speakers included Vice-President Mike Pence, who shared a video message from President Trump. Forty-six years after Roe *v.* Wade, the hundreds of thousands of participants in Washington, DC, clearly felt the tide of events might be turning their way.

Mike Pence had made a definitive appeal to evangelicals in his acceptance speech as Donald Trump's running-mate in 2016. 'As this election approaches,' Pence declared, 'every American should know that while we're filling the presidency for the next four years, this election will define the Supreme Court for the next forty. For the sake of the sanctity of life … We must ensure the next President … is Donald Trump.'[10]

At the March for Life 2019, Pence was equally forthright:

> You can be confident you do not stand alone. You are joined by tens of millions across this nation. And know that you have an unwavering ally in this Vice-President, in our family, and you have a champion in the President of the United States of America, President Donald Trump. The truth is, Donald Trump is the most pro-life President in American history.[11]

Pence proceeded to list the Trump administration's efforts to prevent tax dollars from funding organisations that advocate for abortion rights, appointing conservative judges and backing the defunding of abortion provider Planned Parenthood.

Writing in the *Washington Post* on 18 January 2019, Eugene Scott argued that the administration's positions 'on immigration, foreign policy, the economy or other issues' were less important to 'white evangelicals and other conservative Christians than issues related to abortion'.[12]

Support for Trump among white evangelicals at the time was nearly thirty points higher than the national average, according to a NPR-PBS NewsHour-Marist poll published on 17 January.[13]

By the start of 2019, Trump kept his word by successfully nominating likely pro-life justice Neil Gorsuch to the Supreme Court and then securing the elevation of the Catholic and likely pro-life Brett Kavanaugh, after one of the most bitter and divisive Senate Judiciary Committee hearings the country had seen. On 27 September 2018, the only witnesses were Kavanaugh and Christine Blasey Ford, who had accused Kavanaugh of sexual misconduct during his high-school days. Kavanaugh's youthful behaviour and habits were scrutinised in detail. The full Senate vote was delayed for a week, to allow a 'limited, supplemental' FBI investigation into the allegations. Senators were allowed to read the FBI report in secrecy, one by one, on 4 October, and on 6 October they confirmed Kavanaugh to the Supreme Court by a 50 to 48 vote.

The confirmation was seen as a victory for Trump, Kavanaugh and the pro-life movement in equal measure. The Democrats sensed, rightly, that they were seeing the beginnings of an attempt to overturn Roe *v.* Wade, and that the battle lines were drawn.

The contest between a woman's right to choose and the right to life of an unborn child took hold across individual states. Blue Democratic states began to push for the right to abort a child up to the very end of the third trimester. Red Republican states pushed in the opposite direction, attempting to outlaw abortions early in the first trimester, sometimes without exceptions in cases of rape or incest.

The contested issue of life, which had been a major factor in pulling evangelical support behind Donald Trump in 2016, has increased in intensity since then and has become one of the defining points of contention between supporters and opponents of the Trump White House.

On the Blue side, New York was one of the first states to act. On 22 January 2019, Democratic Governor Andrew Cuomo signed into state law the Reproductive Health Act, a statute designed to expand the rights permitting abortion, and to limit restrictions. Before Roe *v.* Wade in 1973, New York was already one of the four states that granted certain abortion rights. In 1970, while affirming that abortion was a crime, it had delineated some exceptions to allow abortion in certain circumstances. Moreover, of the four states – the others were Washington, Hawaii and Alaska – New York was the only one that did not stipulate a residency requirement. Between 1970 and the passing of Roe *v.* Wade in 1973, roughly 350,000 women had abortions in New York, with more than half of these coming from outside the state.

An article by Julia Jacobs in the *New York Times* of 19 July 2018, 'Remembering an Era Before Roe', carried a photo of a billboard from the early 1970s in Pennsylvania advertising 'Legal Abortions, usually under $250' in New York City.[14]

By 2018 abortion was still regulated in the state's criminal code, which stated that it was a crime in New York for an abortion to be performed after twenty-four weeks, unless the mother's life was in immediate jeopardy. This meant, for example, that if a woman discovered late in her pregnancy that her baby had abnormalities and would be unlikely to survive outside the womb, she would have to go outside the state if she wanted an abortion.

New York aimed to facilitate abortions for the 'small percentage' of women faced with such choices. In New York City in 2015, there were 63,610 abortions as reported by the Centers for Disease Control and Prevention's Morbidity and Mortality weekly report, Abortion

Surveillance United States 2015. Of these, 2.3 per cent were carried out after twenty-one weeks. The actual figure was 1,485.[15]

In the 2018 mid-terms, the Democrats picked up eight seats in the New York State Senate, establishing a 40 to 23 majority, and Governor Andrew Cuomo promptly made a promise about his legislative priorities. In the face of 'a federal government intent on rolling back Roe *v.* Wade and women's reproductive rights', he would enact 'critical legislation' to protect these rights in the first thirty days of the new term. He kept his promise and, in the State Senate in Albany on 22 January 2019, he signed into law the Reproductive Health Act, along with a Comprehensive Contraception Coverage Act. Next to him, as he signed, was Sarah Weddington. 'Thank you for what you've done for women,' she told the governor. To mark the signing of the Acts, Cuomo directed that the spire of One World Trade Center, the Governor Mario M. Cuomo Bridge, the Kosciuszko Bridge and the Alfred E. Smith Building in Albany be lit up in pink to 'shine a bright light forward for the rest of the nation to follow'.[16]

A few days earlier, on 7 January, Cuomo had been joined by Hillary Clinton at a rally at Barnard College, a leading women's liberal arts college in Manhattan. Representatives of Planned Parenthood, the largest single abortion provider in the US, also attended. The State Senate Majority Leader Andrea Stewart-Cousins introduced Clinton as 'our should-have-been President'. Clinton told the rally:

The struggle for women's equality is not simply something to be read about in the pages of your history books. It continues to be the fight of our lifetime. Women's ability to get basic healthcare, or right to make the most deeply personal decisions, is facing the most significant threats in recent memory.[17]

She introduced Cuomo as a 'lifelong champion of women's rights'. Cuomo referred to the Trump administration as 'insane' and said the nation had made a terrible mistake in 2016 by electing Trump rather than Clinton. He said that two years before, he had been told by the Republican State Senate that New York did not need a state law codifying Roe *v.* Wade, because the federal precedence that was enshrined in the decision would not be overturned. But times had changed, he said: 'I have no doubt that Gorsuch is going to reverse Roe *v.* Wade. So, what do we do? Protect ourselves. Pass a law that is a prophylactic to federal action.'[18]

Before 22 January 2019, abortion after twenty-four weeks in New York was limited to protecting the mother's life. The new law introduced by Cuomo allowed abortions past twenty-four weeks if the baby was not viable or to protect the mother's health, and removed all criminal penalties for abortion. 'Every individual who becomes pregnant has the fundamental right to choose to carry the pregnancy to term, to give birth to a child, or to have an abortion, pursuant to this article,' it read.[19]

New York was not the only state that took pre-emptive measures. On 29 January, Democratic delegate Kathy Tran proposed the Repeal Act (HB 2491) before a subcommittee of the Virginia state legislature. Under the Bill, there would be fewer restrictions on third-trimester abortions. As the law stood, such an abortion was only allowed to prevent a woman's death, or 'substantial and irremediable' damage to her mental or physical health, following the judgement of three physicians. The proposed Bill allowed the judgement to be made by one physician, and removed the words 'substantial and irremediable', so that there was no reference to the possible extent of the damage. This meant that a single physician would need to believe there was some possibility of damage to the mother's health to allow an abortion to go ahead.

The chairman of the subcommittee, Republican delegate Todd Gilbert, asked Tran, 'How late in the third trimester could a physician perform an abortion?' Tran replied, 'Through the third trimester. The third trimester goes all the way up to forty weeks … I don't think we have a limit in the Bill.' 'Where it's obvious a woman is about to give birth?' asked Gilbert. Even when 'she has physical signs that she is about to give birth … She's dilating?' 'My Bill would allow that, yes,' responded Tran.[20]

In an interview on the Virginia radio station WTOP the next day, Democratic Governor Ralph Northam, a paediatric neurologist who supported the Bill, was asked about Tran's remarks by WTOP reporter Julie Carey. 'Do you support her measure?' Carey asked. 'Explain her answer.' 'This is why decisions such as this should be made by providers, physicians, and the mothers and fathers that are involved,' Northam said. 'When we talk about third-trimester abortions, it's done in cases where there may be severe deformities. There may be a foetus that's non-viable.'

The governor went on to explain what would happen if labour had already begun. 'If a mother is in labour, I can tell you exactly what would happen,' he said. 'The infant would be delivered. The infant would be kept comfortable. The infant would be resuscitated if that's what the mother and the family desired, and then a discussion would ensue between the physicians and the mother.'[21]

President Trump was asked by the Daily Caller later that day about the unfolding controversy in Virginia. 'I'm surprised that he [Northam] did that, I've met him a number of times,' Trump told the news and opinion website. He had seen a video of Tran discussing the Bill earlier that morning, but hadn't yet heard Northam's remarks. 'I thought it was terrible,' Trump said of Tran's statements, adding, 'Do you remember when I said Hillary Clinton was willing to rip the baby out of the womb? That's what it is, that's what they're doing, it's terrible.'[22]

Trump was not the only one to express outrage. 'This literally makes me sick to my stomach,' former United Nations Ambassador and former Republican Governor of South Carolina Nikki Haley tweeted on 29 January, adding '#AdoptionIsAlwaysAnOption'.[23]

The Daily Wire editor-in-chief Ben Shapiro, who had joined Mike Pence to address the March for Life rally on 18 January, responded to Northam's comments with his own tweet: 'My wife (who, it is rumoured, is a doctor) stayed up all night with my five-year-old because my girl has a brutal cough due to flu (tonight is my turn). My wife then got up and went to work to care for her patients. That's feminism. Not murdering babies outside the womb.'[24] The ferocity of the debate was clearly apparent.

On 31 January, Tran, a mother of four who came to the US as an infant Vietnamese refugee in the 1970s, corrected her answer to the question of whether an abortion could occur when a woman was in labour. 'I should have said: "Clearly, no, because infanticide is not allowed in Virginia, and what would have happened in that moment would be a live birth.'"[25]

The Bill had already been tabled – its passage had been suspended – before the controversy exploded across the country. Tran said that she did not expect it to be taken up again during that current session.

Northam's spokeswoman, meanwhile, said his words were taken out of context, and that he was not trying to say that discussions between a woman and her doctor after a baby is born would include options for terminating the baby's life. His spokeswoman emphasised that the notion that Northam would approve of killing infants was 'disgusting'. She emphasised that his comments were 'absolutely not' a reference to infanticide, and explained that they were made in reference to 'the tragic and extremely rare case in which a woman with a nonviable pregnancy or severe foetal abnormalities went into labour'.[26]

The controversy was challenging for Northam but his remarks on abortion and new-born babies were not going to end his governorship. Evidence of racial insensitivity, on the other hand, that arose a day or two later, could have done just that. Photos emerged of Northam's school yearbook page from 1984 that featured an image of someone wearing blackface next to someone wearing a Ku Klux Klan costume. Northam later denied actually being in the picture (despite the fact he initially apologised for it). Hillary Clinton herself led the chorus of Democratic demands for his resignation.[27]

Fortunately or unfortunately for Northam, the two Democrats who were next in line to succeed him also turned out to be tainted by past behaviour or recent allegations. Virginia Attorney General

Mark R. Herring admitted that he had also worn blackface when at college, while Lieutenant Governor Justin Fairfax faced an accusation from Vanessa Tyson, a professor at Scripps College in Claremont, California, that Fairfax forced her to perform oral sex in a Boston hotel room during the Democratic National Convention in 2004.

Buried under these cascading dramas was a 31 January story by Tom Pappert of Big League Politics that alleged under the headline 'Governor Who Endorsed Infanticide Received $2 Million From Planned Parenthood' that the Northam campaign received '$1.996 million from Planned Parenthood Virginia over the course of five years, with most of the donations coming during his 2017 election campaign. These included massive cash injections of $338,852, $278,247, $255,641, and other similar amounts in the final days before the election.'[28] The allegation revealed how heated and intense the issue was becoming.

On 5 February 2019, President Trump delivered the State of the Union address, his second, to a joint session of Congress in the Chamber of the House of Representatives. The government shutdown had prompted exchanges between newly elected House Speaker Nancy Pelosi, whose prerogative it was to invite the President to the House Chamber, and the President himself, over the date of the constitutionally ordained occasion. The suspension of the shutdown on 25 January allowed Pelosi to invite Trump for 5 February, and Trump accepted.

Behind Trump as he gave his address were Pelosi and Vice-President Pence. A striking presence in the audience to his right were rows of women in white: Democrats and their guests wearing the colour of the women's suffrage movement. A record 117 women had been elected to Congress in the 2018 mid-terms.

When Trump declared: 'No one has benefited more from our thriving economy than women, who have filled 58 per cent of the newly created jobs last year', he appeared genuinely taken aback by the loud applause that ensued on both sides of the aisle.

'You weren't supposed to do that,' he ad-libbed to the women in white, before winning more applause for another tribute: 'All Americans can be proud that we have more women in the workforce than ever before – and exactly one century after the Congress passed the Constitutional amendment giving women the right to vote, we also have more women serving in the Congress than ever before.'

The shared celebrations did not last long. As far as many of the women in white were concerned, female progress in the workforce and abortion rights were connected. So, familiar divisions were re-established when the President turned to the recent legislation in New York and Virginia.

'There could be no greater contrast to the beautiful image of a mother holding her infant child than the chilling displays our nation saw in recent days,' said Trump.

Lawmakers in New York cheered with delight upon the passage of legislation that would allow a baby to be ripped from the mother's womb moments before birth. These are living, feeling, beautiful babies who will never get the chance to share their love and dreams with the world. And then, we had the case of the Governor of Virginia where he basically stated he would execute a baby after birth.

To defend the dignity of every person, I am asking the Congress to pass legislation to prohibit the late-term abortion of children who can feel pain in the mother's womb. Let us work together to build a culture that cherishes innocent life. And let us reaffirm a fundamental truth: all children – born and unborn – are made in the holy image of God.

The Republican side of the chamber gave a standing ovation. The women in white remained seated and stony-faced.[29]

The words that Trump used in that last sentence made it clear that his opposition to recent proposals was being crafted so as to appeal to religious beliefs and particularly to the Judeo-Christian tradition, since these words paraphrased Genesis 1: 26–27 ('God created humankind in his image'). For evangelical listeners this spoke to traditional Christian sexual outlook and practices which rooted the 21st-century pro-life position in the Christian traditions stretching back to the original founding fathers and founding mothers of seventeenth-century New England. In its simplest form: 'To the colonial Puritans, abortion was a sin.'[30] This was because it clashed with the concept of God-given sanctity of life and the role of procreation as a key feature of marriage; a central part of Puritan, and indeed mainstream traditional Christian sexual outlook. Pro-life seemed very much aligned with the Christian (and originally Puritan) cultural DNA of the United States.

However, the situation was originally more complex. Although abortion was condemned by the Puritans, they continued to uphold the English common law position that life in the womb only started at 'quickening' (when a woman felt a baby kick).[31] Termination prior to this was not illegal, although it was frowned upon. In short, Puritans practised limited early-stage abortion. In addition, Puritans never considered procreation the sole purpose of marriage. Consequently, sexual pleasure – although not traditionally associated with them – was promoted by Puritan thinkers as integral to good marriage.[32] In colonial North America, some 40 per cent of brides were pregnant on their wedding day. And it was not until 1821 that the first laws on abortion appeared in the USA and as late as the 1860s that abortion prior to 'quickening' became illegal.[33] Clearly, the Puritan heritage was originally less clear than it is now understood and presented as part of American Puritanism.

Regardless of these historical complications, the President's words were music to the ears of evangelical Christians, and represented a gauntlet being thrown down, not only to pro-choice Democrats but to abortion providers like Planned Parenthood, who knew that their funding was safe under the Democrats, but in jeopardy under the Trump administration.

In a statement issued the next day, Planned Parenthood pointed out that 'the ability of women to succeed is directly tied to their ability to control their own bodies', and claimed President Trump had 'flat-out lied, in a shocking attempt to demonize abortion care later in pregnancy and create controversy where absolutely none should exist'.[34]

Vincent Russell, president and CEO of Planned Parenthood Hudson Peconic (PPHP), which runs ten centres in three counties in New York, stated:

The comments from President Trump were extremely misleading

and disappointing. We will not apologize for protecting the rights of individuals to make the best decisions for themselves with their healthcare providers or enshrining the same protections as Roe *v.* Wade into New York State law. PPHP trusts our patients to make their own healthcare decisions. Our lawmakers should do the same … Reducing access to reproductive healthcare does not protect individuals but instead puts their health and lives at risk.[35]

The position presented by Russell was one that Trump had once broadly endorsed. Speaking to NBC News on 24 October 1999, he had strongly affirmed his pro-choice credentials, while at the same time saying with some ferocity that he hated 'the concept of abortion and everything it stood for'. 'I am pro-choice but I just hate it,' he said, speculating that if he had lived in Iowa rather than New York all his life, he might have held a different position.[36]

His views may have evolved since then, but the emotional antipathy with which Trump described abortion in 1999 arguably foreshadowed the strength of his pro-life position since 2016. Few would discount political calculation to secure his evangelical base as a motivating factor in his later highly charged remarks, which have been described as 'incendiary' by many opponents. Nevertheless, according to the evidence of his 1999 interview, the feelings that he drew on to charge these remarks have been a constant since then.

On 27 April 2019, Trump addressed a rally near Green Bay, Wisconsin. The Republican-majority state Senate was in the process of sending four abortion Bills to Democratic Governor Tony Evers for approval. One of them required that if a baby was born alive after an abortion attempt, then doctors should give the baby medical care and would face criminal penalties if they did not. Evers vowed to veto all the Bills, including this one, and the Republicans did not have the numbers to override his veto.

When Trump raised the issue at the rally at the Resch Center in Ashwaubenon, boos erupted from the crowd. 'Your Democrat governor here in Wisconsin shockingly stated that he will veto legislation that protects Wisconsin babies born alive,' Trump told the rally. He went on to lay out a controversial scenario, taking advantage of the earlier furore surrounding Northam's comments on abortion. 'The baby is born,' Trump explained. 'The mother meets with the doctor. They take care of the baby. They wrap the baby beautifully and then the doctor and the mother determine whether or not they will execute the baby. I don't think so.'[37]

Governor Evers responded at a Milwaukee Press Club event the following Tuesday afternoon. 'The President is the President,' he told the reporters. 'He's going to do this kind of crap as long as he's President.' 'It doesn't happen,' Evers said, with reference to doctors killing babies. 'We already have [statutes] on the book. This is nothing more than a distraction from the work that we need to do.'

He called Trump's remarks 'irresponsible' and comments by the Bill's author, Assembly Majority Leader Jim Steineke, blasphemous. 'For one of the Republican leaders in our state legislature to say "yeah he [Trump] is right, this is extreme on Evers' part", that is blasphemy.'[38]

Journalist Ryan Everson pointed out in the *Washington Examiner* of 6 June that neither Trump nor Evers was correct. Wisconsin doctors were not allowed to kill babies born after an attempted abortion, but neither were they required to care for such a baby as if he or she were a patient. Evers had called the SB175 Bill redundant, but in fact it offered new protections to the baby who survived an abortion. It would require

> any healthcare provider present at the time an abortion or attempted abortion results in a child born-alive to exercise the same degree of professional skill, care, and diligence to preserve the life and health of the child as they would render to any other child born-alive at the same gestational age.[39]

No such requirement existed in Wisconsin, so arguably the Bill was not redundant.

Trump was incorrect to say abortion doctors were 'executing' babies born alive. Aside from state statutes, a federal law – the Born-Alive Infants Protection Act of 2002 – makes it illegal to actively kill babies, regardless of how they are born. What Trump knew, however, was that to pro-life activists the difference between allowing a baby to die and actively killing one, while legally material, was in moral terms a specious technicality. A baby born alive had a right to all the medical help that any other person was entitled to.

LIFE AND THE ROAD TO THE 2020 PRESIDENTIAL ELECTION

When Trump officially launched his re-election campaign on 18 June 2019, in Orlando, Florida, he was still talking about the 'execution' of babies, even if this time his phrasing was slightly nuanced. 'Leading Democrats have even opposed measures to prevent the execution of children after birth,' he said. Condemning those who refused to legislate to prevent a baby's 'execution' stopped short of imagining deliberations on whether or not to execute a baby; but Trump had hardly changed his position. His opponents continued to express outrage over his use of the word. His supporters felt that at last they had a President ready to call out what they considered to be wilful obfuscation on the part of the abortion lobby.[40]

The way the pro-life and pro-choice positions had become polarised along party lines by 2019 is well illustrated by a sudden volte-face performed by Democratic presidential candidate Joe Biden, with regard to the Hyde amendment on abortion funding. The amendment, first passed in 1976, is named after former Representative Henry Hyde, an Illinois Republican. It bans the federal funding of abortion, with exceptions for rape, incest and when the life of the mother is in danger. Its opponents argue that it disadvantages poorer women and racial minorities, because it affects Medicaid funding. Its defenders point out that federal funding of abortion violates the conscience rights of pro-life Americans, who pay for abortion through their taxes if federal funding is allowed.

In his decades as a Democratic Senator, Biden, a Catholic, always supported the Hyde amendment, and opposition to it had not always been required by his party. It was only ahead of the 2016 election that the Democratic Party re-wrote its platform to oppose the amendment.

On 25 April 2019, Biden declared his candidacy for the Democratic presidential nomination. On 5 June, his campaign declared that he still supported the Hyde amendment. However, on the night of 6 June, at a gala hosted by the Democratic National Committee in Atlanta, he reversed his position. He said Republicans in a number of states were introducing 'extreme laws' to restrict abortion, and 'if I believe health care is a right, as I do, I can no longer support an amendment that makes that right dependent on someone's ZIP code'.[41]

Ilyse Hogue, President of the abortion rights group NARAL Pro-Choice America, said on the same evening that she was glad to see Mr Biden had changed his position. 'At a time where the fundamental freedoms enshrined in Roe are under attack, we need full-throated allies in our leaders,' she said. 'We're pleased that Joe Biden has joined the rest of the 2020 democratic field in coalescing around the party's core values – support for abortion rights, and the basic truth that reproductive freedom is fundamental to the pursuit of equality and economic security in this country.'[42]

Biden cemented his new position at Planned Parenthood's 'We Decide: 2020 Election Membership Forum' at the University of South Carolina's Alumni Center in Colombia on 22 June. He explained that his overall healthcare plan – which he had not released at the time – would rely on expanding access to federally funded health insurance, and if the Hyde amendment remained in place, the new beneficiaries would not have access to abortion coverage.

Twenty of the then twenty-three Democratic presidential candidates were at the Planned Parenthood event, which followed a pattern in which attendees would deliver testimonies to illustrate the importance of reproductive rights and candidates responded by promising to expand these rights, while resisting measures in conservative states designed to restrict abortions.

Earlier, Vermont's 2018 gubernatorial election provided an illustration of the Planned Parenthood approach to political engagement. The first openly transgender nominee, Christine Hallquist, ran for the Democrats against Republican incumbent Phil Scott.

In 2016 Planned Parenthood had come out strongly against Scott and spent $458,000 on behalf of his Democratic opponent, Sue Minter.[43] The reason was that, even though he affirmed abortion rights, he had said in the past that it might be appropriate to inform parents of minors if their child was having an abortion, and he had expressed reservations about some late-term abortions.

Hallquist was not in favour of these restrictions and expected an endorsement from Planned Parenthood. However, Vermont's Planned Parenthood branch announced a month before the election that it was declining to support either candidate as they were both equally deserving of the endorsement, which was highly prized in the liberal state. Lucy Leriche, the vice-president of public policy for Planned Parenthood of northern New England, confessed to 'an embarrassment of riches', adding, 'we're very lucky to have two candidates who are solidly in our corner'.

As state senator, Scott had cast some votes 'that gave people concern that he might be inclined to limit access to abortion', Leriche said, but Planned Parenthood had no reservations about his performance over his two years as governor.[44] In response to the Planned Parenthood survey both he and Hallquist had scored 100 per cent, meaning that neither of them supported any restrictions on abortion access. Beyond this, Leriche added, Scott had fought attempts at the federal level to restrict Planned Parenthood's funding. Scott won the race, taking 151,261 votes to Hallquist's 110,335.

The scale of federal funding for Planned Parenthood is considerable, and it is easy to see why the organisation is concerned about any threat of defunding. The Government Accountability Office report on healthcare funding for 2013 to 2015 showed that over this three-year period the Planned Parenthood Federation of America received $89.69 million from the Department of Health and Human Services (HHS), while the International Planned Parenthood Federation received $2.21 million from the HHS and $11.59 million from USAID. But this is not the whole picture. The report also explains that the HHS made additional awards to states that were then passed on to Planned Parenthood and that Planned Parenthood received $1.2 billion for services provided under Medicaid, Medicare and the Children's Health Insurance Program.[45]

The contention that Planned Parenthood's support for political candidates contravenes legislation on political funding – because tax-exempt organisations are not allowed to fund political activities – cannot be sustained. Planned Parenthood is affiliated with two offshoot political entities (Planned Parenthood Votes and Planned Parenthood Action Fund) separate from the main organisation that are allowed to engage in this kind of funding.

Nevertheless, on 20 June 2019, Planned Parenthood's worst fears began to be realised. The Federal Court of Appeals for the Ninth Circuit allowed the enforcement of a Trump administration ban affecting federally funded family planning clinics. The ruling impacted on the Title X family planning programme, under which Title X grants are made to clinics offering contraceptive services to low-income individuals across the country. The Ninth Circuit ruled that the Trump ban issued earlier in the year on abortion providers participating in the Title X programme, and disallowing their participation in abortion counselling and abortion referrals, could go into effect nationwide.

The HHS Secretary, Alex Azar, was delighted. 'This decision is a major step toward the Trump Administration being able to ensure that all Title X projects comply with the Title X statute and do not support abortion as a method of family planning,' he said.[46]

Planned Parenthood, that serves 40 per cent of Title X patients and receives $60 million a year in Title X funding, was less pleased. It had vowed to leave the programme if the bans went into effect, and Planned Parenthood president Leana Wen said in a statement: 'The news out of the Ninth Circuit this morning is devastating for the millions of people who rely on Title X health centres for cancer screenings, HIV tests, affordable birth control and other critical primary and preventive care.'[47]

In the Red states, momentum was also building. On 11 April Ohio's Republican Governor Mike DeWine signed into law a 'foetal heartbeat' Bill, banning abortion once a baby's heartbeat could be detected – which normally occurs between five and a half and six weeks gestation. The Bill had no exceptions for rape or incest, but allowed abortions 'to prevent the death of the pregnant woman' or if there was 'a serious risk of the substantial and irreversible impairment of a major bodily function of the pregnant woman'. Doctors who did not check for a heartbeat, or who performed an abortion after a heartbeat was detected, could face suits for civil damages. The Bill was set to take effect on 11 July, but on 3 July a federal judge, Michael Barrett of the US Court for the Southern District of Ohio, issued a temporary block on its going into effect until a case was finished that had been brought by the American Civil Liberties Union on behalf of Planned Parenthood and other abortion providers, arguing that the Bill violated Roe *v.* Wade.[48]

On 21 March, Mississippi's Republican Governor Phil Bryant had also signed into law a foetal heartbeat Bill, with exceptions similar to those in Ohio, and rendering a doctor who performed an abortion after the heartbeat was detected in danger of losing his or her licence. The day before signing the Bill, Bryant tweeted: 'We will all answer to the good Lord one day. I will say in this instance, "I fought for the lives of innocent babies, even under the threat of legal action."'[49]

In Georgia, the Bill that Republican Governor Brian Kemp signed into law on 7 May banned abortion when a heartbeat could be detected, but allowed an abortion at up to twenty weeks in cases of rape or incest, provided that the victim had filed a police report. Abortion was also allowed if the baby had a 'profound and irremediable congenital or chromosomal anomaly that is incompatible with sustaining life after birth'. 'We protect the innocent, we champion the vulnerable. We stand up and speak for those unable to speak for themselves,' Kemp said as he signed HB 481, the Living Infants Fairness and Equality (LIFE) Act. 'I realise that some may challenge it in the court of law, but our job is to do what is right – not what is easy. Through the LIFE Act, we will allow precious babies to grow up and realise their full God-given potential.' Georgia offers generous tax exemptions to filmmakers, and many Hollywood voices called for productions to be moved to locations in more abortion-friendly states.[50]

Missouri's Republican Governor Mike Parson signed a Bill on 24 May banning abortion after eight weeks of pregnancy, with exceptions if the mother's life is in danger, but not for rape or incest. Doctors performing later abortions faced five to fifteen years in prison. 'All life has value and is worth protecting,' Parson tweeted on 24 May after signing House Bill 126.[51]

In Louisiana, on 30 May, John Bel Edwards, the only pro-life

Democratic governor in the country, signed into law a Bill banning abortion if a foetal heartbeat can be detected. Exceptional circumstances included if the mother's life was in danger, if the baby had anomalies judged so serious they would not survive after birth, but not for victims of rape or incest. 'I have been true to my word and beliefs on this issue,' Edwards said in a statement after the signing.[52]

On 15 May Alabama's Republican Governor Kay Ivey signed a Bill that amounted to an almost total ban on abortion. The Alabama Human Life Protection Act defined the child in the womb as a legal person 'for homicide purposes', although a woman who had an abortion would not be held 'criminally culpable or civilly liable'. Abortion would only be permitted if there was a 'lethal anomaly' affecting the child, or to prevent 'serious health risk' to the mother, but not in cases of rape or incest. In a statement, Ivey acknowledged the wider intent of this highly controversial Bill. 'The sponsors ... believe it is time, once again, for the US Supreme Court to revisit this important matter,' she said, 'and they believe this Act may bring about the best opportunity for this to occur'.[53]

President Trump spotted the danger, and called for all those aiming to overturn Roe *v.* Wade to rally around a position that all pro-life campaigners could embrace. In three linked tweets on 18 May he set out his own position:

As most people know, and for those who would like to know, I am strongly Pro-Life, with the three exceptions – Rape, Incest and protecting the Life of the mother – the same position taken by Ronald Reagan. We have come very far in the last two years with 105 wonderful new...

Federal Judges (many more to come), two great new Supreme Court Justices, the Mexico City Policy [that blocks federal funding for abortion-supporting NGOs], and a whole new & positive attitude about the Right to Life. The Radical Left, with late term abortion (and worse), is imploding on this issue. We must stick together and Win…

For Life in 2020. If we are foolish and do not stay UNITED as one, all of our hard fought gains for Life can, and will, rapidly disappear![54]

This was confirmation of a strategy that went to the top of the Trump administration, and at the same time a warning from the President that pro-life could lose, if its champions did not act as team players, and speak with one voice. And it is clear that in this battle evangelicals will be at the forefront of the battle line.

Pro-life members of the evangelical religious right would hold their views even if they were unaware of Puritan history. But the presence of that Puritan deep story (shorn of the actual historical complications) only adds to the sense of being part of an historic American spiritual and moral tradition that is at war with aspects of modernity. Nowhere is this seen more vividly than in the field of abortion. Here an existential conflict is embodied in the opposition to Roe *v.* Wade. To achieve victory in that conflict, compromises are accepted (supporting a less-than-Puritan Trump) and long-games deployed that will influence future decades (Supreme Court nominations). On this front of the culture war, the reason for evangelical support for Trump is seen in sharp focus: nothing less than a battle for the soul of America.

CHAPTER NINE

LAW AND THE CONSTITUTION

On 18 June 2019 in Orlando, Florida, the forty-fifth President of the United States, Donald Trump, compared himself to the first President, George Washington. He injected flippancy into his remark, thereby sidestepping all but the most churlish allegations of grandiosity. But the fact that he made the very same point, in the very same way, when addressing the Faith and Freedom Coalition on 26 June, suggested a degree of calculation and intent. The comment worked on two levels. The former TV host of many years standing was well aware of the power of subliminal suggestion. President Trump could be mentioned in the same breath as President Washington. And then there was the substantive point. Trump was launching his 2020 re-election campaign, and presenting his record of achievements since 2016. He mentioned his signature issues – the booming economy with record low unemployment, notably for Latin-Americans and African-Americans, the ongoing battle to restrict illegal immigration – but among these, with equal pride of place, was his appointment of judges, and it was on this issue that he made a concession to Washington: Donald Trump would never beat his record![1]

COURTING THE EVANGELICALS

For evangelical Christians who see America as standing at a cross-roads, with one road following the rapid erosion of what they consider the country's founding values, and the other road leading to the securing of these values for decades to come, the issue of maintaining a robust judicial system is paramount. Conservative judges are considered to be a bulwark against residence and welfare rights of illegal immigrants – a cost borne by the American taxpayer who would be obliged, under the Democrats, to contribute from their personal income to what is viewed as a potential block vote for Democrats as the years go by – and they are a battering ram in the battle against Roe *v.* Wade.

Trump made it plain on 18 June that the appointment of judges had been a priority for him from his first day in office: 'I get there the first day. "How many judges do I have to appoint?" They said, "Sir, 139." Now it's 145 and we've just finished number 107, already approved sitting on the bench, how about that?'

And this, he promised, was just the beginning:

By the time we're finished with the rest, we will have record percentages. Our percentage will be a record except for one person. One person has a higher percentage than your favourite President Donald Trump. You know who that President is? He's got a higher percentage than me and it's devastating. His name is George Washington.

Referring to 'George' as if he had been a friend of his in New York, he went on: 'George is at 100 per cent and there's no way I'm going to get there no matter what I tell you. Got 100 per cent. Well, he was first, so he just appointed them all and that was it. That's going to be a hard record to beat.'

Having prepared the ground with knowing humour, he shifted gear, to pour opprobrium on the Democrats: 'They want to take away your judges. They want to pack the court with far-left ideologues and they want to radicalise our judiciary.'²

It was a powerful narrative and it became one of the main pillars of the Trump re-election campaign. One pillar was 'three words: jobs, jobs and jobs'; another was controlling illegal immigration; he was still formulating his policy on healthcare, but was determined to establish a popular successor to Obamacare; he had already turned around the decline in military spending, to the satisfaction of the majority of voters and of the armed services, and he would continue to trumpet this achievement; but equal to all these – because these individuals would define the future of America for the children and grandchildren of current voters – was the building of a conservative judiciary. In the Trump narrative, he could offer prosperity; properly defined and policed borders; security; choice and affordability in healthcare; but through judicial nominations, he would also construct the framework of the real America on the foundations of the Declaration of Independence and the US Constitution. And America would always come first.

It was this last pillar that allowed him to develop – recklessly or ruthlessly depending on your perspective – possibly the most potent weapon in his anti-Democrat armoury. The Democrats consistently and repeatedly relied on the narrative that Trump was a racist. Trump and his supporters could point out that back in the

1990s in New York he had worked closely with – and been regaled by – the likes of Jesse Jackson for the financial support he gave to causes promoting the advancement of African-Americans; they could name the African-American leaders, many of them evangelical Christians, that supported him today; they could point to African-American economic progress in general under his presidency; and to historic appointments such as his nomination in April 2019 of Lorna M. Mahlock to be the first African-American woman promoted to the rank of brigadier general in the US Marine Corps. But none of this dented the 'Trump is a racist' narrative. And this was not surprising since Trump's tweets often encouraged these views, or consciously triggered them, depending on how observers analysed and judged his motivations.

However, Trump was aware that he needed something as potentially lethal as the racist narrative used against him to use against the Democrats. It was not enough simply to deny the accusations; he needed to turn the tables on his opponents, and to do so in a way that inspired his support base, among whom Christian evangelicals dominated, but also reached into decisive and wavering 2020 constituencies. In his defence of the constitutional legacy of the founding fathers, he found the keystone he was looking for.

It was one he clearly felt had been presented to him by the Democratic Party, in more or less every comment of the presidential contenders for 2020 who had declared by mid-2019. His narrative, as the campaigns began the run to November 2020, was that the Democratic Party had been captured by socialists and, as such, were the enemies of US prosperity, liberty and constitutional safeguards.

The clearest evidence, from the Trump perspective, was provided for him in the MSNBC Democratic presidential primary debate nine days after the Orlando rally, on 26 and 27 June. Co-moderator Savannah Guthrie asked the candidates to raise their hand if their healthcare plan would cover undocumented immigrants. 'This is a show of hands question and hold them up so people can see. Raise your hand if your government plan would provide coverage for undocumented immigrants,' Guthrie said to the candidates.[3] Joe Biden, Bernie Sanders, Kamala Harris, Andrew Yang, Pete Buttigieg, Kirsten Gillibrand, Michael Bennet, Marianne Williamson, John Hickenlooper and Eric Swalwell all raised their hands.

A few hours later Trump tweeted: 'All Democrats just raised their hands for giving millions of illegal aliens unlimited healthcare. How about taking care of American Citizens first!? That's the end of that race!'[4]

One of the congresswomen many conservatives considered most responsible for this shift to the left was not on the platform. Alexandria Ocasio-Cortez, from New York, had quickly established a higher media profile than most of her more seasoned colleagues. She teamed up with the newly elected Ilhan Omar of Minnesota, Rashida Tlaib of Michigan and Ayanna Pressley of Massachusetts; the four congresswomen have been collectively referred to as 'the Squad'. Ocasio-Cortez used the media's focus on her to promote big government policies that were usually to the left of House Speaker Nancy Pelosi's. The group's foreign policy positions centred on pro-Palestinian criticism of policies adopted by America's foremost ally, Israel. These four women came to international prominence in July 2019 when they were subjected to an intense Twitter attack launched by Donald Trump. This was the Twitter storm which culminated in Trump supporters chanting 'Send her back! Send her back!' at a rally held at Greenville, North Carolina, on 17 July, aimed at the Muslim congresswoman Ilhan Omar, who was born in Somalia.⁵

To return to the Democrat show of hands on 27 June; this was powerful ammunition for Trump and his supporters, for whom it implied socialism and represented government appropriation of social, economic and religious freedoms, which were written into the US Constitution and the Bill of Rights. The erosion of these principles was incompatible with everything that America – the 'real' America – stood for. 'Tonight, we renew our resolve that America will never be a socialist country,' Trump had declared in his State of the Union address, as the cameras panned over to the self-declared socialist, Bernie Sanders. 'We are born free and we will stay free.'⁶ He would repeat this assurance many times. Kevin McCarthy, the House Minority Leader, told reporters on 12 July that the choice for voters in 2020 was straightforward: 'Socialism versus freedom.'⁷

Socialism, the right contended, was not only good at spending other people's money (in Margaret Thatcher's words); it could be ruthless with those who threatened its precepts. This alleged tendency, too, was laid out by President Trump in Orlando on 18 June 2019.

Trump reminded his audience of the late September day when the Senate Democrats attempted to prevent the appointment of Brett Kavanaugh to the Supreme Court:

> Look at what they did to a great gentleman, Justice Kavanagh, highly respected. They didn't just try to win. They tried to destroy

him with false and malicious accusations. And thank you, Marco [Rubio], and thank you Lindsey [Graham] wherever you may be. Thank you, great job, thank you.[8]

The dramatic intervention of Lindsey Graham, in particular, on the day of the hearing, had turned the tide for Kavanaugh. 'What you want to do is destroy this guy's life, hold this seat open and hope you win in 2020 – you've said that, not me,' Graham had told the Democratic senators. 'This is the most unethical sham since I've been in politics, and if you really wanted to know the truth [about Kavanaugh's school years and his fitness for office] you sure as hell wouldn't have done what you've done to this guy.'[9]

After asking Kavanaugh whether he thought the hearing was a job interview, Graham said: 'This is not a job interview. This is hell, this is going to destroy the ability of good people to come forward because of this.' Finally, he declared: 'To my Republican colleagues, if you vote no [to Kavanaugh's appointment], you are legitimising the most despicable thing I've seen in my time in politics.' Graham, then sixty-three, had been a South Carolina senator since 2003, and a representative for the state in the House from 1995.

Trump kept the memory of this moment alive not only because it allowed him to portray the Democrats as vicious. It also allowed him to portray them as opposed to the 'real' America. He continued:

They tried to ruin the family of now, Justice Kavanagh. They tried to ruin his career, they tried to ruin his life. They even wanted to impeach him on fraudulent charges … Those charges were a fraud. He did nothing wrong. All in pursuit of political domination and control. Just imagine what this angry left-wing mob would do if they were in charge of this country. Imagine if we had a Democrat President and a Democrat Congress in 2020. They would shut down your free speech, use the power of the law to punish their opponents, which they're trying to do now anyway, they'll always be trying to shield themselves.[10]

In 2016, when promising to 'Make America Great Again', he had targeted what he termed the Washington 'swamp', the allegedly corrupt individuals who held power but did not in his view act in the interest of the country and its people. Since his election he had found few friends in the media willing to go along with this narrative. But as he moved into the second half of his first term, he seized the opportunity to move from defence into attack. The release of the Mueller Report (into Russian interference in the 2016 election) after almost two years, on 18 April 2019, found no evidence of Trump campaign collusion with the Russian interference in the election – so, no constitutional case for impeachment on the basis of 'high crimes and misdemeanours'.[11] Friends in the media were still extremely difficult to find, but through his chosen vehicles of packed, adulatory rallies, and Twitter, he could remind people of what America's lost greatness, that he was now reclaiming, had been built on.

Real America had been built – with a wisdom and foresight that weathered the storms and horrors of the Civil War, facilitated the end of slavery and anticipated the malign in political human nature as well as the benign, building in safeguards against the first and making best use of the second – on the US Constitution. America's greatness was founded on the Declaration of Independence, signed – without Washington, who was defending Manhattan against the British at the time – in Pennsylvania on 4 July 1776, and on the Constitution approved in Pennsylvania on 17 September 1787, by all twelve state delegations to the Constitutional Convention, after almost four months of deliberations, under the presidency of Virginia deputy George Washington. This was a deep story indeed.

The choice before the voters in 2020, Trump has declared, is about saving or losing America, and if America is to be saved the Constitution has to be defended. Trump would defend it and the Democrats, he claimed, would destroy it.

'They would strip Americans of their constitutional rights while flooding the country with illegal immigrants in the hopes it will expand their political base, and they'll get votes someplace down the future. That's what it's about,' he told his Orlando audience in June 2019. This was a key strategy, by which Trump sought to connect the issue of illegal immigration with that of constitutional probity and the long game of defending traditional America.

Then Trump harked back to the most resonant promise of his earlier campaign: 'And we are building the wall. We're going to have over 400 miles of wall built by the end of next year.' For evangelical Christians, this transition from the Constitution to the wall on the southern border was unforced and logical. The unspoken link was self-evident: it was not possible to define a country unless you could define – and police – the borders. According to Trump's, and most evangelicals', shared view of the 'real America', illegal immigrants and undocumented migrants were evading the due and established process by which immigrants could legally become American. And they were entering America by colluding with the Democrats. In the 27 June MSNBC debate, co-moderator José Díaz-Balart had said: 'Raise your hand if you think it should be a civil offense rather than a crime to cross the border without documentation.'[12] Most US immigration laws are part of the civil code, similar to tax laws. However, Section 1325 of the Immigration Code makes entering without authorisation, or 'improper entry', a federal misdemeanour. A conviction is punishable by a fine and up to six months in prison. Eight candidates raised their hands, some more eagerly than others. Former Vice-President Joe Biden raised a finger.

The arraignment in a Los Angeles court in July 2019 of twenty-two MS-13 gang members accused of killing seven people did not help the Democratic cause. In March 2017, MS-13 members allegedly targeted a rival gang member who they believed had defaced MS-13 graffiti. After abducting, choking and driving the victim to a remote location in the Angeles National Forest, six members fatally attacked him with a machete, the indictment alleged.

A *Los Angeles Times* editorial of 18 July averred in its headline that 'MS-13 was born in L.A. No wall can keep it out'. 'The violent gang was born on the streets of L.A. in the 1980s among young refugees from the civil war in El Salvador,' the editorial claimed. They had subsequently returned and spread their brand of violence 'throughout not just El Salvador but Guatemala and Honduras as well', and continued to recruit young men and women by force. President Trump 'has at times tried to press his case against illegal immigration by spotlighting violent acts here by MS-13 members', the editorial said, admitting that 'criminals from Central America (but with deep ties to southern California) are implicated in brutal murders around the country ... The killers include people who entered the United States illegally. It makes sense to keep such violent criminals out. It also makes sense to deport some violent criminals already here.'

But the editorial concluded with a plea for understanding of the plight of the people on the border:

It's also important to remember that the vast majority of immigrants and would-be immigrants to the US are not the criminals but more often their victims. They flee their countries to get away from the violence, and then once here – regardless of their immigration status – most try to live their lives, raise their families and operate their businesses without threats or shakedowns. No wall can keep them out, because they are us.

It is difficult to imagine this final statement cutting much ice with evangelical Christians, or many other Republicans for that matter. As we have seen, for these Christians the wall had a double meaning that Trump well understood. It was a physical wall, built to establish a physical boundary. And it was a figurative wall, conjured up to slay the demons that haunted the evangelical mind. For, while most of the immigrants on the southern border come from Latin-American Christian traditions, they are not evangelical Protestants. But, more fundamentally, they are seen as part of a complex set of change factors that challenge the traditional white, conservative evangelical vision of the USA. For many evangelicals, a whole series of cultural changes threaten all that is familiar to them and illegal immigration symbolises this, since such people (they fear) will make it possible for future Democrats to irreversibly change US constitutional arrangements and, as a result, change America itself.

Evangelicals have felt that the rug of America – woven with the images of the founding fathers, the words of the Declaration of Independence, the US Constitution and the Bill of Rights and bound by an unwritten assumption of Protestant Christian principles – has become ever more threadbare in recent years; and the new generation of allegedly 'progressive-socialist' Democrats is poised to yank it entirely from under their feet. Alongside this idea is an anxiety that the evangelical vision of a Christian America is threatened by a combination of big government, secularism, liberalism and Islamic influences. Trump was and is seen as the last hope. Evangelicals began to believe that it may take time, but given another six years, the America that had been so 'threadbare' in 2016 could be not only patched up, but restored to its original condition, the condition that God had always intended for this exceptional country. Constitutional arrangements could be safeguarded in order to protect America from progressive change. No, illegal immigrants were not 'us'.

THE ORIGINS OF THE SOUL OF AMERICAN NATIONALISM

The differences over whether the founding US documents were Christian continue to fuel passionate debates. In his book *The Founding Myth: Why Christian Nationalism is Un-American*, Andrew L. Seidel mounted what he called 'an assault on the Christian nationalists' identity'.[13] Not only are they wrong, he claimed in an interview with Paul Rosenberg in May 2019, but 'their policies and their identity run counter to the ideals on which this nation was founded'. 'The Judeo-Christian God demands obedience,' Seidel claimed. 'So here you have a country that was built on rebellion [against the King of Great Britain], versus a book that is all about obedience, and the two are in fundamental conflict'.[14]

A different case was argued in June 2011 by Mark David Hall, the Herbert Hoover Distinguished Professor of Political Science at George Fox University. Asking 'Did America Have a Christian Founding?', Hall pointed out that 'to understand the story of the United States of America, it is important to have a proper appreciation for its Christian colonial roots. The colonists of European descent who settled in the New World were serious Christians whose constitutions, laws and practices reflected the influence of Christianity'. However, while these [Puritan] settlers 'planted' what became the United States, its 'founding' came later, in the War of Independence and in the creation of the Constitutional order. By the late eighteenth century, a theocratic approach to the political order had evolved into a determination to protect religious liberty.[15]

So, while Christianity is not mentioned in the US Constitution or the Bill of Rights, Hall insists that the founders of the republic were still influenced by Christian ideas, brought to their shores a century and a half earlier. This faith taught them that human beings are sinful, and this Christian-inspired realism meant that they avoided utopian experiments, such as those pursued during the French Revolution. As James Madison wrote in 'Federalist No 51': 'If men were angels, no government would be necessary. If angels were to govern men, neither external or internal controls on government would be necessary.'[16]

This understanding of the necessity of accountability, according to Hall, led to 'a constitutional system characterised by separated powers, checks and balances, and federalism'.[17]

In the eyes of modern conservatives, the eighteenth-century founders (themselves building on seventeenth-century Puritan foundations) were clearly anticipating and pre-empting the utopian tendencies inherent in socialism that led inexorably to the erosion of individual liberty. For Hall, moreover, Christianity informed the founders' understanding of the very concept of liberty. They would have rejected the way the concept elides into licentiousness in the contemporary Western world, and would rather have seen freedom as 'the liberty to do what is morally correct', as Hall put it, quoting Supreme Court Justice James Wilson's 'marvellous' dictum: 'Without liberty law loses its nature and its name, and becomes oppression. Without law, liberty also loses its nature and its name, and becomes licentiousness.'[18]

Again, according to Hall, the founders believed that humans were created in the image of God. This led them to conclude that humans are rational beings, and so, in his words, 'we the people (as opposed to the elite) can order our public lives together through politics rather than force'. This belief 'also helped inform early (and later) American opposition to slavery'. In other words, the first three resounding words of the US Constitution, 'We the People', were derived from a Christian understanding of the nature of the person. Moreover, and crucially, religious liberty was not something granted to ordinary people by their governing superiors, but an inherent right. George Mason's 1776 draft of Article XVI of Virginia's Declaration of Rights betrayed a flawed view of liberty that James Madison spotted. 'All Men shou'd enjoy the fullest Toleration in the Exercise of Religion', Mason wrote. Not good enough, said Madison, and Article XVI was amended 'to make it clear that "the free exercise of religion" is a right and not a privilege granted by the state'.[19]

This led to the first Congress proposing, and the states ratifying in 1791, the First Amendment that prohibited Congress from restricting religious observance: 'Congress shall make no law respecting an establishment of religion, or prohibiting the free exercise thereof.'

Even Thomas Jefferson, who favoured a strict separation of church and state, closed his second inaugural address on 4 March 1805 by encouraging all Americans to join him in seeking 'the favour of that Being in whose hands we are, who led our forefathers, as Israel of old...'.[20] These were words that implicitly led back to the *Mayflower* (1620) and the Winthrop Fleet (1630).

Washington, for his part, in his 1789 Thanksgiving Day Proclamation, referred to 'the duty of all Nations to acknowledge the providence of Almighty God', recommended the 'People of these States to the service of that great and glorious Being, who is the beneficent Author of all the good that was, that is or that will be' and urged unity in 'most humbly offering our prayers and supplications to the great Lord and Ruler of Nations'.

While this last statement was couched in rather unspecific terminology, without explicit Christian detail, the spiritual heritage that Washington was drawing on seems clear; even if it was not as scripturally referenced as that of Jefferson.

Hall concluded his essay with the carefully measured words: 'We ignore at our peril the Founders' insight that democracy requires a moral people and that faith is an important, if not indispensable, support for morality. Such faith may well flourish best without government support, but it should not have to flourish in the face of government hostility.'[21]

Since taking office, Trump has framed his support for Christian evangelicals in the context of overall support for religious liberty, as demanded by the US Constitution. A White House dinner for evangelical leaders, on 27 August 2018, included key figures Paula White, Alveda King, Franklin Graham, Jerry Falwell, Darrell Scott, Robert Jeffress, Ralph Reed, Tony Perkins, Lester Warner and Dr James and Shirley Dobson. Trump welcomed his guests with the following words:

> America is a nation of believers. And tonight, we're joined by faith leaders from across the country who believe in the dignity of life, the glory of God, and the power of prayer. Everybody agree with that? … We're here this evening to celebrate America's heritage of faith, family, and freedom … As you know, in recent years, the government tried to undermine religious freedom. But the attacks on communities of faith are over. We've ended it. We've ended it. (Applause.) Unlike some before us, we are protecting your religious liberty … We sent the entire executive branch guidance on protecting religious liberty. Big deal.[22]

For Trump's support base, this really was a big deal. What mattered was that the US Constitution defended their religious freedom, which they perceived to be under assault. If they were to survive in an America they recognised, it was essential that the judiciary read the documents in this way too. This was because their religious freedoms – as they understood them – required judicial safeguards with regard to specific rights and restrictions, which impacted on US society.

TRIALS OF STRENGTH

The judges Trump was referring to in his address on 18 June in Orlando were those commonly referred to as 'Article III' judges, so named because Article III of the US Constitution states that 'the judicial Power of the United States shall be vested in one Supreme Court and in such inferior Courts as the Congress may from time to time ordain and establish'. The judges, in effect, hold lifetime appointments.

Article III judges are nominated by the President and confirmed by the Senate. The number of Supreme Court justices has been fixed at nine since 1869. Appellate court judges, the next federal tier, sit in one of the twelve regional 'circuits' or the federal circuit, and for this reason are also known as circuit judges. The third tier, district court judges, sit in one of ninety-four district or trial courts across the country, and handle civil and criminal cases.

There are 179 judges who sit on the circuit courts, and 673 on the district courts (the number of active judges is lower than these numbers, because of the career paths within the system). Given that the Supreme Court can only deliver around 100 decisions a year, circuit and district appointees are vitally important in terms of shaping the future of the country – they are the final decision-makers in many fiercely disputed cases. Circuit and district judges usually sit in a panel of three, so the decisions of one or two individuals can have an impact on the whole country.

This is something that President Trump understands. On
1 November 2017, he tweeted: 'Thanks to @SenateMajLdr McConnell and the @SenateGOP we are appointing high-quality Federal
District … and Appeals Court Judges at a record clip! Our courts
are rapidly changing for the better!'[23]

In his Orlando speech eighteen months later, the Senate Republican leader Mitch McConnell was not accorded a presidential
namecheck, but his efforts in this regard had been unstinting.

McConnell had made it his mission in the last two years of Obama's presidency to delay the filling of any judicial openings, up to
and including the Supreme Court seat for which Obama nominated Merrick Garland, but which finally fell to Trump nominee Neil
Gorsuch. After Trump took office, McConnell kept conservative
judicial nominees moving through the Senate with unremitting
vigour, aided by the increase in the GOP Senate majority after the
2018 mid-terms.

As of 13 November 2018, Trump had already appointed almost
twice as many judges as Obama had at the same point in his presidency. According to the Heritage Foundation's Judicial Tracker, as
of that date in his second year in office, Trump had made eighty-
four appointments; Obama had made forty-three.[24]

McConnell revealed the secret of this success at the annual
meeting of the Federalist Society on Thursday 15 November 2018.
The society, founded during the Reagan administration, advocates
for 'originalist' and 'textualist' interpretations of the US Constitution. This approach is very significant regarding an understanding
of how the Constitution should be approached, since 'originalism'
or 'textualism' asserts that 'the Constitution means no more or less

than what it meant to those who originally wrote and ratified it. This is seen as a counter-approach to the "living Constitution" idea where the text is interpreted in light of current times, culture and society.'[25] 'Confirmation is a political decision based on who controls the Senate,' McConnell told the gathering. 'My goal is to confirm as many circuit judges as possible.'

McConnell went on to praise the President's 'political instinct' in creating and publicising a list of possible Supreme Court nominees during his 2016 campaign for the presidency. The list was partly compiled by Federalist Society Executive Vice-President Leonard Leo and was composed primarily of Federalist Society members. The single biggest reason Republicans who had reservations about Trump as their nominee ultimately voted for him was 'the list', McConnell said.[26]

According to Alliance for Justice, 83 per cent of Trump's nominees confirmed as circuit judges by November 2018 were members of the Federalist Society.[27] Of those whose nominations were pending, 90 per cent were Society members, too.

On 8 May 2019, at the Mayflower Hotel in Washington, DC, Vice-President Mike Pence addressed the Federal Society's Seventh Annual Executive Branch Review Conference. His speech was divided into an ideological setting of the stage, and a practical delineation of the programme ahead.

He began with a joke. Washington, DC, Kennedy had said, 'is a place that combines southern efficiency with northern charm'. Pence praised the society for its stand on constitutional principle: 'That the state exists to preserve freedom [and] that the separation of government powers is central to our Constitution, and that it is emphatically the province and duty of the judiciary to say what the law is, not what it should be.'

Pence quoted James Madison, to help him segue into the practical necessities of the moment: 'Accumulation of all powers, legislative [and] executive and judicial,' as Madison wrote in the Federalist Papers, '[is] the very definition of tyranny'.

'As we've seen all too often, federal agencies in the modern era frequently have exerted just that type of control,' Pence said, referring to federal injunctions. These orders are issued by federal district court judges on issues ranging from national security to immigration, from border security to healthcare reform, and can prevent the enforcement of a statute, regulation or policy on a national basis.

'It's remarkable to think,' said Pence, 'a Supreme Court justice has to convince four of their colleagues to uphold a nationwide injunction, but a single district court judge can issue one, effectively preventing the duly elected President of the United States from fulfilling what he believes is a constitutional duty.' He was especially concerned at federal injunctions that affected policies on border security and which, he claimed, undermined the constitutional rule of law and separation of powers. 'This era of judicial activism must end!' he announced to loud applause.

In a resounding conclusion, Pence returned to the historic choice facing the nation. It was, he said, between socialism, which had failed economically and in terms of liberty, and free markets and limited government. The choice was, he claimed, between freedom and socialism, and it was activist judges who by default or design were enabling the latter and undermining the former. 'It's not going to be enough for us just to win the next election,' said Pence, echoing his 2016 acceptance speech. 'We have to win the next generation.' This would only be achieved by returning to the founding principles of the USA and embedding them in the courts, economy and national culture.[28]

On 21 May Attorney General William P. Barr brought his heavyweight judicial stature to the fight. In remarks to the American Law Institute on Legal Injunctions, he quoted Justice Antonin Scalia's 'colourful' quip that 'every banana republic has a bill of rights'. His point and mine, said Barr, is that 'the bulwark against tyranny in America has always been our structure of government, most notably the Separation of Powers'. 'Hamilton had promised in Federalist 78,' continued Barr, 'that the least democratic branch would always be the "least dangerous" because courts have no influence over either the sword or the purse ... neither force nor will but merely judgment'. 'Today,' Barr said, 'that assurance did not instil much confidence'. Over time, he said, there had been an expansion of judicial willingness to review executive action, along with the use of nationwide injunctions.[29]

Since Trump took office, Barr claimed, federal district courts had issued thirty-seven nationwide injunctions against the Executive Branch, more than one a month. By comparison, during President Obama's first two years, the district courts issued two nationwide injunctions against the Executive Branch, both of which were vacated by the Ninth Circuit. And according to the best estimates of the Justice Department, courts issued only twenty-seven nationwide injunctions in all of the twentieth century. 'Some say this proves that the Trump Administration is lawless,' he said. 'Not surprisingly, I disagree.'[30]

But his purpose was not to take sides in the way the Vice-President had done a few days earlier. He explained:

> When a court grants a nationwide injunction, it renders all other litigation on the issue largely irrelevant. Think about what that means for the Government. When Congress passes a statute or the President implements a policy that is challenged in multiple courts, the Government has to run the table – we must win every case. The challengers however, must find only one district judge – out of an available 600 – willing to enter a nationwide injunction. One judge can in effect cancel the policy with the stroke of the pen.

Barr mentioned the President's attempts to push through a revised immigration policy as falling foul of these trends, but he said the problem was not one of 'partisanship', rather one of 'the rule of law'. One could easily imagine a future administration's policies on, say, climate change or employee rights, being paralysed by nationwide injunctions for years, he said. Nationwide injunctions 'undermine the democratic process, depart from history and tradition, violate constitutional principles, and impede sound judicial administration, all at the cost of public confidence in our institutions'.

Not everyone agreed. Sasha Buchert, a senior attorney for the LGBT rights group Lambda Legal, had told The Hill on 11 May, in response to Mike Pence's address to the Federal Society: 'When the extent of the harm is nationwide, the relief should be nationwide.' She cited the case of a ban on transgender service members as an example of a national policy her group was able to fend off by persuading a judge to issue a nationwide injunction. They simply argued that more soldiers than those filing the lawsuit would have been impacted by the ban.[31]

On 6 May, in an article timed to coincide with the Senate's confirmation of Trump's 100th judge, Thomas Jipping, Deputy Director of the Edwin Meese III Center for Legal and Judicial Studies, poured a big bucket of cold water on any triumphalism that Trump supporters might be feeling over the milestone appointment. The 849 days it took for Trump to reach the 100 mark was almost exactly the average 848 days it took the previous five Presidents. And to keep up with them he had had to make many more nominations. 'Trump's 57.3 per cent confirmed to date is well below the average of 80.5 per cent for the previous five presidents at this point,' said Jipping. 'Between January 2009 when Obama took office and 6 May of his third year, the Senate confirmed eighty-three judges. Republican senators serving during that period each opposed an average of 7 per cent of Obama's nominees.' Jipping went on: 'Between January 2017 when Trump took office and May 6 [of 2019], the Senate confirmed 100 judges. Democratic senators serving during that period each opposed an average of 47 per cent of Trump's nominees.'[32]

The precise path to the Supreme Court of any proposed legislation was not clear at the time of the Barr and Pence addresses, but one thing was discernible: behind Jipping's cold, raw arithmetic the battle for America's soul and for its future was lurking.

It is a battle which, for all the Enlightenment terminology of the eighteenth-century US Constitution and its later secular legal interpretation, draws on Christian concepts and themes whose roots extend beyond the American Revolution and into the origins of the settlement of New England and the foundational Puritan concepts of 'Americanness'. The conflict certainly excites religious passions among many of those who regard themselves as the staunchest defenders of constitutional and judicial traditions. For, not only do such conservative evangelicals consider themselves to be guardians of a constitutional framework which is – debatably perhaps – seen as moulded by Christian principles; they also understand its critical role in guarding the kind of America they wish to preserve. And in defining the America to which they wish to return.

From the future of Roe *v.* Wade to challenging the role of federal injunctions, the make-up and function of the US judiciary and the interpretation of the US Constitution lies at the heart of the culture war gripping the United States of America. What at first glance may appear to be arcane debates over legal procedures and contested candidatures for judicial appointments, is in reality a front-line in that war. Occupation of this legal high ground may make victory possible to whoever seizes those commanding heights, and Trump has been energetic in both promising and delivering in this area. Understanding this situation goes a long way towards explaining the support of the religious right for Donald Trump in 2016 and its continued support for him as the battlefield of 2020 looms on the horizon.

CHAPTER TEN

TRUMP, ISRAEL AND
THE MIDDLE EAST

President Trump's time in office has been marked by many striking foreign policy moves. Threats of trade wars with China; antagonism towards the European Union; enthusiasm for Brexit; the ups and downs of relations with Putin's Russia; and the one-on-one diplomacy conducted with North Korea's Kim Jong-un, have all left commentators debating the nature of the Trump Doctrine when it comes to foreign policy.

A number of features have emerged throughout these varied areas of US interaction with the wider world: an apparent personal predilection for populist hardmen; an aggressive pursuit of 'America First' in all areas; the desire to undermine transnational institutions capable of challenging US dominance; aggressive brinkmanship; and a personal belief that the President is a deal-maker who can break with orthodox diplomacy.

However, there is one area of Trump's foreign policy that strikes a chord with US evangelical voters more than any other; and that is with regard to Israel. Trump's relations with Israel represent an acceleration of a long-established US policy which, for many within the Christian right, goes far beyond a simple conservative agenda concerning the Middle East. For this is where policy and apocalypse meet. What Trump promises for US–Israeli relations exceeds anything offered by US neoconservatives of the past.

For here, more than in any other foreign policy area, members of the evangelical religious right firmly believe that, in the words of Oliver Cromwell in 1653, they stand 'at the edge of promises and prophecies'.[1] In this area of US foreign policy Christian millenarianism is influential in a way that it has not been since the seventeenth century. Past meets present in the actions of the Trump administration. And without some awareness of the former, the full ramifications of the latter will be missed.

THE US RELATIONSHIP WITH ISRAEL: A MODERN PHENOMENON WITH DEEP ROOTS

Christians United For Israel (CUFI) was established in its present form by Texas-based evangelical pastor John Hagee in 2006. The organisation claims more than 7.1 million members, and is dedicated to supporting Israel for biblical reasons: it believes that the Bible requires Christians to give unequivocal support to Israel because Jews are God's chosen people. Its mission statement states its aim of 'transforming millions of pro-Israel Christians into an educated, empowered, and effective force for Israel'. CUFI exercises this support through engagement in the political sphere. The Israeli Prime Minister Benjamin Netanyahu has said: 'I consider CUFI a vital part of Israel's national security'.[2]

In a little over a quarter of a century, CUFI has been buffeted by changing political winds, but has managed to maintain its direction of travel. The 2016 election, however, saw a dramatic change in the weather for the group for the better. After struggling against the headwinds of the Obama presidency for eight years, it found itself pushed along by the tailwind of the Trump administration.

So benign was this effect that in July 2019 at the time of their Washington conference, the CUFI leaders found themselves invited to the White House to discuss Israel with Trump's son-in-law Jared Kushner, while five senior members of the administration, including the Vice-President, came to address its conference.

But in 2015, with the Obama years ending and Hillary Clinton's beckoning, only the true prophets among the organisation could have entertained the possibility of a Trump presidency. Their resources were devoted to defending their brand of Christian values in what was seen as a culture war between tradition and progressivism – a war in which they seemed to be permanently on the defensive.

After the victory of Benjamin Netanyahu in the March 2015 election in Israel, CUFI issued the following statement:

> CUFI is a bipartisan organisation. We have gone out of our way to acknowledge President Obama when he has stood by Israel. But now we must note that President Obama has crossed the line. His disrespect of the Israeli people and the leader they just re-elected by a wide margin are simply unacceptable. The fact that he blasts Israel while embracing and forgiving Iran only adds salt to the wound.

Clearly, CUFI felt that they had reached a decisive turning point. In case anyone had missed it, the point was emphasised as the statement continued:

> The Israeli people have spoken. In this time of enormous danger in the Middle East, they want a pragmatic leader who does not conjure peace partners out of thin air or base their security on a foundation of shifting sands. Meanwhile, President Obama continues to live in a fairy-tale world where there could be peace and security tomorrow if only Israel left the West Bank. To believe in this nice story, the President must ignore all of the Israeli peace offers that the Palestinians have rejected.[3]

The mutual distaste between Obama and Netanyahu had been a political given for years, and there had even been allegations that Obama had interfered in the elections to try to prevent Netanyahu's re-election.

John McLaughlin, an American Republican who served as Netanyahu's pollster in the 2015 elections, claimed after the victory of Netanyahu's right-wing Likud party that Obama had intervened in the campaign, to try to prevent that very outcome. 'What was not well reported in the American media is that President Obama and his allies were playing in the election to defeat Prime Minister Netanyahu,' McLaughlin said in an interview on John Catsimatidis's *The Cats Roundtable* radio show broadcast on 22 March 2015 on AM 970 in New York. 'There was money moving that included taxpayer US dollars, through non-profit organisations. And there were various liberal groups in the United States that were raising millions to fund a campaign called V15 against Prime Minister Netanyahu,' McLaughlin claimed.[4]

After the election, the V15 co-founder Nimrod Dweck said in an interview with Ronan Farrow on MSNBC's *Jose Diaz-Balart* that 'not a single cent' of State Department or taxpayer money had gone to their campaign. 'These are false allegations and they have nothing to do with reality,' Dweck said.[5]

The truth came out in a report released a year later. The Obama administration was cleared of wrongdoing – a taxpayer-funded grant had not been used for political purposes – but as soon as the terms of the grant expired, the money that had been provided by the State Department was put to use against Netanyahu's re-election.

On 12 July 2016 Jennifer Rubin wrote in the *Washington Post* about the report from the Permanent Subcommittee on Investigations (PSI) under the chairmanship of Republican Senator Rob Portman for Ohio, that had been released on that day. The report 'confirm[ed] allegations that an NGO with connections to President Obama's 2008 campaign used US taxpayer dollars attempting to oust Israeli Prime Minister Benjamin Netanyahu in 2015'. The *Washington Post* quoted the PSI press release in full, and it merits some exploration: 'OneVoice – a non-governmental organization operating in Israel and the Palestinian Territories … received nearly $350,000 in grants from the U.S. State Department to support peace negotiations between Israelis and the Palestinian Authority over a 14-month grant period ending in November 2014.'

A significant stage in this process occurred in December 2014. It was then that Israeli elections were called following the collapse of peace negotiations.

The Subcommittee's investigation concludes that OneVoice Israel complied with the terms of its State Department grants. Within days after the grant period ended, however, the group deployed the campaign infrastructure and resources created, in part, using U.S. grant funds to support a political campaign to defeat the incumbent Israeli government [i.e. Netanyahu] known as V15. That use of government-funded resources for political purposes after the end of the grant period was permitted by the grant because the State Department failed to adequately guard against the risk that campaign resources could be repurposed in that manner or place limitations on the post-grant use of resources.[6]

Things were clearly complex, but the bottom line was that there appeared to be growing estrangement between key players in Washington and the Israeli right in the run-up to the 2016 US presidential election.

As it happened, Netanyahu outfoxed them. Exit polls forecast a result close to a dead heat between Netanyahu's right-wing Likud party and the centre-left Zionist Union. In the event Likud won thirty seats in the 120-seat Knesset, the highest number, with the Zionist Union gaining twenty-four.

Shortly after the elections Netanyahu made an apology. He regretted saying just before the election that 'Arab voters are heading to the polls in droves'. Addressing an event at his official residence for community leaders from the Arab sector, he said: 'I know the things I said a few days ago hurt some citizens in Israel, the Israeli Arab citizens. This was not my intention and I am sorry.' But, by then, he had won.

CUFI had not spent the Obama years in the wilderness, but had pursued advocacy from the sidelines, sometimes pulling embarrassment from the jaws of influence.

In the 2008 campaign that resulted in Obama's election, Hagee had initially supported Republican John McCain, but McCain rejected Hagee's endorsement after a sermon that Hagee delivered in 1999 came to light in which he appeared to suggest that the Holocaust was part of God's plan for Jews to return to Israel. A leaked transcript read:

God says in Jeremiah 16: 'Behold, I will bring them – the Jewish people – again unto their land that I gave to their fathers ... Behold, I will send for many fishers, and after will I send for many hunters, And they the hunters shall hunt them.' That would be the Jews ... Then God sent a hunter. A hunter is someone who comes with a gun and he forces you. Hitler was a hunter.[7]

In a statement at the time, McCain said: 'Obviously, I find these remarks and others deeply offensive and indefensible, and I repudiate them. I did not know of them before Reverend Hagee's endorsement, and I feel I must reject his endorsement as well.'

Hagee then withdrew his own endorsement, citing critics who had been 'grossly misrepresenting' his positions. 'I am tired of these baseless attacks and fear that they have become a distraction in what should be a national debate about important issues,' he said in a statement. 'I have therefore decided to withdraw my endorsement of Senator McCain for President effective today, and to remove myself from any active role in the 2008 campaign.' Hagee added that 'to assert that I in any way condone the Holocaust or that monster Adolf Hitler is the biggest and ugliest of lies. I have always condemned the horrors of the Holocaust in the strongest of terms.'[8]

A spokesman for Hagee's organisation, Ari Morgenstern, explained to CNN that Hagee had preached the sermon basing it on the writings of a Jewish theologian named Rabbi Yissachar Shlomo Teichtal, who had been persecuted by the Nazis. According to Morgenstern, Teichtal had written that the horrors that befell the Jewish population of Europe during the Second World War were meant to initiate a return of the Jews to the Holy Land. Teichtal was murdered by the Nazis, during the brutal evacuation of Auschwitz in January 1945.[9]

Despite his insistence that he had been misunderstood, Hagee apologised for the sermon. 'In a sermon in 1999, I grappled with the vexing question of why a loving God would allow the evil of the Holocaust to occur,' Hagee wrote in a letter to Anti-Defamation League Director Abraham Foxman. 'I know how sensitive the issue of the Holocaust is and should be to the Jewish community and I regret if my Jewish friends felt any pain as a result.'[10]

Foxman issued a statement welcoming the apology. 'Pastor Hagee has devoted his life to combating anti-Semitism and supporting the State of Israel,' he said. 'We are grateful for his efforts to eradicate anti-Semitism and to rally so many in the Christian community to stand with Israel.'

Hagee continued his political efforts on behalf of Israel, but for eight years he was swimming against a strong current. After the Trump victory in 2016 there were signs that the tide was beginning to turn under the new presidency. This change in political climate was soon apparent.

Several US Presidents had promised to move the US embassy to Jerusalem, but none has quite managed it. On 14 May 2018, the seventieth anniversary of the Israeli Declaration of Independence, and in the face of fierce opposition from Palestinians and their supporters, the American embassy was officially opened in the contested holy city. Pastor Hagee delivered the following benediction at the ceremony: 'We thank you, O Lord, for President Donald Trump's courage in acknowledging to the world a truth that was established 3,000 years ago – that Jerusalem is and always shall be the eternal capital of the Jewish people,' Hagee prayed. 'And because of that courage of our President, we gather here today to consecrate the ground upon which the United States Embassy will stand reminding the dictators of the world that America and Israel are forever united.'[11]

In an interview with Breitbart News the Friday before the embassy opening, Hagee said he had told President Trump of the significance of what he was doing: 'I told him that the moment that you do that [move the embassy], I believe that you will step into political immortality. Because you are having the courage to do what other presidents did not have the courage to do.'[12]

Also praying at the opening of the embassy was Southern Baptist evangelical pastor Robert Jeffress. 'Heavenly Father we come before you, the God of Abraham, Isaac and Jacob, thanking you for bringing us to this momentous occasion in the life of your people and in the history of our world,' Jeffress prayed.

He went on to praise the leadership of Israeli Prime Minister Benjamin Netanyahu, the US Ambassador to Israel David Friedman, and, of course, President Trump: 'We want to thank you for the tremendous leadership of our great President, Donald J. Trump. Without President Trump's determination, resolve and courage we would not be here today,' he prayed. 'I believe I speak for every one of us when I say I thank you every day that you have given us a President who boldly stands on the right side of history but more importantly stands on the right side of you, O God, when it comes to Israel.'[13]

Jeffress's words clearly articulated how this highly controversial relocation was perceived by US evangelicals and, as a consequence, expressed a wider verdict on the Trump presidency itself.

On the night before the opening (13 May 2018) the unsuccessful 2012 Republican presidential contender Mitt Romney, a Mormon, had tweeted that Jeffress was 'a bigot' and that he should not 'be giving the prayer that opens up' the embassy. 'Robert Jeffress says "you can't be saved by being a Jew", and "Mormonism is a heresy from the pit of hell." He's said the same about Islam. Such a religious bigot should not be giving the prayer that opens the United States Embassy in Jerusalem.'[14]

That tweet occurred at 6.42 p.m. At 7.46 p.m. on the same day, Jeffress responded: 'Historic Christianity has taught for 2,000 years that salvation is through faith in Christ alone. The fact that I, along with tens of millions of evangelical Christians around the world, continue to espouse that belief, is neither bigoted nor newsworthy.'[15]

In their belief that the fates of America and Israel were intertwined, Jeffress and Hagee were standing in a centuries-old tradition.

On 11 November 1620, as the *Mayflower* sat at anchor in the shelter of Cape Cod, the Pilgrim colonists and their fellow passengers signed the Mayflower Compact. This was not just a contract or agreement between men, but also a covenant. They promised to 'Covenant and Combine ourselves together into a Civil Body Politic, for our better ordering and preservation'.[16] For the Pilgrims, the word 'Covenant' acknowledged a divine presence, the same presence that was manifest in the Old Testament covenant between God and Abraham. They saw themselves as a New Israel. Having crossed their 'River Jordan' (the Atlantic), they were forming a New Jerusalem in the New World. They also looked to the imminent, literal, second coming of Christ, but in their day there was no literal Israel in the Holy Land to fulfil biblical prophecy. So, for them, Israel was primarily a spiritual state which had devolved upon themselves as Christian believers. Others took up this theme: North America was, in a sense, Israel.

Thomas Jefferson, author of the Declaration of Independence, in his second inaugural address as third US President in 1805, proclaimed: 'I shall need too the favour of that Being in whose hands we are, who led our forefathers, as Israel of old, from their native land and planted them in a country flowing with all the necessaries and comforts of life.'[17]

And George Washington, in his 1790 letter to a Hebrew congregation in Newport, Rhode Island, wrote: 'May the children of the stock of Abraham, who dwell in this land, continue to merit and enjoy the good will of the other inhabitants; while everyone shall sit in safety under his own vine and fig tree, and there shall be none to make him afraid'. The last reference being an exact quotation from the Old Testament book of the prophet Micah 4: 4.

So when, in 1799, Abiel Abbot, a Massachusetts minister,

preached a Thanksgiving sermon entitled 'Traits of Resemblance in the People of the United States of America to Ancient Israel', he was not putting new ideas into the heads of his congregation. Rather, he was giving scriptural and cultural ballast to ideas that were already common currency: 'It has been often remarked that the people of the United States come nearer to a parallel with Ancient Israel than any other nation upon the globe,' he proclaimed. 'Hence "OUR AMERICAN ISRAEL" [capitals in the original] is a term frequently used; and common consent allows it apt and proper'.[18]

'This parallel with biblical Israel', according to Amy Kaplan in her 2018 book *Our American Israel*, 'conferred an exceptional identity on the United States right from the start'.[19] Long before the formation of the State of Israel in 1948, North America and the idea of Israel were inextricably mixed in the Puritan mind and in the minds of those who came after them. This would bear remarkable fruit in the twentieth and twenty-first centuries, through US support for the State of Israel. For evangelicals this has brought together a sense of an exceptional – spiritual – 'American Israel' (rooted in Puritan ideology) and active support for an 'actual Israel' in the Middle East. And in this, the millenarian beliefs of the seventeenth century have become focused on modern US support for a state that is considered to be the fulfilment of biblical prophecy. The two 'Israels' have become deeply intertwined. Policy has met apocalypse. And this support for Israel has significantly increased under President Trump.

President Trump knew where to look for support for his pro-Israel policy. In an interview on the Christian Broadcast Network with Mike Huckabee, former governor of Arkansas and the father of Trump's then press secretary Sarah Huckabee Sanders, Trump said he had received more notes of thanks from the American evangelical Christian community than the American Jewish community over his decision to move the embassy. The Jewish community historically tends to vote Democrat. 'You know who really likes it the most is the evangelicals,' Trump said. 'I'll tell you what, I get more calls of "thank you" from evangelicals, and I see it in the audiences and everything else, than I do from Jewish people. And the Jewish people appreciate it, but the evangelicals appreciate it more than the Jews, which is incredible.'[20]

Huckabee, an evangelical Christian who had pushed for the embassy move throughout his own political career, replied by suggesting the move particularly affected Christians. 'It's not a surprise though, Mr President, because evangelicals are people of the Book [i.e. the Bible],' Huckabee said. 'And they believe you kept a promise, were fulfilling really a 3,000-year-old commitment to recognise Jerusalem as the capital.'[21] Huckabee attended the embassy opening in May.

Robert P. Jones, CEO of the Public Religion Research Institute, quoted in an article in NBC News, put this in political perspective:

> The end goal isn't what's good for the Jewish community, the end goal is what's good for the second coming of Christ. If you're purely thinking from a tactical point of view, you've got a bigger group in white evangelicals, and you've got a group that as a whole has a theological orientation that thinks that this is an important thing for their theological worldview.[22]

'What's good for the second coming of Christ': few US foreign policy decisions have been so described and the millenarian dimensions of this policy could not be more clearly stated.

In a survey of the American Jewish community taken before the 2012 presidential election, the Public Religion Research Institute had found that 45 per cent said support for social equality was most important to their Jewish identity, while only 20 per cent named Israel and only 4 per cent said Israel was their top consideration in deciding how to vote in that year's election.[23]

Trump's style of support for Israel is not driven by the US Jewish community, but by the US evangelical Christian community.

In 2016, according to the Pew Research Center, 24 per cent of Jewish voters backed Trump, and 71 per cent backed Clinton, compared with the much-trumpeted 81 per cent of white evangelical Christians voting for Trump rather than Hillary Clinton, who managed 16 per cent in this group. Jews made up 3 per cent of the overall voting electorate, compared with 26 per cent for white evangelical Christians.[24]

TRUMP AND MIDDLE EASTERN PEACE: A NEW CYRUS?

The move of the US embassy to Jerusalem did not make it any easier for Trump to cut what was being referred to – with tongue in cheek by sceptics – as the 'deal of the century'.

Trump's son-in-law Jared Kushner had been making strenuous efforts since 2017 to bring together the main actors in the Middle East to affirm an Israel–Palestine peace deal. He managed to generate enough interest on the part of a number of Arab states, to the extent that a gathering took place in Manama, Bahrain, from 25 to 26 June 2019.

The main Palestinian actors – the Palestinian Authority, Fatah, Islamic Jihad and Hamas – strongly opposed the conference. They argued that the Trump administration – which had unilaterally declared Jerusalem as the capital of Israel, cut aid to the United Nations Relief and Works Agency for Palestinian Refugees in the Near East and recognised Israeli sovereignty over the Golan Heights – had ruled itself out as a power broker.

Lebanon, dominated by the Iranian-backed Hezbollah militias that deny Israel's right to exist, and Iraq also refused to attend. Qatar, the main supporter of Hamas in Gaza, did attend under pressure from Saudi Arabia and the United Arab Emirates, while Kushner maintained he had been well received by King Mohammed VI of Morocco and King Abdullah II of Jordan when touring the region to build up support, though King Abdullah declared that any plan must provide for a Palestinian state.[25] Morocco sent a staff member from the Ministry of Economy and Finance. A Jordan foreign ministry spokesman confirmed that his country would dispatch the secretary-general of the Finance Ministry to Manama, without giving a name. Egypt attended but President Abdel Fattah al-Sisi promised his country would not agree to any plan the Palestinians rejected, and the country sent a delegation headed by a deputy finance minister, again without specifying the name.

Speaking at the conference, UAE Minister of State for Financial Affairs Obaid al-Tayer said: 'We should give this initiative a chance.'[26] Saudi Finance Minister Mohammed al-Jadaan said Riyadh would support whatever economic plan would bring prosperity to the Palestinians. Saudi Minister of State Mohammed al-Sheik expressed support for the plan and stated that it could succeed since it included the private sector and 'there is hope of peace'. 'I truly believe it can be done if people do believe that it can be done,' he said. 'And the way to make the people on the ground believe is to give them hope that this will be sustainable, that this will be everlasting and that ultimately there will be prosperity and there will be sustained development.'[27]

The Palestinians staged demonstrations against the meeting in Hebron, Bethlehem, Jenin, Nablus, Tulkarm, Salfit, Qalqilia and Jericho, while Hamas organised a general strike in the Gaza Strip. 'Any plan that includes the liquidation of the Palestinian cause … is rejected by the Palestinians and is not debatable or negotiable,' Saeb Erekat, secretary-general of the Palestine Liberation Organization's executive committee, said in a statement.[28]

The main proposal in the plan, published in English and Arabic, was a $50 billion pledge that was, in effect, a start-up fund for the region's Palestinians. The plan carefully avoided any mention of political realities, and so there was no discussion of the internationally supported two-state solution to the conflict. The Palestinians suspected that the Kushner agenda was not only heavily favourable to the Israelis, but that when the political discussions began after this purely economic meeting, that solution would be off the table.

Given that any deal would have to make concessions to the Palestinians, and because Israeli backing for a plan would immediately raise alarm bells with the Arabs, the Israelis curbed any enthusiasm for the process that they might have felt, and did not attend at government level.

On 10 July Jared Kushner met with a group of CUFI leaders in Washington, to brief them on the Manama meeting. He knew that if the plan did come to any sort of fruition, the Trump team would be shooting itself in the foot if success abroad was at the cost of lost votes at home.

CUFI was holding its annual conference in Washington that week, and dozens of its top brass came over to the White House. Kushner assured them that the administration's Middle East peace plan would make Israel's security needs a priority. According to two sources who attended the White House conversation, reported by the Israeli *Haaretz* newspaper, Kushner spoke to the leadership group that met with him for half an hour, and also took questions.[29] He thanked those in attendance for supporting Trump's policies in the Middle East.

Some evangelical supporters of Israel had expressed concerns about the plan. Many evangelicals are strong supporters of Israeli settlements in the West Bank, and oppose any Israeli territorial concessions as part of a future peace deal. According to the sources who spoke with *Haaretz*, Kushner did not provide new details about the peace plan during the meeting, but he did reaffirm that Israel's security is a major priority for the administration.

Israeli elections were to be held on 17 September 2019, and the political chapter of the plan would be withheld until after that date. The chapter was only seen by a very small group of advisers that included Kushner and his close aide Avi Berkowitz, as well as

Trump's Middle East envoy, Jason Greenblatt, and US Ambassador to Israel David Friedman.

No fewer than five senior Trump advisers addressed the CUFI conference. Greenblatt and Friedman gave speeches, as did Vice-President Mike Pence and fellow evangelical Christian, Secretary of State Mike Pompeo. Pompeo said during his speech that 'Israel is a majority Jewish nation, but the government doesn't force Jewish beliefs on others'.

Pence said in his speech that 'we stand with Israel because her cause is our cause, her values are our values'. Pence also referred to God's promise to Abraham that 'I will bless those who bless you'. 'We stand with Israel because we cherish that ancient promise that those who bless her will be blessed,' Pence said.

Trump's national security adviser, John Bolton, spoke and pointed out that 'Israel's security is central to the stability of the Middle East' and that 'the relationship between the United States and Israel under President Trump is stronger than ever'.

The conference also shared some tweets by members of Congress who met with CUFI activists during the event. The only Democrat who appeared in one of the tweets, meeting a delegation of CUFI activists, was Senator Chuck Schumer of New York.

Israeli Prime Minister Netanyahu spoke by video link to the conference and after delivering a warm message was interviewed by Pastor Hagee.

Speaking 'to Washington, DC, from "Jerusalem, DC" – Jerusalem, David's capital', Netanyahu thanked Hagee for the support of 'millions and millions of devout Christians'. Speaking of Trump's transfer of the US embassy to Jerusalem, he compared it in historic magnitude to the British government's 1917 Balfour Declaration, which announced its support for the establishment of a 'national home for the Jewish people' in Palestine, then under Ottoman rule with just a small Jewish population; and to the recognition of the new State of Israel by US President Harry Truman in 1948. He mentioned the uncovering by archaeologists of the 'same road that Jesus walked from the Siloam Pool to the Temple ... 3,000 years, that's some connection ... you can't bury the truth for ever'.

Netanyahu also made an eyebrow-raising reference to King Cyrus. 'You remember the Cyrus Declaration that said to the exiles in Babylon "you can come back to Jerusalem"? I think this is [what we are seeing].' Netanyahu's reference was to Isaiah 45: 13: 'I have aroused Cyrus in righteousness, and I will make all his paths straight; he shall build my city and set my exiles free, not for price or reward, says the Lord of hosts.'[30]

After recognising Israel in 1948, Harry Truman had said, 'I am Cyrus.' And we have already seen the comparisons made by some of Trump's evangelical supporters between Cyrus the Great of Persia and President Trump. Netanyahu had certainly provided food for thought to accompany the CUFI dinner that evening. In a slightly different key, Netanyahu's references in the video call were also made to the contemporary manifestation of Persia: Iran.

THE MATTER OF IRAN

The Joint Comprehensive Plan of Action (JCPOA) was signed by China, France, Germany, Russia, the UK and the USA (the P5+1) with Iran in July 2015. Its purpose was to restrict Iran's capacity to develop nuclear weapons. The negotiators deliberately and explicitly made no reference to Iran's sponsorship of terrorism in the region, and no reference to its often-stated aim of the destruction of the State of Israel. The aim was clearly to deal with Iran, one step at a time; first dealing with the highest level of potential threat: nuclear capability.

The plan prescribed in detail restrictions on Iran's capacity to enrich uranium, and included a strict regime of inspections of its facilities. Even the deal's most determined defenders, however, had to admit that there was no guarantee that Iran's inability to develop nuclear weapons would last more than ten years. The benefits to all the signatories were obvious: for the P5+1, reduction in Middle Eastern tensions, and investment opportunities in a country brought low, economically, by sanctions; and for Iran, economic development – although there was no guarantee that the benefits would feed through to ordinary Iranians, who had already been thwarted in their attempts to vote out the regime. Supreme Leader Ali Khamenei's protector, the Islamic Revolutionary Guard Corps, which is tasked with militarily protecting the Islamist ideals of the 1979 revolution, has far-reaching tentacles in the major aspects of the economy, and its leaders are unlikely to release their grip.

The JCPOA made no reference to Iran's determination to destroy Israel, even though its leaders had never hidden this ambition. In November 2014, Ali Khamenei issued a statement that the 'barbaric' Jewish state 'has no cure but to be annihilated' and posted a plan entitled '9 key questions about the elimination of Israel'.[31] In 2001, he had said: 'It is the mission of the Islamic Republic of Iran to erase Israel from the map of the region.'[32] In 2012: 'The Zionist regime is a cancerous tumor and it will be removed.'[33] In 2014: 'This barbaric, wolflike and infanticidal regime of Israel which spares no crime has no cure but to be annihilated.'[34]

And on 3 June 2018 he tweeted: 'Our stance against Israel is the same stance we have always taken.'[35]

In 2013 Hezbollah leader Hassan Nasrallah said: 'The elimination of Israel is not only a Palestinian interest. It is the interest of the entire Muslim world and the entire Arab world.'[36]

And Khamenei's representative in the Revolutionary Guard, Hojatoleslam Ali Shirazi, said in 2013: 'The Zionist regime will soon be destroyed, and this generation will be witness to its destruction.'[37]

The threat to Israel was clear; but so was the P5+1 determination to deal with Iran in a staged fashion, starting with nuclear containment. The P5+1 were confident that their deal was fit for purpose and the deal was signed on 14 July 2015. However, the signatories failed to persuade Israel that Iran would not be able to eventually carry out its ambitions, and Israel opposed the signing.

On 8 May 2018, President Trump kept a campaign promise and announced that America was withdrawing from the Iran nuclear agreement. The deal was so poorly negotiated, he said in his White House statement, that 'even if Iran fully complies, the regime can still be on the verge of a nuclear breakout in just a short period of time'. 'If I allowed this deal to stand,' he predicted, 'there would soon be a nuclear arms race in the Middle East. Everyone would want their weapons ready by the time Iran had theirs.' He did not, though, explain how Iran's nuclear capability was to be contained outside of the deal.

Trump referenced what he regarded to be crucial elements that should have been addressed in any deal with Iran: the welfare of the ordinary people of the country, and the regime's sponsorship of terror.

> The Iranian regime has funded its long reign of chaos and terror by plundering the wealth of its own people ... In the years since the deal was reached, Iran's military budget has grown by almost 40 per cent, while its economy is doing very badly ... Finally, the deal does nothing to constrain Iran's destabilizing activities, including its support for terrorism. Since the agreement, Iran's bloody ambitions have grown only more brazen.[38]

Since Trump considered the Iran deal 'defective at its core', he claimed that Iran – 'the world's leading state sponsor of terror' – would soon have nuclear capability. He was mainly successful in deterring the US partners (not that they were happy at his actions) from lifting their sanctions against Iran, and invited the government in Tehran to phone him if they wanted to talk about negotiating a more satisfactory deal.

Netanyahu spoke to the CUFI conference at a time of increased tension with Iran, which had shot down a US drone a few weeks before, on 20 June, and was interfering with shipping in the Gulf of Hormuz. In his remarks, Netanyahu applauded Trump for pulling the US out of the Iran deal, and said: 'We should stand up to Iran's aggression now. It's important to respond to their actions by increasing the pressure, not by reducing the pressure.'[39]

However the Iranian crisis develops, it is clear that the USA and Israel stand shoulder to shoulder, while other partners and allies can be marginalised or ignored by the US, which has ramifications for international agreements generally.

THE USA AND SAUDI ARABIA

It is important not to view Trump's withdrawal from the Iranian nuclear deal and his subsequent squaring up to the country in isolation. It is inseparable from his early establishment of good relations with Saudi Arabia and Crown Prince Mohammed bin Salman. The President visited Riyadh with the First Lady in March 2017. A Reuters news agency report read: 'Saudi Arabia hailed a "historical turning point" in U.S.-Saudi relations after a meeting between U.S. President Donald Trump and Crown Prince Mohammed bin Salman highlighted the two leaders' shared view that Iran posed a regional security threat.'[40]

The meeting appeared to signal a drawing together of the US and Saudi Arabia after previous tensions under the Obama administration, following the 2015 Iran nuclear deal.

An adviser to Prince Mohammed issued a statement that referred to the meeting as a 'historical turning point'. It had restored the relationship to the right path, on 'political, military, security and economic issues'.

What Trump had established was an alliance between the USA, Riyadh and Saudi Arabia's Gulf allies, that would help contain Sunni Muslim Saudi Arabia's adversary in the region, Shia Muslim majority Iran. Prince Mohammed viewed the nuclear deal as 'very dangerous', the senior adviser said, and both Trump and the man the world would come to know as MBS had 'identical views' on the danger of Iran's 'regional expansionist activities'.

As a bonus, at a time when Trump's so-called Muslim travel ban was coming in for criticism, the adviser said that MBS had 'expressed his satisfaction after the meeting on the positive position and clarifications he heard from President Trump on his views on Islam'.[41]

The previous year (2016) Obama had suspended certain US arms sales to Saudi Arabia, in reaction to the high toll of civilian casualties in the proxy war in Yemen between Iran and Saudi Arabia. US officials under Trump signalled that the ban would come to an end.

Trump stayed true to his word when the US–Saudi relationship came under its severest pressure. Following the murder of International Saudi dissident Jamal Khashoggi, a *Washington Post* columnist, at the Saudi consulate in Istanbul on 2 October 2018, opprobrium was heaped on Saudi Arabia and there were calls for international sanctions. Trump resisted all pressure to take measures that would damage the alliance he had cemented with MBS.

The fact that there was Saudi support at the Manama summit in June 2019 was clearly no accident. Trump, since 2017, had been putting together the pieces of a grand plan. It was also, ultimately – if regime changes took effect in Iran – a peace plan. But as always with Trump, this was a high-risk game. And support for Saudi Arabia in the boxing-in of Iran was entirely consistent with US defence of Israel. Only time will tell whether such strategies will survive the turbulent realities of the Middle East, in a world where international agreements now have a very short shelf-life.

But one thing is certain: US evangelicals are more than happy with the President. Support for Israel is the foreign policy equivalent of domestic opposition to Roe *v.* Wade. At home and abroad, the President seems set to deliver.

JULY 2019: MILITARY MIGHT AND PROVIDENTIAL HISTORY

On Independence Day 2019 President Trump led celebrations in a 'Salute to America' at the Lincoln Memorial in Washington, DC. His address covered decisive events in American history, then offered a tribute to the country's armed forces.

An aerial photograph that Trump tweeted after the event showed massive crowds that filled both sides of the Reflecting Pool that stretched back to the Washington Monument. 'A great crowd of tremendous Patriots this evening, all the way back to the Washington Monument!' he said.[42]

It was the first time since President Harry Truman addressed a crowd on the Monument grounds in 1951 – on the 175th anniversary of American Independence – that a President made an Independence Day speech to such a large crowd. American nationalism had rarely seemed so confident.

Democratic candidate Pete Buttigieg expressed his antipathy to this gathering; a feeling that was shared by most of Trump's opponents. 'This business of diverting money and military assets to use them as a kind of prop, to prop up a presidential ego, is not reflecting well on our country,' he complained.[43]

But even critics had to respect the choreography of the event. Trump's tribute to each of the five armed services – army, navy, air force, marines and coast guard – was followed with precise timing

by a flypast of their respective aircraft, including B-23 stealth bomb-
ers, F-22 Raptors and F-18 Super Hornets.

As he ended his address, the army band launched into the 'Battle
Hymn of the Republic', composed in 1861 by dedicated abolitionist
Julia Ward Howe. The final verse performed was:

> In the beauty of the lilies
> Christ was born across the sea,
> With a glory in His bosom
> That transfigures you and me;
> As He died to make men holy,
> Let us die to make men free;
> While God is marching on.

As the chorus reached its climax – 'Glory! Glory! Hallelujah! His
truth is marching on', followed by a resounding 'Amen' – six Blue
Angel aircraft, in formation, soared over the crowd and wheeled
back again over the Lincoln Memorial. The display was designed to
affirm a link between military might and freedom. But beyond that,
there was a concluding mention of Jesus Christ, and a reminder
that he was 'born across the sea'.

Where then was he born? For many, that place was Palestine.
But for the majority of those tens of thousands who stretched back
to the Washington Monument, the place was Israel. For many of
those singing and listening there was a profound connection between the State of Israel and their own 'American Israel'. President
Trump had certainly understood that.

CONCLUSION

TRUMP, US EVANGELICALS AND PURITANS

For many critics of Donald Trump – especially as revealed in his frequent tweets – what stands out to a remarkable degree is his rudeness and pomposity. For example, on 11 July 2019 – after disparaging possible Democratic presidential candidates, including describing Massachusetts Democratic Senator Elizabeth Warren as 'a very nervous and skinny version of Pocahontas' – he described himself as being 'great looking and smart, a true Stable Genius!'[1] Other critics might point out his rudeness towards the British ambassador in July 2019, when he described him as being 'a very stupid guy' and 'a pompous fool'. Trump had every reason to be unhappy with the ambassador's leaked memos, in which he described the Trump administration as dysfunctional, but the tone in response was far from elevated. Others would highlight the way he described Theresa May as going 'her own foolish way', in the same tweet, because she had ignored his advice over Brexit.[2] Rudeness towards opponents, and general pomposity, have become frequent features of such tweets. Trump's insults are never particularly presidential in tone or terminology.

Some have the capacity to arouse alarm. A striking example would be his attack in July 2019 on, as he put it, '"Progressive" Democratic Congresswomen, who originally came from countries whose governments are a complete and total catastrophe', who he invited to 'go back and help fix the totally broken and crime infested places from which they came'.[3] The women in question were not named in Trump's tweets but were understood to be four congresswomen of colour: Alexandria Ocasio-Cortez, Rashida Tlaib, Ayanna Pressley and Ilhan Omar.[4] The President's 'originally came from' statement was particularly ill-informed given that Ocasio-Cortez, Tlaib and Pressley were all born in the USA and, consequently, are as American as Trump. Only Omar, who came to the USA as a refugee when she was aged twelve, had been born elsewhere.

Trump's emphasis of the congresswomen's alleged non-US origins as justification for the attacks was reminiscent of the claims he had made for years that former President, Barack Obama, was not born in the USA; encouraging the so-called 'birther' conspiracy.

On 17 July Trump supporters at a rally held at Greenville, North Carolina, chanted 'Send her back! Send her back!' after the President singled out Ilhan Omar of Minnesota. It had echoes of previous Trump rally chants such as 'Lock her up!' and 'Build the wall!' Trump did not lead this chant, but many critics felt he had primed the situation through his own intemperate language.

In response to the accusations of racism that followed this, Trump supporters would, no doubt, claim that the issues in question were over perceived loyalty to the United States, not racial origin; opposition to Omar's views on Israel; that Trump's economic policies were benefiting African-Americans; and that the chants did not spread to subsequent rallies. In short, it was politics, not racism, that lay behind the chants at the Greenville rally.

However, to conclude as Sarah Sanders, the White House press secretary, did in February 2019: 'I think that he [God] wanted Donald Trump to become President, and that's why he's there', will not be how many assess the situation.[5] Even less will these many critics of the current occupier of the White House be persuaded by the more recent evaluation voiced on Twitter by Brad Parscale, the President's campaign manager, on 30 April 2019: 'Only God could deliver such a savior to our nation, and only God could allow me to help. God bless America!'[6]

This tweet, written just before the White House hosted religious leaders for the annual National Day of Prayer, is only the latest in such extreme declarations regarding the divine calling of Donald Trump.

However, it is not just US Democrats who find the idea that Donald Trump is a saviour sent by God to save America difficult to square with much of the actions and rhetoric of the Trump presidency. In the UK and across the world many share their incomprehension. To many millions – who do not agree with the outlook of Sarah Sanders and Brad Parscale – the question remains: Why do millions of US evangelical Christians determinedly support a man who falls far short of the Christian ideal, in terms of personal ethics and behaviour? They are, though, asking the wrong question.

ASKING THE RIGHT QUESTION

There is plenty of evidence to indicate that huge numbers within the Trump base approve of the President's language and tone.[7] It is difficult to interpret this as anything other than that he has given voice to their own outlook on US society and has (from their perspective) legitimised language and views that many others find divisive, racist and misogynistic. For these supporters, all criticisms of his language and outlook can be dismissed as mere 'political correctness'. In this, we can see the normalisation of terminology and outlooks that would have been unthinkable under recent Presidents (both Democrat and Republican). A voice has been provided for what many would regard as an alarming side to the US national character. The discourse has coarsened and the debate has become more polarised as a result. As a consequence, the USA is deeply divided as the nation gears up for the 2020 presidential election.

However, to assume that evangelical Christians sign up to all this is an assumption too far. The extreme rhetoric used by the President and the crowd reactions at Trump rallies represent interaction with only a tiny section of his base. They do not speak for the majority of Americans. Polling by the respected Pew Research Center, in June 2019, found that a surprisingly high percentage of those polled said that 'Trump's comments often or sometimes make them feel concerned (76 per cent), confused (70 per cent), embarrassed (69 per cent) and exhausted (67 per cent)'.[8]

Overall, a majority (55 per cent) felt that Donald Trump had personally changed both the tone and nature of political debate for the worse; while only 24 per cent felt he had changed it for the better. Concern that 'heated or aggressive' language by elected officials could make violence more likely towards targeted groups was felt more keenly by Democrat or Democrat-leaning respondents (91 per cent) than by those who identified as Republican or Republican-leaning (61 per cent). Nevertheless, concern still occupied a clear majority position among Republicans.

What this means is that Trump-inclined voters are not necessarily approving of the extreme nature of Trump rhetoric. On 15 July 2019 – early on in the Twitter storm over the four congresswomen – Arlie Russell Hochschild, Emeritus Sociology Professor at the University of California, Berkeley, and author of *Strangers in Their Own Land: Anger and Mourning on the American Right*,[9] explained in a radio interview that, from her research, Trump supporters (including evangelicals) were often unhappy at Trump's language and his use of Twitter.[10] This reinforces a poll by Pew Research in August 2018 – of direct relevance to the outlook of evangelical Christians – which found that about half of white evangelicals thought that Trump had not set a high moral standard since becoming President. Despite this, in January 2019, 69 per cent of the same sub-set of US electors approved of the way Trump was handling his job as President.[11]

How to square this circle? How can almost 70 per cent of white evangelicals approve of the job Trump is doing, while about 50 per cent of the same group feel he has lowered the moral tone? Surely morality is what evangelicals 'do'?

This takes us back to asking the 'right question'; an issue posed earlier, regarding those who cannot understand why evangelicals support Trump. If we detach the sub-clause relating to Trump's personal behaviour we will get a very different answer to the question and will come close to solving the conundrum of why evangelicals support him. Given US evangelical Christian attitudes in the past towards the personal morality demanded of a leader (and roundly denounced in its absence), the ability of the evangelical religious right to live with the personal shortcomings of Donald Trump may come as something of a surprise to many observers. However, the key thing is that Trump delivers; or is perceived as being amenable to deliver. And this outweighs most other issues.

Evangelicals consider themselves engaged in a culture war against many aspects of modern US society. This idea of a culture war did not arise with Donald Trump, but has been several decades in the making. At the same time, the polarisation of US politics, which accompanied the rise of the Tea Party movement after 2009, has accelerated this sense of political conflict, has shrunk or abolished the middle ground and has meant that any moderate Republican candidate for elected office risks being outflanked on the right, while many Democrats have shifted leftward in response. The polarisation is undeniable. And in such an atmosphere it seems clear that certain things (personal slurs, and negative discourse) have become accepted by many evangelicals as undesired but tolerable, in order to achieve victory in key areas of the culture war.

Of these, abortion is probably the key issue. The desire to roll back Roe *v.* Wade means that appointments to the Supreme Court are crucial if this is to be achieved. Long after the Trump presidency is over, his judicial nominations will be deciding issues coming before the court. In many ways this is the ultimate long-game being played by evangelicals. The same may apply to LGBT rights too.

Although in this issue Trump's evangelical credentials are not readily apparent, this deficiency is made up by Mike Pence.

This whole area is where the Cyrus Factor comes into play: the idea that God will use an unlikely leader (i.e. Donald Trump) in order to achieve godly goals. Some evangelicals will go further and claim that Trump himself has changed over time and become more open to Christian influence, which in itself shows the actions of God on the man.

The evangelical commitment to viewing Trump through this providential lens is clear, both implicitly and explicitly. His moral and behavioural shortcomings, therefore, do not bar him from receiving their committed support. In fact, it may even reinforce the concept of the Cyrus Factor.

As the Trump presidency has progressed, the concept of the Cyrus Factor has become increasingly prevalent. A striking example is that of the film *The Trump Prophecy*, released in October 2018. The film, allegedly representing real events, claimed that in 2011 a retired firefighter named Mark Taylor received a message from God that Trump had been chosen to become President. It has become known as the 'Commander-in-Chief Prophecy' and is consistent with pronouncements concerning Trump's divine calling made by a number of leading evangelicals.[12] The film was a collaboration between ReelWorksStudios and Liberty University's Cinematic Arts programme. Liberty University is the Christian evangelical college originally founded by the Southern Baptist pastor, televangelist and conservative activist Jerry Falwell; whose son, Jerry Falwell Jr, is a leading Trump supporter.

Taylor has also made other claims: Trump will serve two terms; Roe *v.* Wade will be overturned; the November 2018 mid-terms will produce a 'red [i.e. Republican] tsunami'; Obama will be charged with treason; thousands of corrupt officials, involved in a massive paedophile ring, will be arrested; and cures for cancer and Alzheimer's disease will be forced out of big pharmaceutical companies by Trump's actions.[13] This reads like a conservative evangelical wish-list, or hit-list. And belief in it is unlikely to have been dented by the failure of the prophecy regarding the 'red tsunami'. However, the key point is that Trump's divine mandate is based on heavenly approval, not on his own personal behaviour.

The Trump commitment to Israel can be seen in a similar light. The President himself may personally be drawn to tough politicians – in a way that is evident from his affinity with Russia's Vladimir Putin and North Korea's Kim Jong-un – but for evangelicals the increasing support for current Israeli hard-line nationalist politicians and policies fits with a particular Christian-Zionist and millenarian view of the State of Israel. It arises from a focus on the second coming of Christ and the impending apocalypse that can be traced back to seventeenth-century New England, which has accelerated in the twentieth and twenty-first centuries, following the establishment of the State of Israel in 1948. This particular way of viewing (and simplifying) the politics of the Middle East – rooted in Puritan origins – is now hard-wired into the US evangelical outlook and is intensifying. Once again, despite being personally flawed, Trump delivers.[14] It should be noted that the film *The Trump Prophecy* makes specific reference to a closer relationship between the USA and

Israel and sees the movement of the US embassy to Jerusalem as evidence of Trump's divine anointing.

At the same time, Trump is not inclined to disturb any of the other ingredients in the cocktail of ideas that have long been associated with Republicans and the religious right in the USA. His climate-change denial chimes with an outlook that God, not human agency, will decide the global future and again is consistent with a particular apocalyptic outlook. His inaction on gun control (by no means unique to his presidency) is approved of by those who possess a deep individualistic antipathy towards the liberal federal state, as well as the more extreme members of the evangelical right who are ready to oppose worldly government in an End Time conflict. Christian conspiracy theories (e.g. the antichrist is guiding the EU, the UN and the Catholic Church) are popular within the evangelical right and correspond with Trump's antagonism towards such international bodies.[15] That many of these bodies may limit American freedom of action only adds to his belief in and commitment to 'America First'. Among white evangelicals (and one must remember that many evangelicals are not white) racial anxiety also plays a part and shows itself in unease over an ethnically changing USA and a shifting ethno-demographic balance. It should also be remembered that most immigrants from Mexico and Central America are Catholics and are therefore the 'wrong kind of Christian' to many evangelical Protestants. They are therefore frequently seen as being Democrat voters in waiting.

While Trump is no Puritan, his appeal to evangelicals has seventeenth-century roots. It draws on a deep story of American exceptionalism, providential calling, elimination of the alien other, distrust of foreign states and the jeremiad against current sinfulness. We might call these 'foundational phenomena', and they reverberate with Puritan resonances.

The Mayflower Compact and the later covenanting agreements of the Puritan congregations of Massachusetts Bay contributed a profound sense of 'calling' and moral self-confidence to a community which saw itself as an 'American Israel'. This fed into the, arguably, more secular concepts of the Declaration of Independence and the US Constitution; and still informs much of the deep story of many people concerning what it means to be an American today. And among modern evangelicals there has occurred a revitalising of the theocratic and providential aspects inherent in many of the original concepts. Consequently, though it is a secular state, the USA contains millions of voters who harbour theocratic ambitions that would have been readily understood in seventeenth-century New England.

As a result, the current manifestations of these foundational phenomena can be traced back through a very American style of imperialism and nationalism, to manifest destiny and frontier expansion, which has its ultimate roots in the seventeenth-century drive to create a New Jerusalem in the New World. 'America First' and 'Make America Great Again' may be 21st-century slogans, but they appeal to something very deep within the US psyche and cultural mythology.

Much cultural water has passed under the bridge since the seventeenth century, and many tributaries have flowed into and diluted that primordial Puritan stream. Despite this, that original current has, arguably, played a greater role in forming a sense of American exceptionalism – both in terms of political culture and religious identity – than any other single causal factor. From the 1620 *Mayflower* landing and the 1630 Winthrop Fleet to the 2016 election of Donald Trump, from the 1692 Salem witch hunts to the divided USA of today, the Puritans have left a unique and complex legacy that helps explain the role of the evangelical religious right in modern US politics and, ultimately, the phenomenon that is the Trump presidency. This Puritan-derived influence and energy is far from exhausted. Seventeenth-century Puritan history has not finished with the USA.

FURTHER READING

There is a large and growing literature on the Trump presidency and related themes. The following give just a flavour of some of these reflections (both positive and negative), which provide additional insights into the Trump presidency, US conservatives and evangelicals, the Puritans and the wider religious background.

Ahlstrom, Sydney Eckman, *A Religious History of the American People*, 2nd edn (New Haven, CT, and London: Yale University Press, 1972)

Alberta, Tim, *American Carnage: On the Front Lines of the Republican Civil War and the Rise of President Trump* (New York: HarperCollins, 2019)

Anton, Michael, *After the Flight 93 Election: The Vote that Saved America and What We Still Have to Lose* (New York: Encounter Books, 2019)

Bercovitch, Sacvan, *The American Jeremiad* (Madison, Wisconsin: University of Wisconsin Press, 2012)

Bradford, William, *Of Plymouth Plantation, 1620–1647*, Samuel E. Morison edn (New York: Alfred A. Knopf, 2015)

Bremer, Francis J., *The Puritan Experiment: New England Society from Bradford to Edwards* (Hanover, NH, and London: University Press of New England, 1995)

Buck, Christopher, *Religious Myths and Visions of America: How Minority Faiths Redefined America's World Role* (Westport, CT, and London: Praeger Publishers, 2009)

Buck, Christopher, *God & Apple Pie: Religious Myths and Visions of America*, revised edn (Kingston, NY: Educator's International Press, 2015)

Coffey, John and Lim, Paul C. H. (eds), *The Cambridge Companion to Puritanism* (Cambridge: Cambridge University Press, 2008)

Fea, John, *Believe Me: The Evangelical Road to Donald Trump* (Grand Rapids, MI: Eerdmans, 2018)

Fischer, Claude S., *Made in America: A Social History of American Culture and Character* (Chicago, IL: University of Chicago Press, 2010)

Gingrich, Newt, *Trump's America: The Truth about Our Nation's Great Comeback* (New York: Center Street, 2019)

Grossman, Matt and Hopkins, David A., *Asymmetric Politics: Ideological Republicans and Group Interest Democrats* (New York and Oxford: Oxford University Press, 2016)

Hanson, Victor Davis, *The Case for Trump* (New York: Basic Books, 2019)

Hochschild, Arlie Russell, *Strangers in Their Own Land: Anger and Mourning on the American Right* (New York and London: The New Press, 2018)

Hurt, Charles, *Still Winning: Why America Went All In on Donald Trump – And Why We Must Do It Again* (New York: Center Street, 2019)

Kaplan, Amy, *Our American Israel: The Story of an Entangled Alliance* (Cambridge, MA, and London: Harvard University Press, 2018)

Kidd, Thomas S., *The Protestant Interest: New England After Puritanism* (New Haven, CT, and London: Yale University Press, 2004)

Kranish, Michael and Fisher, Mark, *Trump Revealed* (London and New York: Simon & Schuster, 2016)

Lewandowski, Corey R. and Bossie, David N., *Let Trump Be Trump: The Inside Story of His Rise to the Presidency* (New York: Center Street, 2017)

Morgan, Edmund S. (ed.), *Puritan Political Ideas 1558–1794* (Indianapolis, IN: Hackett Publishing Company, 2003)

Naden, Corinne J., *Open for Debate: Abortion* (New York: Marshall Cavendish, 2008)

Norris, Pippa, *Cultural Backlash: Trump, Brexit, and Authoritarian Populism* (Cambridge: Cambridge University Press, 2019)

Rozell, Mark J. and Whitney, Gleaves (eds.), *Religion and the Bush Presidency* (London and New York: Palgrave Macmillan, 2007)

Scott, Catherine V., *Neoliberalism and US Foreign Policy: From Carter to Trump* (London and New York: Palgrave Macmillan, 2018)

Seidel, Andrew L., *The Founding Myth: Why Christian Nationalism is Un-American* (New York: Sterling, 2019)

Sim, Stuart, *Twenty-First Century Puritanism: Why We Need It and How It Can Help Us* (Champaign, IL: Common Ground Publishing, 2018)

Sopel, John, *If Only They Didn't Speak English: Notes From Trump's America* (London: BBC Books, 2018)

Stewart, Katherine, *The Good News Club: The Christian Right's Stealth Assault on America's Children* (New York: Public Affairs, 2017)

Strang, Stephen E., *God and Donald Trump* (Lake Mary, FL: Charisma House Book Group, 2017)

Taylor, Mark, *The Trump Prophecies: The Astonishing True Story of the Man Who Saw Tomorrow … and What He Says Is Coming Next* (Crane, MO: Defender, 2017)

Trump, Donald and Schwartz, Tony, *The Art of the Deal* (New York: Random House, 1987)

Viguerie, Richard A., *The New Right: We're Ready to Lead* (Falls Church, VA: Viguerie Co., 1980)

Volle, Jeffrey J., *Donald Trump and the Know-Nothing Movement: Understanding the 2016 US Election* (London and New York: Palgrave Macmillan, 2018)

Williams, Daniel K., *God's Own Party: The Making of the Christian Right* (Oxford: Oxford University Press, 2010)

Winship, Michael, *Hot Protestants: A History of Puritanism in England and America* (New Haven, CT, and London: Yale University Press, 2019)

Wolff, Michael, *Fire and Fury: Inside the Trump White House* (London: Little, Brown, 2018)

Wolff, Michael, *Siege: Trump Under Fire* (London: Little, Brown, 2019)

Wong, Janelle S., *Immigrants, Evangelicals, and Politics in an Era of Demographic Change* (New York: Russell Sage Foundation, 2018)

Woodward, Bob, *Fear: Trump in the White House* (London and New York: Simon & Schuster, 2018)

Wuthnow, Robert, *The Restructuring of American Religion: Society and Faith Since World War II* (Princeton, NJ: Princeton University Press, 1988)

NOTES

INTRODUCTION: A RATHER UNEXPECTED ALLIANCE

1   Marlow Stern, 'John Oliver: We must fight Trump, a "Klan-backed misogynist internet troll"', Daily Beast, 13 April 2017, https://www.thedailybeast.com/john-oliver-we-must-fight-trump-a-klan-backed-misogynist-internet-troll?ref=scroll (accessed November 2018).

2   The speech, according to a pool report, reported by *Time* at: http://time.com/4486502/hillary-clinton-basket-of-deplorables-transcript/ (accessed November 2018).

3   Genesis 1: 27, *Holy Bible, New Revised Standard Version*, Anglicised Edition (Oxford: Oxford University Press, 1995). All Bible quotations in this book are from this version of the Bible, unless otherwise stated.

4   Michael S. Williamson/the *Washington Post* via Getty Images, https://www.vox.com/policy-and-politics/2018/10/29/18015400/2018-midterm-elections-results-white-evangelical-christians-trump (accessed November 2018).

5   One of the factors feeding into the so-called 'birther' conspiracy theories in 2008 and after, which falsely claimed that Barack Obama was not actually born in the USA, alongside related claims designed to undermine his credentials as a US citizen.

6   Witness the impact of Front National in France, Jobbik in Hungary, Law and Justice in Poland, AfD in Germany and the rise of the far right in Austria, Sweden and elsewhere; also, the vote to leave the European Union in the UK.

7   In the UK, these particular Christians would describe themselves as 'Bible-based evangelicals' but certainly do not represent all those who would also use the same descriptor of themselves. This is because there is not the same degree of theological and political homogeneity among this group of believers as in the USA.

8   Ruth Gledhill, '"Most Importantly, We Will Be Protected By God." Donald Trump Inauguration', Christian Today, 20 January 2017, https://www.christiantoday.com/article/trump-inauguration-live-blog/104035.htm (accessed July 2019).

9   Leah MarieAnn Klett, 'Televangelist Paula White Says Opposition to Donald Trump Stems from "Demonic Spirits"', The Gospel Herald Society, 22 August 2017, https://www.gospelherald.com/articles/71284/20170822/televangelist-paula-white-opposition-donald-trump-stems-demonic-spirits.htm (accessed July 2019).

10 *Holy Bible, New International Version* (Colorado Springs, CO: Biblica (worldwide), Grand Rapids, MI: Zondervan (USA), 1973, 1978, 1984, 2011).

11 Harriet Sherwood, 'Muslim group calls for preacher linked to Trump to be denied UK

visa', *The Guardian*, 9 September 2018, https://www.theguardian.com/world/2018/sep/09/muslim-council-insists-evangelical-preacher-franklin-graham-be-denied-uk-visa (accessed November 2018).

12 Ibid.

13 For the full speech transcript see https://factba.se/transcript/donald-trump-speech-maga-rally-pensacola-fl-november-3-2018 (accessed November 2018).

14 This is based on figures indicating that, in 2016, white evangelical Christians constituted 17 per cent of the US adult population and 26 per cent of actual voters (so the figures quoted above could be higher since not all evangelicals are white). See Dylan Scott, 'White evangelicals turned out for the GOP in big numbers again', Vox, 7 November 2018, https://www.vox.com/policy-and-politics/2018/10/29/18015400/2018-midterm-elections-results-white-evangelical-christians-trump (accessed November 2018). The size of the Trump vote from this section of society is based on figures from the exit poll conducted by Edison Research, for the National Election Pool, a consortium of ABC News, Associated Press, CBS News, CNN, Fox News and NBC News. These voters responded by self-identifying under the category: 'Would you describe yourself as a born-again or evangelical Christian?' Some later reports suggested that this response only reflected the views of 'white evangelicals'. However, there was no ethnic characteristic in the wording of the exit poll question.

15 Dylan Scott, 'White evangelicals turned out for the GOP in big numbers again'.

16 Stephen E. Strang, *God and Donald Trump* (Lake Mary, FL: Charisma House Book Group, 2017), p. xii.

CHAPTER ONE: CREATING A PURITAN BRAND

1 'America's changing religious landscape', Pew Research Center, 12 May 2015, http://www.pewforum.org/2015/05/12/americas-changing-religious-landscape/#fn-23198-1(accessed November 2018).

2 Charles Fleetwood, quoted in Austin Woolrych, *Britain in Revolution: 1625–1660* (Oxford: Oxford University Press, 2002), p. 755.

3 Laura Lunger Knoppers, *Constructing Cromwell: Ceremony, Portrait, and Print 1645–1661* (Cambridge: Cambridge University Press, 2000), p. 184, gives a detailed description from contemporary accounts, including the payment of 6d (6 pennies) per person to see the corpse.

4 Neil Forsyth, *John Milton: A Biography* (Oxford: Lion Hudson, 2008), p. 148.

5 Ed Stetzer and Andrew Macdonald, 'Why evangelicals voted Trump: debunking the 82%', 18 October 2018, https://www.christianitytoday.com/ct/2018/october/why-evangelicals-trump-vote-81-percent-2016-election.html (accessed November 2018).

6 As in the pamphlet entitled 'The Humble Petition of the Brownists' of 1641. See: David Cressy, *England on Edge: Crisis and Revolution 1640–1642* (Oxford: Oxford University Press, 2006), p. 231.

7 William H. Brackney, *Historical Dictionary of Radical Christianity* (Lanham MD, Plymouth: Scarecrow Books, 2012), p. 67.

8 Samuel E. Morison (ed.), *Winthrop Papers, Volume II: 1623–1630* (Boston, MA: Massachusetts Historical Society, 1931).

9 Election Eve Address: 'A Vision for America', 3 November 1980, The American Presidency Project, https://www.presidency.ucsb.edu/documents/election-eve-address-vision-for-america (accessed November 2018).

10 'Farewell Address to the Nation', 11 January 1989, https://www.nytimes.com/1989/01/12/news/transcript-of-reagan-s-farewell-address-to-american-people.html (accessed November 2018).

11 Claude S. Fischer, *Made in America: A Social History of American Culture and Character* (Chicago, IL: University of Chicago Press, 2010), Chapter Four, 'Groups'.

12 Quoted by Claude S. Fischer, 'Pilgrims, Puritans, and the ideology that is their American legacy', Berkeley Blog, 24 November 2010, http://blogs.berkeley.edu/2010/11/24/pilgrims-puritans-and-their-american-legacy/ (accessed November 2018).

13 Quoted in Catherine Armstrong, *Writing North America in the Seventeenth Century: English Representations in Print and Manuscript* (Aldershot: Ashgate Publishing, 2007), p. 67.

14 Ibid., p. 68.

15 'Native Americans and Massachusetts Bay Colony, History of American Women, http:// www.womenhistoryblog.com/2007/10/native-americans-and-massachusetts-bay.html (accessed November 2018).

16 Quoted in Bob Blaisdell, *Essential Documents of American History, Volume I: From Colonial Times to the Civil War* (Mineola, NY: Courier Dover Publications, 2016), p. 19.

17 Quoted in Steven M. Wise, *An American Trilogy: Death, Slavery, and Dominion on the Banks of the Cape* (Philadelphia, PA: Da Capo Press, 2009), p. 33.

18 For more information on the war see 'The Pequot War', Battlefields of the Pequot War, http:// pequotwar.org/about/ (accessed November 2018).

19 Some accounts number this as high as seventeen.

20 See http://www.womenhistoryblog.com/2007/10/native-americans-and-massachusetts-bay. html (accessed October 2019).

21 Claude S. Fischer, 'Pilgrims, Puritans, and the ideology that is their American legacy'.

22 David Cody, 'Puritanism in New England', The Victorian Web, http://www.victorianweb. org/religion/puritan2.html (accessed November 2018).

23 Francis J. Bremer, *The Puritan Experiment: New England Society from Bradford to Edwards* (Hanover, NH, and London: University Press of New England, 1995), p. 117.

24 Ibid.

25 William Bradford and Samuel E. Morison (ed.), *Of Plymouth Plantation, 1620–1647, by William Bradford, Sometime Governor Thereof, A New Edition* (New York: Alfred A. Knopf, 2015), p. 76.

CHAPTER TWO: THE PURITAN LEGACY IN THE EIGHTEENTH CENTURY

1 Claude S. Fischer, *Made in America: A Social History of American Culture and Character* (Chicago, IL: University of Chicago Press, 2010), p. 106.

2 E. Brooks Holifield, 'Peace, Conflict, and Ritual in Puritan Congregations', *The Journal of Interdisciplinary History*, Vol. 23, No. 3, Religion and History (Winter 1993), pp. 551–70.

3 Sydney Ahlstrom, *A Religious History of the American People*, 2nd edn (New Haven, CT, and London: Yale University Press, 1972), pp. 280–330.

4 Henry Warner Bowden, 'What is Puritanism?', Scholastic, https://www.scholastic.com/ teachers/articles/teaching-content/what-puritanism/ (accessed April 2019).

5 Emory Elliott, 'The Legacy of Puritanism', Divining America, TeacherServe, National Humanities Center, http://nationalhumanitiescenter.org/tserve/eighteen/ekeyinfo/legacy. htm (accessed November 2016).

6 The so-called Boston Tea Party was a protest against the Tea Act of 1773, which allowed the British East India company to sell tea in the American colonies without paying taxes, apart from those recently imposed on the colonies, which were objected to by the American patriots.

7 Emory Elliott, 'The Legacy of Puritanism'.

8 Modern-day targets, well evidenced in modern millenarian literature and online sources emanating from the USA, and to a lesser extent the UK, include: the papacy (a historical target); the European Union (a modern target); a worldwide conspiracy of complex form involving liberalism, political elites of varied political persuasions, international finance and a supposed anti-Christian worldwide religion (a modern target). These form a shifting pattern of conspiracy-theory accusations and suppositions.

9 The Lexico definition for 'testament', https://en.oxforddictionaries.com/definition/testament (accessed April 2019).

10 Thomas Hobbes, *Leviathan*, published in 1651, and John Locke, *Two Treatises of Civil Government* and *A Letter Concerning Toleration*, both published in 1689.

11 Jean-Jacques Rousseau, *The Social Contract*, first published as *On the Social Contract; or, Principles of Political Rights* (in French, *Du contrat social; ou Principes du droit politique*) in 1762.

12 John Winthrop, *A Model of Christian Charity*, 1630, redacted and introduced by John Beardsley, The Winthrop Society, https://www.winthropsociety.com/doc_charity.php (accessed April 2019).

13 Voters approved this document in 1780.

14 Joseph Parker Warren, 'The Confederation and the Shays Rebellion', *The American Historical Review*, No. 11 (October 1905), pp. 42–67.

15 Robert J. Taylor, 'Construction of the Massachusetts Constitution', *American Antiquarian Society*, 15 October 1980, https://www.americanantiquarian.org/proceedings/44517652.pdf (accessed April 2019), p. 317.

16 Ibid., p. 320.

17 Ibid., p. 321.

18 'The Declaration of Independence', US History, http://www.ushistory.org/declaration/document/ (accessed April 2019).

19 William Bradford, *Of Plymouth Plantation, 1620–1647, by William Bradford, Sometime Governor Thereof, A New Edition*, p. 76.

20 'George Washington and Religion: Interview with Mary V. Thompson', Mount Vernon, https://www.mountvernon.org/george-washington/religion/george-washington-and-religion/ (accessed April 2019).

CHAPTER THREE: AN ENDURING PEOPLE – PURITAN INFLUENCE IN THE NINETEENTH CENTURY

1 'The Barbary Treaties 1786–1816: Treaty of Peace and Friendship, Signed at Tripoli November 4 1796', The Avalon Project, http://avalon.law.yale.edu/18th_century/bar1796t.asp (accessed May 2019).

2 For an overview of Unitarian beliefs on a range of subjects see: 'Frequently asked questions (FAQ) – Unitarians', www.unitarian.org.uk (accessed May 2019).

3 For an overview of the beliefs of both Unitarians and Universalists see: David Robinson, *The Unitarians and the Universalists* (Westport, CT: Greenwood Press, 1985).

4 Visiting this very church in May 2018, the author was interested to overhear a guide telling another tourist that the creeds, painted on wooden boards at the front of the church, were 'part of the history of this church but we don't believe them anymore'.

5 Although they were not strict adherents to official creeds, and this would cause a real problem for their later descendants in maintaining orthodoxy.

6 Michael G. Hall, *The Last American Puritan: The Life of Increase Mather, 1639–1723* (Middletown, CT: Wesleyan University Press, 1988).

7 A thought-provoking reflection on this fall from Puritanism from a Catholic perspective can be found at: Joe Heschmeyer, 'How did the Puritans become Unitarians?', Shameless Popery, http://shamelesspopery.com/how-did-the-puritans-become-unitarians/ (accessed May 2019).

8 'Page 143 US 465', https://supreme.justia.com/cases/federal/us/143/457/ (accessed May 2019).

9 'Page 143 US 466'.

10 'Page 143 US 471'.

11 John R. Vile, 'People *v.* Ruggles (N.Y.) (1811) Related cases in Blasphemy and Profane Speech', The First Amendment Encyclopedia, https://www.mtsu.edu/first-amendment/article/94/people-v-ruggles-n-y (accessed May 2019).

12 Thomas Jefferson, 'Jefferson's Letter to the Danbury Baptists: The Final Letter, as Sent', *The Library of Congress Information Bulletin*, June 1998 (Washington, DC: Library of Congress).

13 Daniel Dreisbach, *Thomas Jefferson and the Wall of Separation Between Church and State* (New York: New York University Press, 2003), p. 77.

14 Randall Herbert Balmer, *Encyclopedia of Evangelicalism* (Louisville, KY: Westminster John Knox Press, 2002), pp. vii–viii.

15 'Proclamation of Thanksgiving', 3 October 1863, Abraham Lincoln Online, http://www.abrahamlincolnonline.org/lincoln/speeches/thanks.htm (accessed May 2019).

16 An accessible overview can be found at: 'Thanksgiving 2019', History.com, https://www.history.com/topics/thanksgiving/history-of-thanksgiving (accessed April 2019).

17 Emory Elliott, 'The Legacy of Puritanism'.

CHAPTER FOUR: THE EMERGENCE OF THE 'EVANGELICAL RELIGIOUS RIGHT'

1 If so – and evidence from a number of later surveys supports this view – then they were in line with Republican support generally for Donald Trump, as the exit poll suggested that the majority of Republicans responded that the best description of their voting decision was 'I dislike the other candidates' (51 per cent).

2 It does, of course, allow for the contribution of other significant factors. But it singles out the Puritan legacy as being most important.

3 Grant Wacker, 'The Christian Right, The Twentieth Century, Divining America: Religion in American History', National Humanities Center, http://nationalhumanitiescenter.org/tserve/twenty/tkeyinfo/chr_rght.htm (accessed May 2019).

4 Sarah Pulliam, 'Phrase "Religious Right" Misused, Conservatives Say', Christianity Today, 12 February 2009, https://www.christianitytoday.com/ct/2009/februaryweb-only/106-42.0.html (accessed October 2019).

5 A succinct overview of the complexity can be found at: Grant Wacker, 'The Christian Right'.

6 Daniel K. Williams, *God's Own Party: The Making of the Christian Right* (Oxford: Oxford University Press, 2010), p. 3.

7 Ibid.

8 Neal R. Pierce, *The Deep South States of America: People, Politics, and Power in the Seven States of the Deep South* (New York: W. W. Norton, 1974), pp. 123–61. See also Shaun Casey, *The Making of a Catholic President: Kennedy vs. Nixon 1960* (Oxford: Oxford University Press, 2009), pp. 3–11.

9 Shaun Casey, *The Making of a Catholic President*, pp. 101–22.

10 Ibid., p. 103.

11 Grant Wacker, 'The Christian Right'.

12 Robert Wuthnow, *The Restructuring of American Religion: Society and Faith Since World War II* (Princeton NJ: Princeton, University Press, 1988), p. 281.

13 Richard A.Viguerie, *The New Right: We're Ready To Lead* (Falls Church, VA: Viguerie Co., 1980).

14 As of May 2019.

15 Obituary for Jerry Falwell, *The Guardian*, 17 May 2007.

16 Ibid.

17 Ibid.

18 Ibid.

19 According to the Christian Coalition (which calculated it as 42 per cent), and Sydney Blumenthal, 'Letter from Washington: Christian Soldiers', *The New Yorker*, 18 July 1994, http://www.cs.cmu.edu/~jab/pol/christian-soldiers.txt (accessed October 2019).

20 A very accessible overview of the Bush Sr presidency, which has assisted this brief exploration, can be found at: Neil J. Young, 'How George H.W. Bush enabled the rise of the religious right', *Washington Post*, 5 December 2018, https://www.washingtonpost.com/outlook/2018/12/05/how-george-hw-bush-enabled-rise-religious-right/?utm_term=.8449694e8825 (accessed May 2019).

21 Grant Wacker, 'The Christian Right', in an article revised in October 2000 and looking at the Christian right as it had developed since 1980.

22 Mark J. Rozell, 'Bush and the Christian Right: The Triumph of Pragmatism', in Mark J. Rozell and Gleaves Whitney (eds), *Religion and the Bush Presidency* (New York: Palgrave Macmillan, 2007), p. 12.

23 Rich Lowry, editor of the *National Review*, writing in the *Washington Post*, 10 August 2003.

24 Mark J. Rozell, 'Bush and the Christian Right: The Triumph of Pragmatism', pp. 11–28.

25 Karen Tumulty and Matthew Cooper, 'Does Bush Owe the Religious Right?', *Time*, 7 February 2005, http://content.time.com/time/specials/packages/article/0,28804,1993235_1993249_1993321,00.html (accessed May 2019).

26 By 2013, 33 per cent of self-identified Republicans also identified with the religious right: Valerie Richardson, 'Libertarians: Don't call us tea partyers; survey finds blocs often clash', *Washington Times*, 29 October 2013, https://www.washingtontimes.com/news/2013/oct/29/libertarians-dont-call-us-tea-partyers-survey-find/ (accessed May 2019).

27 Ibid.

28 Robert P. Jones, CEO of the Public Religion Research Institute, quoted in the *Washington Times*, 29 October 2013.

29 Arlie Russell Hochschild, *Strangers In Their Own Land: Anger and Mourning on the American Right* (New York and London: The New Press, 2018).

30 Claude S. Fischer, 'Pilgrims, Puritans, and the ideology that is their American legacy'.

31 Emory Elliott, 'The Legacy of Puritanism'.

32 From Richard Kyle's review of Christopher Buck's *Religious Myths and Visions of America* (Westport, CT: Praeger Publishers, 2009), and quoted in Christopher Buck, *God & Apple Pie: Religious Myths and Visions of America* (Kingston, NY: Educator's International Press, revised edn 2015), p. 72.

33 Christopher Buck, *God & Apple Pie: Religious Myths and Visions of America*, pp. 83–4.

34 Martyn Whittock, 'How Puritanism explains Trump: Why the 17th century taught the US and UK different lessons', Christian Today, 18 May 2018, https://www.christiantoday.com/article/how-puritanism-explains-trump-why-the-17th-century-taught-the-us-and-uk-different-lessonsexecute1/129250.htm (accessed May 2019).

CHAPTER FIVE: THE POLITICS OF RACE

1   These words are quoted here: 'Civil Rights Act of 1964', History.com, https://www.history.com/topics/black-history/civil-rights-act. However, they are impossible to trace back to a source. Dr Steven J. Allen insists there is no record of LBJ ever having uttered them: '"We have lost the South for a generation": What Lyndon Johnson said, or would have said if only he said it', Capital Research Center, https://capitalresearch.org/article/we-have-lost-the-south-for-a-generation-what-lyndon-johnson-said-or-would-have-said-if-only-he-had-said-it/ (accessed March 2019).

2   Ronald Kessler, *Inside The White House* (New York: Pocket Books, Simon & Schuster, 1995).

3   Ibid., p. 3.

4   Ibid., p. 33. Many accusations regarding LBJ's racist language are contained in Robert Parker (with Richard Rashke), *Capitol Hill in Black and White* (New York: Dodd, Meade & Co., 1986).

5   In a Fox News poll reported on by Dylan Scott, 'White evangelicals turned out for the GOP in big numbers again'.

6   Janelle S. Wong, *Immigrants, Evangelicals, and Politics in an Era of Demographic Change* (New York: Russell Sage Foundation, 2018).

7   Janelle S. Wong, 'Untapping the Potential of Black, Latino and Asian American Evangelical Voters', American Prospect, 6 June 2018, https://prospect.org/article/untapping-potential-black-latino-and-asian-american-evangelical-voters (accessed March 2016).

8   Arlie Russell Hochschild, *Strangers In Their Own Land*.

9   Speaking at a meeting of inner-city pastors with President Trump in the Cabinet Room of the White House on 1 August 2018, 'Pastor praises Trump as "pro-black" at prison reform event', Associated Press, 1 August 2018, https://apnews.com/e807334359144684bf23f0f89ff750c0 (accessed November 2019).

10 Chandelis R. Duster, 'Trump praised as "pro-black" at White House prison reform event', NBC News, 2 August 2018, https://www.nbcnews.com/news/nbcblk/trump-praised-pro-black-white-house-prison-reform-event-n896526 (accessed November 2019). The following day WBLS.com

ran news a story by Marie David headlined 'Pastor John Gray SLAMMED for his meeting with President Donald Trump', 3 August 2018, https://www.wbls.com/news/ann-trip/pastor-john-gray-slammed-his-meeting-president-donald-trump-video (accessed November 2019).

11 Tweet by @BishopPMorton, 2 August 2018, 6.28 a.m.

12 Ian Schwartz, 'Don Lemon Interviews Black Pastor that Met With Trump, Doesn't Understand Why He Did', RealClear Politics, 2 August 2018, https://www.realclearpolitics.com/video/2018/08/02/don_lemon_interviews_black_pastor_that_met_with_trump_doesnt_understand_why_he_did.html (accessed November 2019).

13 Ben Sisario and Steve Friess, 'Aretha Franklin's Funeral: Stars, Dignitaries and Fans Honor the Queen of Soul', New York Times, 31 August 2018, https://www.nytimes.com/2018/08/31/arts/music/aretha-franklin-funeral.html (accessed November 2019).

14 'Reverend Al Sharpton calls Aretha Franklin "soundtrack of the civil rights movement"', AP Archive, 5 September 2018, 2:40 to 3:49, https://www.youtube.com/watch?v=dnMJ8blxvV8 (accessed October 2019).

15 'Remarks by President Trump in Cabinet Meeting', 16 August 2018, https://www.whitehouse.gov/briefings-statements/remarks-president-trump-cabinet-meeting-10/ (accessed October 2019).

16 'Georgetown professor Michael Eric Dyson speaks at Aretha Franklin funeral service', AP Archive, 5 September 2018, 1:38 to 2:17, https://www.youtube.com/watch?v=foroiKmZcjM (accessed October 2019).

17 'Omarosa says Trump is a racist who uses N-word – and claims there is a tape to prove it', The Guardian, 11 August 2018, https://www.theguardian.com/us-news/2018/aug/10/omarosa-trump-book-the-apprentice-memoir (accessed October 2019).

18 Ibid.

19 @realDonaldTrump, 14 August 2018, 4.31 a.m.

20 David Livingstone Smith, Less Than Human: Why We Demean, Enslave and Exterminate Others (New York: St Martin's Press, 2011). The Morning Joe interview can be found at: 'President Trump Calls Omarosa Manigault "Dog", "Crying Lowlife" in Tweet', Morning Joe MSNBC, 14 August 2018, https://www.youtube.com/watch?v=8bMD8blET-k (accessed October 2019).

21 Josh Dawsey, 'Trump derides protections for immigrants from "shithole" countries', Washington Post, 12 January 2018, https://www.washingtonpost.com/politics/trump-attacks-protections-for-immigrants-from-shithole-countries-in-oval-office-meeting/2018/01/11/bfc0725c-f711-11e7-91af-31ac729add94_story.html (accessed November 2019).

22 @OfficialCBC, 11 January 2018, 3.17 p.m.

23 Statement reported by Julie Hirschfeld Davis, Sheryl Gay Stolberg, Thomas Kaplan, 'Trump alarms lawmakers with disparaging words for Haiti and Africa', New York Times, 11 January 2018, https://www.nytimes.com/2018/01/11/us/politics/trump-shithole-countries.html (accessed November 2019).

24 Lisa De Moraes, 'Trevor Noah to Donald Trump: "As Someone From South Sh*t Hole, I'm offended"', Deadline, 11 January 2018, https://deadline.com/2018/01/trevor-noah-donald-trump-offended-racist-shit-hole-countries-video-1202241657/ (accessed November 2019). De Moraes reports Noah as saying what really 'put him over the edge' was Trump saying the US should instead let in more people from Norway: 'He didn't just name a white country, he named the whitest – so white they wear moonscreen.'

25 Kyle Swenson, 'Trevor Noah: "As someone from South Shithole, I'm offended Mr. President"', Washington Post, 12 January 2018, https://www.washingtonpost.com/news/morning-mix/wp/2018/01/12/trevor-noah-as-someone-from-south-shithole-im-offended-mr-president/ (accessed November 2019).

26 Statement by the African Union Mission in Washington, Reuters.

27 @realDonaldTrump, 12 January 2018, 4.28 a.m.

28 @SteveKingIA, 12 January 2018, 2.11 a.m.

29 CNN Tonight, 11 January 2018. Reported in Erin Nyren, 'Anderson Cooper, Don Lemon, Call Trump "Racist" Over "S—hole Countries" Remark', Variety, 11 January 2018, https://variety.com/2018/tv/

news/anderson-cooper-don-lemon-donald-trump-racist-shithole-remark-1202662653/ (accessed November 2019).

30 Reported, *inter alia*, by Brent D. Griffiths, 'Trump: "I am the least racist person you have ever interviewed"', Politico, 14 January 2018, https://www.politico.eu/article/donald-trump-i-am-the-least-racist-person-you-have-ever-interviewed/ (accessed November 2019).

31 @WhiteHouse, 15 January 2018, 7.06 a.m., 0:16 to 0:30 on attached video, https://twitter.com/whitehouse/status/952919816888659973?lang=en (accessed November 2019).

32 @ThisWeekABC, 14 January 2018, 6.15 a.m., '@repjohnlewis to @GStephanopoulos on Trump: "I think he is a racist." #ThisWeek'.

33 @scottwongDC, 16 January 2018, 5.38 p.m., reported in Andrew Prokop, 'The "shithouse defense" explained: how Trump's allies are trying to dig him out of his "shithole"', Vox, 16 January 2018.

34 C-SPAN, Homeland Security Oversight, Part 1, 16 January 2018, 1:00:48 to 1:03:50. Senator Leahy refers to Africa as a 'country' at 1:02:30, https://www.c-span.org/video/?c4710934/user-clip-homeland-security-oversight (accessed November 2019).

35 'I love Trump! The Best President ever – Uganda President', Chill Pill, 24 January 2018, https://www.youtube.com/watch?v=srY3fD59MIw (accessed October 2019).

36 John C. Richards Jr, 'For Blacks, Lies Matter: Black Christians, the Trump Presidency and New Research', Christianity Today, 18 October 2018, https://www.christianitytoday.com/edstetzer/2018/october/for-blacks-lies-matter-black-christians-trump-presidency-an.html (accessed November 2019).

37 Nancy D. Wadsworth, 'The racial demons that help explain evangelical support for Trump', Vox, 30 April 2018, https://www.vox.com/the-big-idea/2018/4/30/17301282/race-evangelicals-trump-support-gerson-atlantic-sexism-segregation-south (accessed November 2019).

38 Link to press conference, at 12.34 p.m. ET, 13 August 2017, Dan Merica, 'Trump condemns "hatred, bigotry and violence on many sides" in Charlottesville', CNN Politics, 13 August 2017, https://edition.cnn.com/2017/08/12/politics/trump-statement-alt-right-protests/index.html (accessed November 2019).

39 @SenCoryGardner, 12 August 2017, 9.44 p.m., @IvankaTrump, 13 August 2017, 5.09 a.m.

40 As reported by the *Washington Post*, ABC News, Reuters, *inter alia*, 13 August 2017.

41 @JerryFalwellJr, 16 August 2017, 4.42 p.m., @JerryFalwellJr, 17 August 2017, 7.43 p.m.

42 'Jeffress on Trump: "There is Not a Racist Bone in His Body"', CBN News, 16 August 2017, https://www1.cbn.com/cbnnews/politics/2017/august/jeffress-on-trump-there-is-not-a-racist-bone-in-his-body (accessed November 2019).

43 Statement tweeted by @ARBernard, 18 August 2017, 2.44 p.m.

44 'Aretha Franklin's Full Eulogy by Rev. Jasper Williams Jr.', Jenn L, 1 September 2018, https://www.youtube.com/watch?v=oKh9DlcWaFY (accessed October 2019). The eulogy is in the tradition of the American Jeremiad (see Chapter Three).

45 Jonathan Landrum Jr, 'Aretha Franklin funeral eulogy slammed; pastor stands firm', Associated Press, 2 September 2018, https://apnews.com/32d797c5a5324c7593b44a6d0a1c8f3d (accessed November 2019).

46 'Presidential proclamation on National African American History Month', 31 January 2019, https://www.whitehouse.gov/presidential-actions/presidential-proclamation-national-african-american-history-month-2019/ (accessed October 2019).

47 'Remarks by President Trump at a Reception for National African American History Month', 21 February 2019, https://www.whitehouse.gov/briefings-statements/remarks-president-trump-reception-national-african-american-history-month/ (accessed October 2019).

CHAPTER SIX: IMMIGRATION AND THE WALL

1 'The Historic Results of President Donald J. Trump's First Two Years in Office', 20 January 2019, https://www.whitehouse.gov/briefings-statements/the-historic-results-of-president-donald-j-trumps-first-two-years-in-office/ (accessed October 2019).

2 Donald Trump and Tony Schwartz, *The Art of the Deal* (New York: Random House, 1987).

3 Victor Davis Hanson, 'Private Papers: Mythologies of Illegal Immigration', Hoover Institution, 23 January 2018. Hanson is the author of *The Case for Trump* (New York: Basic Books, 2019).

4 Victor Davis Hanson, 'Private Papers'.

5 The quotes from this important interview are from Diane Rehm, 'Why Evangelical Christians Support Trump's Wall', *On My Mind* podcast, American University Radio, 8 January 2019, https://dianerehm.org/shows/2019-01-08/why-evangelical-christians-support-trumps-wall (accessed November 2019).

6 See Dylan Scott, 'White evangelicals turned out for the GOP in big numbers again'.

7 In a blog published on 24 February 2016, that was expanded into an op-ed for the *Washington Post* on 26 February 2016, Max Lucado wrote, with reference to Trump's conduct in the primaries: 'We appreciate decency. We applaud decency. We teach decency. We seek to develop decency. Decency matters, right? Then why isn't decency doing better in the presidential race?', https://maxlucado.com/decency-for-president/ (accessed November 2019).

8 Julie Lyons, 'Robert Jeffress wants a mean "son of a gun" for President, says Trump isn't a racist', *Dallas Observer*, 5 April 2016, https://www.dallasobserver.com/news/robert-jeffress-wants-a-mean-son-of-a-gun-for-president-says-trump-isnt-a-racist-8184721 (accessed October 2019).

9 Edward-Isaac Dovere, 'Tony Perkins, Trump Gets a "Mulligan" on Life, Stormy Daniels', *Off Message* podcast, Politico, 23 January 2018, https://www.politico.com/magazine/story/2018/01/23/tony-perkins-evangelicals-donald-trump-stormy-daniels-216498 (accessed November 2019).

10 Katherine Stewart is the author of *The Good News Club: The Christian Right's Stealth Assault on America's Children* (New York: Public Affairs, 2012, 2017 edn).

11 Isaiah 45: 5–6.

12 Isaiah 45: 13.

13 Lance Wallnau, 'Is Trump himself a prophet? This businessman says yes!', Charima News, 18 August 2016, https://www.charismanews.com/opinion/59307-is-trump-himself-a-prophet-this-businessman-says-yes (accessed October 2019).

14 Josh Hafner, 'Meet the Evangelicals who Prophesied a Trump win', *USA Today*, 11 November 2016, https://eu.usatoday.com/story/news/nation-now/2016/11/10/meet-evangelicals-prophesied-trump-win/93575144/ (accessed November 2019).

15 Lance Wallnau, 'Our meeting with trump!', Lance Wallnau, https://lancewallnau.com/our-meeting-with-trump/ (accessed April 2019).

16 Published in September 2016, by Killer Sheep Media. The title borrows from a description of Trump by Jeb Bush during the Republican primaries as 'the chaos candidate'.

17 Author of *Believe Me: The Evangelical Road to Donald Trump* (Grand Rapids, MI: William B. Eerdmans, 2018).

18 For this Vox interview see: Tara Isabella Burton, 'Why (white) evangelicals still support Trump', Vox, 5 November 2018, https://www.vox.com/2018/11/5/18059454/trump-white-evangelicals-christian-nationalism-john-fea (accessed November 2019).

19 John Fea, 'Evangelical Fear Elected Trump', *The Atlantic*, 24 June 2018, https://www.theatlantic.com/ideas/archive/2018/06/a-history-of-evangelical-fear/563558/ (accessed November 2019).

20 *Holy Bible*.

21 Robert Kagan, senior fellow at the Brookings Institution wrote the paper as part of a Brookings Foreign Policy series, 'Democracy and Disorder'.

22 Alan Fram, 'Trump border emergency survives as House veto override fails', Associated Press, 27 March 2019, https://apnews.com/056c0ce531a34b999a6a50179e2265ad (accessed October 2019).

CHAPTER SEVEN: SEXUALITY AND GENDER IDENTITY

1 '2020 US presidential candidate speakers at NAN conference', streamed live by *The Guardian* on 5 April 2019, https://www.youtube.com/watch?v=IT9Fe8z324E (accessed November 2019).

2 Tal Axelrod, 'Bernie Sanders calls Trump "most racist, sexist, homophobic, bigoted president

in history"', The Hill, 31 October 2018, https://thehill.com/homenews/campaign/414133-bernie-sanders-calls-trump-most-racist-sexist-homophobic-bigoted-president (accessed November 2019).

3 @BernieSanders, 5 April 2019, 8.16 a.m.

4 Tyler O' Neill, 'Bernie Sanders: Trump is "a Racist, a Sexist, a Homophobe, a Xenophobe, a Religious Bigot"', PJ Media, 5 April 2019, https://pjmedia.com/video/bernie-sanders-trump-is-a-racist-a-sexist-a-homophobe-a-xenophobe-a-religious-bigot/ (accessed November 2019).

5 Colby Itkowitz and Sean Sullivan, 'Why Pete Buttigieg says he stopped using "all lives matter"', Washington Post, 4 April 2019, https://www.washingtonpost.com/politics/why-pete-buttigieg-says-he-stopped-using-all-lives-matter/2019/04/04/eb794242-570b-11e9-8ef3-fbd41a2ce4d5_story.html (accessed November 2019).

6 Matt Stevens, 'Pete Buttigieg Faces Scrutiny Over "All Lives Matter" Remark in 2015', the New York Times, 4 April 2019, https://www.nytimes.com/2019/04/04/us/politics/pete-buttigieg-all-lives-matter.html (accessed November 2019).

7 Kirsten Powers, 'Mayor Pete Buttigieg's countercultural approach to Christianity is what America needs now', USA Today, 4 April 2019, https://eu.usatoday.com/story/opinion/2019/04/03/mayor-pete-buttigieg-christian-right-2020-democratic-primary-trump-column/3342767002/ (accessed November 2019).

8 Tim Hains, 'Pete Buttigieg: "Hypocrisy" of Evangelical Christians Supporting Trump Is "Unbelievable"', RealClear Politics, 7 April 2019, https://www.realclearpolitics.com/video/2019/04/07/pete_buttigieg_hypocrisy_of_evangelical_christians_supporting_trump_is_unbelievable.html (accessed November 2019).

9 Devan Cole, 'Buttigieg to Pence: "If you got a problem with who I am, your problem is not with me … your quarrel, sir, is with my creator"', CNN Politics, 8 April 2019, https://edition.cnn.com/2019/04/08/politics/pete-buttigieg-mike-pence/index.html (accessed November 2019).

10 'CNBC Exclusive: CNBC Transcript: Vice-President Mike Pence Speaks with CNBC's Joe Kernen on CNBC's "Squawk Box" Today', CNBC, 11 April 2019, https://www.cnbc.com/2019/04/11/cnbc-exclusive-cnbc-transcript-vice-president-mike-pence-speaks-with-cnbcs-joe-kernen-on-cnbcs-squawk-box-today.html (accessed November 2019).

11 Scott Morefield, in 'Richard Grenell: Buttigieg Engaging in Smollett-Style "Hate Hoax" Against Pence', posted a video link to the Fox News interview, and quoted from it in the Daily Caller on 18 April 2019, https://dailycaller.com/2019/04/18/richard-grenell-buttigieg-smollett-hate-hoax-pence/ (accessed November 2019). Tre Goins-Phillips, 'Openly Gay US Ambassador Richard Grenell Takes Down Buttigieg's "Hate Hoax" Against "Godly" Pence', quoted from the Fox News interview on Faith Wire, 19 April 2019, https://www.faithwire.com/2019/04/19/openly-gay-us-ambassador-richard-grenell-takes-down-buttigiegs-hate-hoax-against-godly-pence/ (accessed November 2019).

12 Associated Press, 'Jussie Smollett case: special prosecutor to investigate why charges were dropped', The Guardian, 21 June 2019, https://www.theguardian.com/us-news/2019/jun/21/jussie-smollett-case-special-prosecutor-to-investigate-why-charges-were-dropped (accessed July 2019).

13 See also this tweet by Richard Grenell referencing a tweet by Mike Pence in 2015: 'Here's a tweet from 2015 that is barely mentioned. The hate hoax being perpetrated on my friend @VP Mike Pence is sadly tied to a political fundraising strategy. Mayor Pete was silent for years - I'm outraged by his phony outrage.' @RichardGrenell, 19 April 2019. The Pence tweet reads: 'If I saw a restaurant owner refuse to serve a gay couple, I wouldn't eat there anymore.' @GovPenceIN, 31 March 2015.

14 'Remarks by the President on the Supreme Court Decision on Marriage Equality', White House, 26 June 2015, https://obamawhitehouse.archives.gov/the-press-office/2015/06/26/remarks-president-supreme-court-decision-marriage-equality (accessed November 2019).

15 These reactions were reported, inter alia, by Lawrence Hurley, 'Landmark US Supreme Court ruling legalizes gay marriage nationwide', Reuters, 28 June 2015, https://www.reuters.com/article/us-usa-court-gaymarriage/landmark-u-s-supreme-court-ruling-legalizes-gay-marriage-nationwide-idUSKBN0P61SW20150628 (accessed November 2019).

16   Pete Kasperowicz, 'Scalia: Supreme Court now a "threat to American democracy"', *Washington Examiner*, 26 June 2015, https://www.washingtonexaminer.com/scalia-supreme-court-now-a-threat-to-american-democracy (accessed November 2019).

17   Will Drabold, 'Here's What Mike Pence Said on LGBT Issues Over the Years', *Time*, 15 July 2016, https://time.com/4406337/mike-pence-gay-rights-lgbt-religious-freedom/ (accessed November 2019).

18   Frank Bruni, 'Mike Pence, Holy Terror: Are you sure you want to get rid of Donald Trump?', *New York Times*, 28 July 2018, https://www.nytimes.com/2018/07/28/opinion/sunday/mike-pence-holy-terror.html (accessed November 2019).

19   @Franklin_Graham, 8 August 2018, 5.43 p.m.

20   Glenn T. Stanton, 'The New York Times' Hit Piece on Mike Pence is Anti-Christian Bigotry Pure and Simple', *The Federalist*, 6 August 2018, https://thefederalist.com/2018/08/06/new-york-times-hit-piece-mike-pence-anti-christian-bigotry-plain-simple/ (accessed November 2019).

21   David Brody, Jenny Browder, 'VP Pence on Coming Under Fire for His Faith: "I Just Breathe a Prayer of Praise"', CBNNews, 31 August 2018, https://www1.cbn.com/cbnnews/politics/2018/august/vp-pence-on-coming-under-fire-for-his-faith-i-just-breathe-a-prayer-of-praise (accessed November 2019).

22   The video was posted on the *Washington Post* website, 7 October 2016, 5.32 p.m., and was entitled: 'Watch: Donald Trump recorded having extremely lewd conversation about women in 2005', and included the caption: 'In this video from 2005, Donald Trump prepares for an appearance on "Days of Our Lives" with "Access Hollywood" host Billy Bush and actress Arianne Zucker', https://www.washingtonpost.com/gdpr-consent/?destination=%2fblogs%2fpost-partisan%2fwp%2f2016%2f10%2f07%2fdonald-trumps-remarkably-gross-comments-about-women%2f%3f (accessed November 2019).

23   Madeline Conway, 'RNC chairman condemns Trump: "no woman should ever be described in these terms or talked about in this manner. Ever"', Politico, 10 July 2016, https://www.politico.com/story/2016/10/reince-priebus-donald-trump-comments-women-229316 (accessed November 2019).

24   @HillaryClinton, 7 October 2016, 12.55 p.m., Lisa Kagen, Kaine on lewd Trump tapes: 'Makes me sick to my stomach', The Hill, 10 July 2016.

25   Emma Gray, 'Trump's Latest Comments About Women Are Rape Culture In A Nutshell', HuffPostUS, 10 August 2016, https://www.huffingtonpost.co.uk/entry/donald-trump-billy-bush-rape-culture_us_57f80a89e4boe655eab4336c?ri18n=true&guccounter=1&guce_referrer=aHRocHM6Ly9jb25zZW5oaaG9vLmNvbS8S8&guce_referrer_sig=AQAAAHuVz1KpA7V7Mu_ZtvdZyMVOWhMNwbLYUmkSoIkvXZGHqjxSkNZKSkC3rGqbNwtQz-qRayWT2i_7zcWAnWBl5HYVoU49MlRPrsiCELGl9LMqHiTWFX4jjhGyqcgnwoBi6anoOzsYIMxDMJkvorISUJ75siOQg2HsCapqVTyyZH9n (accessed November 2019).

26   Rosie Gray, 'Prominent Evangelicals Still Backing Trump After Lewd Video', Buzzfeed News, 10 October 2016, https://www.buzzfeednews.com/article/rosiegray/prominent-evangelicals-still-backing-trump-after-graphic-vid (accessed November 2019).

27   Oliver Darcy, '"I was offended": Mike Pence breaks his silence on Donald Trump's vulgar comments about women', Business Insider, 8 October 2016, https://www.businessinsider.com/pence-trump-comments-women-video-billy-bush-2016-10/commerce-on-business-insider?r=US&IR=T (accessed November 2019).

28   Allan Smith, 'Melania Trump Responds: "Unacceptable and offensive to me"', Business Insider, 9 October 2016, https://www.businessinsider.com/melania-trump-donald-leaked-tape-2016-10?r=US&IR=T (accessed November 2019).

29   Allan Smith, 'Shocking audio emerges of lewd comments Trump made about women in 2005', Business Insider, 7 October 2016, https://www.businessinsider.com/trump-leaked-recording-women-audio-billy-bush-2016-10?r=US&IR=T (accessed November 2019).

30   Amy Chozick and Michael M. Grynbaum, 'She Has a Name, Alicia Machado, and It Is Everywhere', *New York Times*, 28 September 2016, https://www.nytimes.com/2016/09/29/us/

politics/alicia-machado-presidential-race.html (accessed November 2019). The story records that Machado worked for the Clinton campaign in 2016, and that in the forty-eight hours after the first presidential debate of Monday 26 September 2016, Machado was written about 'in more than 150 print news articles, referred to on TV more than 6,023 times and mentioned on Twitter nearly 200,000 times. She appeared on NBC's 'Today' show, ABC's 'Good Morning America,' CNN, MSNBC, Fox News, Univision and Telemundo'.

31 'Donald Trump: Miss Universe Alicia Machado was "the absolute worst"', Fox News, 27 September 2016, https://www.foxnews.com/entertainment/donald-trump-miss-universe-alicia-machado-was-the-absolute-worst (accessed November 2019).

32 @realDonaldTrump, 22 March 2016, 6.53 p.m.

33 @tedcruz, 22 March 2016, 7.21 p.m.

34 @tedcruz, 23 March 2016, 9.30 p.m.

35 Some analysts have argued this 53 per cent figure is overstated, because it was based on exit polls that have their own biases. Nevertheless, a Pew Research Center study published in August 2018 still found a majority of white women voting for Trump, with 47 per cent supporting Trump compared with 45 per cent supporting Clinton, 'An examination of the 2016 electorate, based on validated voters', Pew Research Center, 9 August 2018, https://www.people-press.org/2018/08/09/an-examination-of-the-2016-electorate-based-on-validated-voters/ (accessed November 2019).

36 Moira Donegan, 'Half of white women continue to vote Republican. What's wrong with them?', The Guardian, 9 November 2018, https://www.theguardian.com/commentisfree/2018/nov/09/white-women-vote-republican-why (accessed November 2019).

37 Andrea Dworkin, Right-Wing Women (New York: Perigee Books, 1983).

38 Moira Donegan, 'Half of white women continue to vote Republican. What's wrong with them?'.

39 Tom Perkins, '"You don't have to date him": the women standing by Trump in 2020', The Guardian, 10 May 2019, https://www.theguardian.com/us-news/2019/may/10/women-for-trump-michigan-supporters-grassroots-organizing (accessed November 2019).

40 Katie Gaddini, 'Donald Trump, why white evangelical women support him', The Conversation, 19 February 2019, http://theconversation.com/donald-trump-why-white-evangelical-women-support-him-112041 (accessed November 2019).

41 Leah MarieAnn Klett, 'Candace Owens Says Left Enjoys "Making Fun" of Jesus Christ, "Wants to Replace God with Gov't"', Christian Post, 9 November 2018, https://www.christianpost.com/news/candace-owens-says-left-enjoys-making-fun-jesus-christ-wants-to-replace-god-with-government.html (accessed November 2019). For the full Owens address at the Liberty University Convocation on 26 September 2018, see 'Liberty Owens, Liberty University Convocation', Liberty University, https://www.youtube.com/watch?v=rrKOnprdcoo (accessed October 2019). The quotation regarding Jesus, God and the left is at 24:00.

42 'Remarks by President Trump Before Marine One Departure', 10 April 2019, https://www.whitehouse.gov/briefings-statements/remarks-president-trump-marine-one-departure-70/ (accessed October 2019).

43 For the full interview see: 'Diamond and Silk: trump is not a racist; he's a realist', Fox News, 14 January 2018, www.youtube.com/watch?v=VK7aauzXsIg (accessed June 2019).

44 @realDonaldTrump, 31 May 2019, 12.12 p.m.

45 Brandon Straka @usminority, 31 May 2019.

CHAPTER EIGHT: THE POLITICS OF LIFE

1 For an overview of the main events see: Joshua Prager, 'Norma McCorvey: The Woman Who Became "Roe" – Then Regretted It, 1947–2017', 28 December 2017, https://www.politico.com/magazine/story/2017/12/28/norma-mccorvey-obituary-216184 (accessed October 2019) and Patricia Bauer, 'Norma McCorvey, American Activist', Encyclopaedia Britannica, updated 18 September 2019, https://www.britannica.com/biography/Norma-McCorvey (accessed October 2019).

NOTES

2 Wording of legal action filed in March 1970 by Weddington and Coffee as quoted in Randolph B. Campbell, *Gone to Texas: A History of the Lone Star State* (Oxford: Oxford University Press, 2003).

3 Section 1, '14th Amendment', Legal Information Institute, Cornell Law School, www.law.cornell.edu/constitution/amendmentxiv (accessed June 2019).

4 'Roe v. Wade: Summary of the Decision, Landmark Cases of the US Supreme Court, https://www.landmarkcases.org/roe-v-wade/roe-v-wade-summary-of-the-decision (accessed October 2019).

5 For example, Leana Wen, president of Planned Parenthood, in an interview with WFAA of Dallas, 6 March 2019, stated: 'We face a real situation where Roe could be overturned. And we know what will happen, which is that women will die. Thousands of women died every year pre-Roe.' Glenn Kessler, 'Planned Parenthood's false stat: "Thousands" of women died every year before Roe"', *Washington Post*, 29 May 2019, https://www.washingtonpost.com/politics/2019/05/29/planned-parenthoods-false-stat-thousands-women-died-every-year-before-roe/ (accessed November 2019), shows Wen making the same claim in interviews and tweets in March, April and May 2019.

6 Elizabeth Noland Brown, 'Planned Parenthood President Wrong on Illegal Abortion Deaths Pre-Roe', Reason, 29 May 2019, https://reason.com/2019/05/29/planned-parenthood-president-wrong-on-illegal-abortion-deaths-pre-roe/ (accessed November 2019).

7 David Sivak, 'Fact Check: Have there been 60 million abortions since Roe v. Wade?', 3 July 2018, https://checkyourfact.com/2018/07/03/fact-check-60-million-abortions/ (accessed July 2019).

8 National Right to Life Committee, 'The State of Abortion in the United States', January 2018 www.nrlc.org/uploads/communications/stateofabortion2018.pdf (accessed June 2019).

9 Ibid., p. 15.

10 Ben Johnson, 'Mike Pence: "For the sake of the sanctity of life" elect Donald Trump', The Right's Writer, 21 July 2016, https://therightswriter.com/2016/07/mike-pence-for-the-sake-of-the-sanctity-of-life-elect-donald-trump/ (accessed June 2019).

11 'Word for Word: VP Pence on President Trump: "Most Pro-Life President in American History"', C-SPAN, 18 January 2019, https://www.youtube.com/watch?v=rXTzw2dDsMs (accessed October 2019).

12 Eugene Scott, 'At the March for Life, Pence reminded white evangelicals why they should stick with Trump', *Washington Post*, 18 January 2019, https://www.washingtonpost.com/politics/2019/01/18/march-life-pence-reminded-white-evangelicals-why-they-should-stick-with-trump/ (accessed November 2019).

13 Marist Poll, 'NPR/PBS NewsHour/Marist Poll Results & Analysis', 17 January 2019, http://maristpoll.marist.edu/npr-pbs-newshour-marist-poll-results-analysis/#sthash.eorPezG6.dpbs (accessed November 2019).

14 Julia Jacobs, 'Remembering an Era Before Roe, When New York Had the "Most Liberal" Abortion Law', *New York Times*, 19 July 2018, https://www.nytimes.com/2018/07/19/us/politics/new-york-abortion-roe-wade-nyt.html (accessed November 2019).

15 Centers for Disease Control and Prevention, Morbidity and Mortality Weekly Report, Abortion Surveillance – United States, 2015, published 23 November 2018, www.cdc.gov/mmwr/volumes/67/ss/ss6713a1.htm (accessed June 2019).

16 Caitlin O'Kane, 'New York passes law allowing abortions at any time if mother's health is at risk', CBS News, 24 January 2019, https://www.cbsnews.com/news/new-york-passes-abortion-bill-late-term-if-mothers-health-is-at-risk-today-2019-01-23/ (accessed November 2019).

17 Shubham Saharan, 'Hillary Clinton, Cuomo call for decriminalization of abortion in New York at rally at Barnard', *Columbia Spectator*, 7 January 2019, https://www.columbiaspectator.com/news/2019/01/07/hillary-clinton-cuomo-call-for-decriminalization-of-abortion-in-new-york-at-rally-at-barnard/ (accessed November 2019).

18 Ibid.

19 The New York State Senate, 'Section 2599-AA Policy and Purpose', www.nysenate.gov/legislation/laws/PBH/2599-AA (accessed July 2019).

20 Leonardo Blair, 'Va. Democrat defends abortion for women in labor: While "she's dilating?" "Yes"', *Christian Post*, 30 January 2019, https://www.christianpost.com/news/va-democrat-defends-abortion-for-women-in-labor-while-shes-dilating-yes.html (accessed November 2019).

21 Terence P. Jeffrey, 'Virginia Governor Says He Doesn't Regret What He Said – or Way He Said It – About Letting Born Baby Die', CNS News, 31 January 2019, https://www.cnsnews.com/blog/terence-p-jeffrey/virginia-governor-says-he-doesnt-regret-what-he-said-or-way-he-said-it-about (accessed November 2019).

22 Vince Coglianese and Saagar Enjeti, 'EXCLUSIVE: Trump Rips Virginia Democrats' Abortion Comments', The Daily Caller, 30 January 2019, https://dailycaller.com/2019/01/30/exclusive-trump-rips-virginia-democrats-abortion-comments/ (accessed November 2019).

23 @NikkiHaley, 29 January 2019.

24 @benshapiro, 30 January 2019.

25 Antonio Olivo, 'Del. Kathy Tran was known for nursing her baby on the House floor. Now she's getting death threats over abortion', *Washington Post*, 31 January 2019, https://www.washingtonpost.com/local/virginia-politics/lawmaker-at-center-of-abortion-bill-firestorm-elected-as-part-of-democratic-wave-that-changed-richmond/2019/01/31/d4f76ecc-2565-11e9-90cd-dedb0c92dc17_story.html (accessed November 2019).

26 Ann North, 'The controversy around Virginia's new abortion bill, explained', Vox, 1 February 2019, https://www.vox.com/2019/2/1/18205428/virginia-abortion-bill-kathy-tran-ralph-northam (accessed November 2019).

27 Dylan Scott, 'Virginia governor's 1984 yearbook page features people in blackface and KKK hood', Vox, 2 February 2019, https://www.vox.com/policy-and-politics/2019/2/1/18207433/ralph-northam-eastern-virginia-medical-school-yearbook-kkk-blackface (accessed October 2019).

28 Tom Pappert, 'Governor Who Endorsed Infanticide Received $2 Million From Planned Parenthood', Big League Politics, 31 January 2019, https://bigleaguepolitics.com/governor-who-endorsed-infanticide-received-2-million-from-planned-parenthood/ (accessed November 2019).

29 'WATCH: Trump says he'll ask Congress to outlaw late-term abortions', PBS NewsHour, 5 February 2019, https://www.youtube.com/watch?v=cXRTnD7JEWQ, (accessed October 2019).

30 Corinne J. Naden, *Open For Debate: Abortion* (New York: Marshall Cavendish, 2008), p. 12.

31 Ibid., p. 12. See also: Ranana Dine, 'Scarlet Letters: Getting the History of Abortion and Contraception Right', 8 August 2013, Center for American Progress, https://www.americanprogress.org/issues/religion/news/2013/08/08/71893/scarlet-letters-getting-the-history-of-abortion-and-contraception-right/ (accessed June 2019).

32 Francis J. Bremer, *The Puritan Experiment: New England Society from Bradford to Edwards* (Hanover, NH, and London: University Press of New England, 1995), p. 114; Leland Ryken, *Wordly Saints* (Grand Rapids, MI: Zondervan, 1986), pp. 43–5; Daniel Doriani, 'The Puritans, Sex and Pleasure', in Elizabeth Stuart and Adrian Thatcher (eds), *Christian Perspectives on Sexuality and Gender* (Leominster: Gracewing Publishing, published jointly with Wm B. Eerdmans, Grand Rapids, MI, 1996), pp. 33–52.

33 Ranana Dine, 'Scarlet Letters: Getting the History of Abortion and Contraception Right'.

34 Preamble to statement by Planned Parenthood Hudson Peconic, 'President Trump Uses State of the Union to Attack Women Planned Parenthood Hudson Peconic Vows to Fight for All New Yorkers', released 6 February 2019, https://www.plannedparenthood.org/planned-parenthood-hudson-peconic/newsroom/president-trump-uses-state-of-the-union-to-attack-women-planned-parenthood-hudson-peconic-vows-to-fight-for-all-new-yorkers (accessed November 2019).

35 Statement from Vincent Russell, President and CEO, Planned Parenthood, Hudson Peconic in Planned Parenthood Hudson Peconic, 'President Trump Uses State of the Union to Attack Women Planned Parenthood Hudson Peconic Vows to Fight for All New Yorkers'.

36 Donald Trump, *Meet the Press*, 24 October 1999, with Tim Russert, NBC News, https://www.youtube.com/watch?v=G_IG07XhT3k (accessed November 2019).

37 Anthony Dabruzzi, 'Gov. Tony Evers Calls President Trump's Abortion Comments During Wisconsin Rally "Horrific"', Spectrum News, 30 April 2019, https://spectrumnews1.com/wi/madison/news/2019/05/01/gov--tony-evers-calls-president-trump-s-abortion-comments-during-wisconsin-rally--horrific-- (accessed November 2019).

38 Ibid.

39 Ryan Everson, 'Trump and Gov. Evers are both wrong about the Wisconsin "born alive" bill', *Washington Examiner*, 6 June 2019, https://www.washingtonexaminer.com/opinion/trump-and-gov-evers-are-both-wrong-about-the-wisconsin-born-alive-bill (accessed November 2019).

40 The 18 June 2019 speech also returned to many of the themes of 2016: immigration, fake news, even Hillary Clinton (at one point the crowd started shouting the 2016 chant of 'Lock Her Up!'. The pro-life rhetoric, though, was sharper than before and Trump also added references to the dangers that 'radical socialism' posed to the American dream (a swipe at Bernie Sanders and Alexandria Ocasio-Cortez), https://factba.se/transcript/donald-trump-speech-maga-rally-reelection-orlando-june-18-2019 (accessed July 2019).

41 Katie Glueck, Jonathan Martin and Alexander Burns, 'Behind Biden's Reversal on Hyde Amendment: Lobbying, Backlash and an Ally's Call', *New York Times*, 7 June 2019, https://www.nytimes.com/2019/06/07/us/politics/biden-abortion-hyde-amendment.html (accessed November 2019).

42 Statement by President of NARAL Pro-Choice America Ilyse Hogue, issued on 6 June 2019.

43 Xander Landen, 'Planned Parenthood declines to endorse in governor's race', VTDigger, 7 October 2018, https://vtdigger.org/2018/10/07/planned-parenthood-declines-endorse-governors-race/ (accessed November 2019).

44 Ibid.

45 US Government Accountability Office, 'Federal Obligation to and Expenditures by Selected Organizations Involved in Health-Related Activities. Fiscal Years 2013–2015', 6 March 2018, https://www.gao.gov/products/GAO-18-204R (accessed June 2019).

46 US Department of Health and Human Services, 'HHS Secretary Statement on Ninth Circuit's Rejection of Nationwide Block on New Family Planning Policy', 20 June 2019, https://www.hhs.gov/about/news/2019/06/20/statement-ninth-circuit-rejection-nationwide-block-new-family-planning-policy.html (accessed October 2019).

47 Jessie Hellmann, 'Appeals court allows Trump abortion referral ban to take effect', The Hill, 20 June 2019, https://thehill.com/policy/healthcare/449524-white-house-plan-to-ban-federally-funded-clinics-from-giving-abortion (accessed November 2019).

48 Ema O'Connor and Zoe Tillman, 'A Federal Judge Has Blocked Ohio's 6-Week Abortion Ban', BuzzFeed News, 3 July 2019, https://www.buzzfeednews.com/article/emaoconnor/ohio-abortion-ban-blocked (accessed November 2019).

49 Calvin Freiburger, 'Mississippi gov. on signing heartbeat abortion ban: "We will all answer to the good Lord one day"', LifeSiteNews, 25 March 2019, https://www.lifesitenews.com/news/mississippi-gov.-on-signing-heartbeat-abortion-ban-we-will-all-answer-to-the-good-lord-one-day (accessed November 2019); @PhilBryant, 20 March 2019.

50 Michael Foust, 'Georgia Gov. Defies Hollywood Threats, Signs Pro-Life Heartbeat Bill', Christian Headlines, 7 May 2019, https://www.christianheadlines.com/contributors/michael-foust/georgia-gov-defies-hollywood-threats-signs-pro-life-heartbeat-bill.html (accessed November 2019).

51 Missouri Governor Michael L. Parson, 'Governor Parson Signs House Bill 126 and Senate Bill 21', 24 May 2019, https://governor.mo.gov/press-releases/archive/governor-parson-signs-house-bill-

126-and-senate-bill-21 (accessed November 2019) and Alexa Lardieri, 'Missouri Governor Signs Ban on Abortion After 8 Weeks of Pregnancy', U.S. News, 24 May 2019, https://www.usnews.com/news/politics/articles/2019-05-24/missouri-gov-mike-parson-signs-ban-on-abortion-after-8-weeks-of-pregnancy (accessed November 2019).

52 Mark Jennings, 'Democrat Louisiana Governor Signs Abortion Ban: "I Have Been True to My Word and Beliefs"', CNS News, 31 May 2019, https://www.cnsnews.com/blog/craig-bannister/democrat-louisiana-governor-signs-abortion-ban-i-have-been-true-my-word-and (accessed November 2019).

53 Caroline Kelly, 'Alabama governor signs nation's most restrictive anti-abortion bill into law', CNN, 16 May 2019, https://edition.cnn.com/2019/05/15/politics/alabama-governor-signs-bill/index.html (accessed November 2019).

54 @realDonaldTrump, 18 May 2019.

CHAPTER NINE: LAW AND THE CONSTITUTION

1   'Speech: Donald Trump Announces His 2020 Candidacy at a Political Rally in Orlando – June 18 2019', https://factba.se/transcript/donald-trump-speech-maga-rally-reelection-orlando-june-18-2019 (accessed July 2019).

2   Ibid.

3   Ian Schwartz, 'All Democrats At Main Debate Agree Illegal Immigrants Should Get Health Care Coverage', RealClear Politics, 27 June 2019 (accessed July 2019), https://www.realclearpolitics.com/video/2019/06/27/all_dem_candidates_raise_hand_when_asked_if_illegal_immigrants_should_get_health_care_coverage_at_debate.html (accessed July 2019).

4   @realDonaldTrump, 27 June 2019, 6.37 p.m.

5   Megan Flynn, '"Malignant, dangerous, violent": Trump rally's "Send her back!" chant raises new concerns of intolerance', Washington Post, 18 June 2019, https://www.washingtonpost.com/nation/2019/07/18/malignant-dangerous-violent-trump-rallys-send-her-back-chant-raises-new-concerns-intolerance/ (accessed November 2019).

6   Video extract of this part of the 2019 State of the Union speech posted by Ian Schwartz, 'Trump: "America Will Never Be A Socialist Country"; "We Were Born Free And We Will Stay Free"', RealClear Politics, 5 February 2019, https://www.realclearpolitics.com/video/2019/02/05/trump_america_will_never_be_a_socialist_country_we_were_born_free_and_we_shall_stay_free.html (accessed July 2019).

7   Interview with Maria Bartiromo on Mornings with Maria, Fox Business Network, 12 July 2019, https://video.foxbusiness.com/v/6058377378001/#sp=show-clips (accessed July 2019).

8   'Speech: Donald Trump Announces His 2020 Candidacy at a Political Rally in Orlando – June 18 2019'.

9   Todd Venezia, 'Graham rips Dems for turning Kavanaugh hearing into "unethical sham"', New York Post, 27 September 2018, https://nypost.com/2018/09/27/graham-rips-dems-for-turning-kavanaugh-hearing-into-unethical-sham/ (accessed November 2019).

10 'Speech: Donald Trump Announces His 2020 Candidacy at a Political Rally in Orlando – June 18 2019'.

11 'Mueller finds no collusion with Russia, leaves obstruction question open', American Bar Association, March 2019, https://www.americanbar.org/news/abanews/aba-news-archives/2019/03/mueller-concludes-investigation/ (accessed July 2019).

12 Joe Berkowitz, 'Biden's feeble hand-raises at the debate told us a lot about his presidential campaign – and generated a lot of comedy', Fast Company, 28 June 2019, https://www.fastcompany.com/90370902/bidens-feeble-hand-raises-at-the-debate-told-us-a-lot-about-his-presidential-campaign-and-generated-a-lot-of-comedy (accessed November 2019).

13 Andrew L. Seidel, The Founding Myth: Why Christian Nationalism is Un-American (New York: Sterling, 2019).

14 Andrew L. Seidel interviewed by Paul Rosenberg, 'Demolishing the Right's "Founding Myth": America was never a "Christian nation"', Salon, 18 May 2019, https://www.salon.

com/2019/05/18/demolishing-the-rights-founding-myth-america-was-never-a-christian-nation/ (accessed November 2019).

15 Mark David Hall, 'Did America Have a Christian Founding?', The Heritage Foundation, 7 June 2011, https://www.heritage.org/political-process/report/did-america-have-christian-founding (accessed November 2019).

16 James Madison, 'The Federalist No 51, to the People of the State of New York: The Structure of Government Must Furnish the Proper Checks and Balances Between the Different Departments', 6 February 1788, www.constitution.org/fed/federa51.htm (accessed July 2019).

17 Mark David Hall, 'Did America Have a Christian Founding?'.

18 James Wilson, 'Of the Study of the Law in the United States', 1790, billofrightsinstitute.org/founding-documents/founders-quotes/ (accessed July 2019).

19 Mark David Hall, 'Did America Have a Christian Founding?'

20 Thomas Jefferson, 'Second Inaugural Address', 4 March 1805, The Avalon Project, avalon.law.yale.edu/19th_century/jefinau2.asp (accessed July 2019).

21 Mark David Hall, 'Did America Have a Christian Founding?'

22 'Remarks By President Trump at Dinner with Evangelical Leaders', 27 August 2018, https://www.whitehouse.gov/briefings-statements/remarks-president-trump-dinner-evangelical-leaders/ (accessed October 2019).

23 @RealDonaldTrump, 1 November 2017, 3.03 p.m.

24 See the Heritage Foundation's Judicial Tracker here: https://www.heritage.org/judicialtracker (accessed October 2019).

25 Graydon Head & Ritchey LLP, 'What is Originalism/Textualism?', 15 February 2016, https://www.lexology.com/library/detail.aspx?g=c9148c01-ae9c-44f5-8ac6-a225f8ca1187 (accessed July 2019).

26 Deanna Paul, '"Keep those judges coming": Conservatives praise Trump's success in filling the courts', *Washington Post*, 16 November 2018, https://www.washingtonpost.com/politics/2018/11/16/keep-those-judges-coming-conservatives-praise-trumps-success-filling-courts/ (accessed November 2019).

27 'AFJ Two-Year Retrospective Highlights Trump's Harm to Federal Judiciary', Alliance for Justice, 3 April 2019, https://www.afj.org/press-room/press-releases/afj-two-year-retrospective-highlights-trumps-harm-to-federal-judiciary (accessed October 2019).

28 'Remarks by Vice-President Pence at the Federalist Society's Seventh Annual Executive Branch Review Conference', 8 May 2019, https://www.whitehouse.gov/briefings-statements/remarks-vice-president-pence-federalist-societys-seventh-annual-executive-branch-review-conference/ (accessed October 2019).

29 'Attorney General William P. Barr Delivers Remarks to the American Law Institute on Nationwide Injunctions', 21 May 2019, https://www.justice.gov/opa/speech/attorney-general-william-p-barr-delivers-remarks-american-law-institute-nationwide (accessed July 2019).

30 Ibid.

31 Jacqueline Thomsen, 'Trump seeks to limit judges' powers on injunctions after legal blows', The Hill, 11 May 2019, https://thehill.com/regulation/court-battles/443211-trump-seeks-to-limit-judges-powers-on-injunctions-after-legal (accessed November 2019).

32 Thomas Jipping, 'The Senate Has Confirmed Trump's 100th Judge. Let's Put That Number In Perspective', The Heritage Foundation, 6 May 2019, https://www.heritage.org/courts/commentary/the-senate-has-confirmed-trumps-100th-judge-lets-put-number-perspective (accessed November 2019).

CHAPTER TEN: TRUMP, ISRAEL AND THE MIDDLE EAST

1 Quoted in Antonia Fraser, *Cromwell: Our Chief of Men* (London: Granada, 1973), p. 424.

2 'Mission and Vision', Christians United For Israel, https://www.cufi.org/impact/about-us/mission-and-vision/ (accessed July 2019).

3 'Talking Points, Christians United For Israel website: Obama, Netanyahu and the Israeli Election', www.cufi.org/obama-netanyahu-israeli-election/ (accessed July 2019).

4   Jesse Byrnes, 'Netanyahu pollster: Obama role in election larger than reported', The Hill, 22 March 2015, https://thehill.com/policy/international/236565-netanyahu-pollster-obama-role-in-election-larger-than-reported (accessed November 2019).

5   McLaughlin & Associates, 'The Hill: Netanyahu pollster: Obama role in election larger than reported', 26 May 2015, mclaughlinonline.com/2015/05/26/the-hill-netanyahu-pollster-obama-role-in-election-larger-than-reported/ (accessed July 2019).

6   Jennifer Rubin, 'NGO connected to Obama's 2008 campaign used U.S. tax dollars trying to oust Netanyahu', Washington Post, 12 July 2016, https://www.washingtonpost.com/blogs/right-turn/wp/2016/07/12/ngo-connected-to-obamas-2008-campaign-used-u-s-tax-dollars-trying-to-oust-netanyahu/ (accessed November 2019).

7   Ben Mathis-Lilley, 'Critics Question Whether Pastor Who Said Hitler Was Sent by God Was Good Choice to Speak at U.S. Embassy in Israel', Slate, 14 May 2018, https://slate.com/news-and-politics/2018/05/israel-embassy-pastor-said-hitler-was-sent-by-god.html (accessed November 2019).

8   Alex Koppelman, 'McCain rejects John Hagee Endorsement', Salon, 23 May 2008, https://www.salon.com/control/2008/05/22/mccain_hagee_2/ (accessed November 2019).

9   Matt Korade, Kevin Bohn and Daniel Burke, 'Controversial US pastors take part in Jerusalem embassy opening', CNN politics, 14 May 2018, https://edition.cnn.com/2018/05/13/politics/hagee-jeffress-us-embassy-jerusalem/index.html (accessed July 2019).

10 Haaretz Service, 'U.S. Pastor Apologizes to Jews for "God Sent Hitler" Comments', Haaretz, 14 June 2008, https://www.haaretz.com/1.4991820 (accessed November 2019).

11 Matt Korade, Kevin Bohn and Daniel Burke, 'Controversial US pastors take part in Jerusalem embassy opening', CNN, 14 May 2018, https://edition.cnn.com/2018/05/13/politics/hagee-jeffress-us-embassy-jerusalem/index.html (accessed November 2019).

12 Joel B. Pollak, 'Exclusive: Hagee says Trump, like Truman, earned "political immortality" by moving embassy to Jerusalem', Breitbart, 11 May 2018, https://www.breitbart.com/politics/2018/05/11/john-hagee-trump-jerusalem-embassy/ (accessed November 2019).

13 The First Baptist Dallas website has the full text of Dr Jeffress's prayer: 'Dr. Robert Jeffress Prays at US Embassy Opening in Jerusalem', 14 May 2018, https://www.firstdallas.org/news/dr-robert-jeffress-prays-at-us-embassy-opening-in-jerusalem-/ (accessed October 2019).

14 @MittRomney, 13 May 2018, 6.42 p.m.

15 @robertjeffress, 13 May 2018, 7.46 p.m.

16 William Bradford, Of Plymouth Plantation, 1620–1647, by William Bradford, Sometime Governor Thereof, A New Edition, p. 76.

17 Thomas Jefferson, 'Second Inaugural Address'.

18 Amy Kaplan, Our American Israel: The Story of an Entangled Alliance (Cambridge, MA, and London: Harvard University Press, 2018), p. 5.

19 Ibid., p. 5.

20 Jewish Telegraphic Agency, 'US Embassy move got more love from Christians than Jews, Trump says', 24 June 2018. The website has a fourteen-minute recording of the 18 June 2018 interview, https://www.jta.org/2018/06/24/politics/evangelical-christians-appreciative-u-s-embassy-move-jerusalem-jews-trump-says (accessed October 2019).

21 Ibid.

22 Jonathan Allen, 'In the Trump era, evangelicals take center stage on Israel policy', NBC News, 15 April 2019, https://www.nbcnews.com/politics/white-house/trump-era-evangelicals-take-center-stage-israel-policy-n994326 (accessed July 2019).

23 Ibid. The Public Religion Research Institute Survey referred to by Allen is called 'Chosen for What? Jewish values in 2012' and was published on 4 March 2012, https://www.prri.org/research/jewish-values-in-2012/ (accessed November 2019).

24 Jessica Martinez and Gregory A. Smith, 'How the faithful voted: a preliminary 2016 analysis', Pew Research Center, 9 November 2016, https://www.pewresearch.org/fact-tank/2016/11/09/how-the-faithful-voted-a-preliminary-2016-analysis/ (accessed November 2019).

25 'US-led Bahrain meeting on Palestine: All the latest updates', Aljazeera, 26 June 2019, https://www.aljazeera.com/news/2019/06/led-bahrain-workshop-palestine-latest-updates-190624092422392.html (accessed November 2019); Stephen Kalin, Suleiman Al-Khalidi and Mohamed Abdellah, 'Kushner's economic plan for Mideast peace faces broad Arab rejection', Reuters, 23 June 2019, https://uk.reuters.com/article/uk-israel-palestinians-plan-arabs/kushners-economic-plan-for-mideast-peace-faces-broad-arab-rejection-idUKKCN1TN0S0 (accessed November 2019); and Amir Tibon and Jack Khoury, 'Jordan, Egypt and Morocco to Attend Bahrain Conference, Says White House Official', *Haaretz*, 11 June 2019, https://www.haaretz.com/middle-east-news/jordan/.premium-jordan-should-take-part-in-bahrain-conference-king-abdullah-reportedly-says-1.7359302 (accessed November 2019).

26 'Saudi Arabia will support whatever economic plan will bring prosperity to the Palestinians: finance minister', Reuters, 26 June 2019, https://www.reuters.com/article/us-israel-palestinians-plan-saudi/saudi-arabia-will-support-whatever-economic-plan-will-bring-prosperity-to-the-palestinians-finance-minister-idUSKCN1TR1WT (accessed November 2019).

27 'Saudi minister says Kushner's plan could succeed if there is "hope for peace"', *Arab Weekly*, 26 June 2019, https://thearabweekly.com/saudi-minister-says-kushners-plan-could-succeed-if-there-hope-peace (accessed November 2019).

28 'US-led Bahrain meeting on Palestine: All the latest updates'.

29 Amir Tibon, 'Kushner Reassures Evangelicals: Israel's Security a Priority in Trump Peace Plan', *Haaretz*, 11 July 2019, https://www.haaretz.com/us-news/.premium-kushner-reassures-evangelicals-israel-s-security-a-priority-in-trump-peace-plan-1.7490199 (accessed November 2019).

30 *Holy Bible*.

31 Stuart Winer and Marissa Newman, 'Iran supreme leader touts 9-point plan to destroy Israel', *Times of Israel*, 10 November 2014, https://www.timesofisrael.com/iran-supreme-leader-touts-9-point-plan-to-destroy-israel/ (accessed November 2019).

32 Quoted by Prof Joshua Teitelbaum and Lt Col (ret.) Michael Segall in: 'The Iranian Leadership's Continuing Declarations of Intent to Destroy Israel', Jerusalem Centre for Public Affairs, 2012. The section on 'The statements of Supreme Leader Ayatollah Ali Khamenei' reports Ali Khamenei saying this on 15 January 2001, at a meeting with organisers of the International Conference for Support of the Intifada. The translation from Farsi is by Iranian journalist Kasra Naji, http://jcpa.org/wp-content/uploads/2012/05/IransIntent2012b.pdf (accessed October 2019).

33 'Khamenei: Zionist regime is a cancer', Ynet News, 2 March 2012. Khamenei was addressing thousands of worshippers at a Tehran University prayer service marking the Fajr celebration of Friday 2 March 2012, https://www.ynetnews.com/articles/0,7340,L-4184838,00.html (accessed November 2019).

34 @khamenei_ir, 8 November 2014, 1.15 p.m. According to Daniel Politi, 'Iran's Khamenei: No Cure for Barbaric Israel but Annihilation', Slate, 9 November 2014. The posting of the tweet came just days after the *Wall Street Journal* alleged that President Obama wrote a secret letter to Khamanei suggesting the two nations could cooperate in fighting against ISIS, but any cooperation would be dependent on Iran reaching a nuclear deal with global powers by 24 November. Mitt Romney harshly criticised the letter according to *Washington Post*. Jay Solomon and Carol E. Lee, 'Obama wrote secret letter to Iran's Khamenei About Fighting Islamic State', *Wall Street Journal*, 6 November 2014, https://www.wsj.com/articles/obama-wrote-secret-letter-to-irans-khamenei-about-fighting-islamic-state-1415295291 (accessed November 2019) and Melinda Henneberger, 'Romney tells Israeli Americans Obama is "divisive and dictatorial and demeaning"', *Washington Post*, 8 November 2014, https://www.washingtonpost.com/politics/romney-tells-israeli-americans-obama-is-divisive-and-dictatorial-and-demeaning/2014/11/08/733fde54-6759-11e4-9fdc-d43b053ecb4d_story.html (accessed November 2019).

35 @Khamenei_ir, 3 June 2018, 10.49 a.m.

36 'Nasrallah, in vicious public address, calls for the destruction of Israel', *Times of Israel*, 2 August 2013, https://www.timesofisrael.com/hezbollah-leader-rallies-shiites-with-highly-sectarian-speech/ (accessed November 20019). Nasrallah was making his first public appearance in over a year, in a southern Beirut suburb, marking 'al-Quds day', which is celebrated across the Islamic world on the last Friday in Ramadan.

37 Lt Col (ret) Nicgael Segall and Daniel Rubenstein, 'Sworn to Destruction: What Iranian Leaders Continue to Say About Israel in the Rouhani Era', Jerusalem Centre for Public Affairs, 7 January 2014.

38 'Remarks by President Trump on the Joint Comprehensive Plan of Action', 8 May 2018, https://www.whitehouse.gov/briefings-statements/remarks-president-trump-joint-comprehensive-plan-action/ (accessed October 2019).

39 'Netanyahu addresses CUFI 2019 summit in Washington', 9 July 2019, www.breakingisraelnews.com/133029/pm-netanyahu-addresses-cufi-2019-summit-in-washington/ (accessed July 2019).

40 'Saudi deputy crown prince, Trump meeting a "turning point": Saudi adviser', Reuters, 14 March 2017, https://www.reuters.com/article/us-saudi-usa-idUSKBN16L2CT (accessed November 2019).

41 Ibid.

42 @realDonaldTrump, 4 July 2019, 5.28 p.m.

43 Darlene Superville, Calvin Woodward and Lynn Berry, 'Trump asks Americans to "stay true to our cause"', Boston25News/AP, 5 July 2019, https://apnews.com/5fef7761f14f4c65a7de982359b87bdo (accessed November 2019). Buttigieg is reported in the 10.30 a.m. slot on this posting as making these comments to a crowd in Sioux City, Iowa, on 3 July 2019.

CONCLUSION: TRUMP, US EVANGELICALS AND PURITANS

1 @realDonaldTrump, 11 July 2019, 4.30 a.m.

2 Ibid., 9 July 2019, 4.48 a.m.

3 Ibid., 14 July 2019, 5.27 a.m.

4 'Trump to congresswomen of colour: Leave the US', BBC, 15 July 2019, https://www.bbc.co.uk/news/world-us-canada-48982172 (accessed July 2019).

5 Discussed by Dana Milbank, 'Trump is on a mission from God', *Washington Post*, 1 February 2019, https://www.washingtonpost.com/opinions/trump-is-on-a-mission-from-god/2019/02/01/dc3a535a-2643-11e9-90cd-dedb0c92dc17_story.html?noredirect=on&utm_term=.679127c14a98 (accessed July 2019).

6 Reported by Andrew Restuccia, 'The sanctification of Donald Trump', Politico, 30 April 2019, https://www.politico.com/story/2019/04/30/donald-trump-evangelicals-god-1294578 (accessed July 2019).

7 On 15 July 2019, at a press conference following his Twitter attack on the four congresswomen, Trump defended his behaviour with telling words: 'As far as I am concerned if you hate our country – if you're not happy here you can leave. That is what I say all of the time. That's what I said in a Tweet which I guess some people think is controversial, *a lot of people love it by the way*' (author's italics), Ryan Teague Beckwith, 'President Trump Doubled Down on "Why Don't They Go Back" Remarks: Read the Transcript', *Time*, 15 July 2019, https://time.com/5626813/donald-trump-racist-tweets-transcript/ (accessed July 2019).

8 'Public Highly Critical of State of Political Discourse in the U.S. Reactions to Trump's rhetoric: Concern, confusion, embarrassment', 19 June 2019, https://www.people-press.org/2019/06/19/public-highly-critical-of-state-of-political-discourse-in-the-u-s/ (accessed July 2019).

9 Arlie Russell Hochschild, *Strangers In Their Own Land: Anger and Mourning on the American Right*.

10 BBC Radio 4, *PM*, 15 July 2019, 5 p.m.

11 Philip Schwadel and Gregory A. Smith, 'Evangelical approval of Trump remains high, but

other religious groups are less supportive', Pew Research Center, 18 March 2019, https://www.pewresearch.org/fact-tank/2019/03/18/evangelical-approval-of-trump-remains-high-but-other-religious-groups-are-less-supportive/ (accessed July 2019).

12 The film is based on Mark Taylor's book, *The Trump Prophecies: The Astonishing True Story of the Man Who Saw Tomorrow… and What He Says Is Coming Next* (Crane, MO: Defender, 2017).

13 Harriet Sherwood, 'The chosen one? The new film that claims Trump's election was an act of God', *The Guardian*, 3 October 2018, https://www.theguardian.com/us-news/2018/oct/03/the-trump-prophecy-film-god-election-mark-taylor (accessed July 2019).

14 Revealingly, Trump's criticism of the four congresswomen and their Democrat defenders included the words: 'That means they are endorsing Socialism, hate of Israel and the USA!', @realDonaldTrump, 15 July, 2.26 p.m.

15 Martyn Whittock, 'How Puritanism explains Trump: Why the 17th century taught the US and UK different lessons'.

INDEX